ABRAHAM WAS THEIR FATHER

Abraham Was Their Father

by Warren Matthews

Mercer University Press
Macon, Ga.

LIBRARY OF CONGRESS CATALOGING IN PUBLICATION DATA

Matthews, Alfred Warren.
    Abraham was their father.

    Includes bibliographies and index.
    1. Judaism—History. 2. Church history.
3. Islam—History. I. Title.
BM155.2.M35   200'.9   81-146
ISBN 0-86554-005-5   AACR2

ACKNOWLEDGEMENTS

To list all of the people and events who have entered my life in preparation for this introduction to religions in the West would require a separate small book. Yet, there are some persons who must be mentioned as contributing especially to the preparation of the text.

Particular appreciation should be expressed for the professional services of Mr. Henry L. Thornburg. While studying this text he voluntarily prepared the illustrative maps to assist other students. I am grateful for his generous services.

Old Dominion University provided the working conditions necessary for writing, and Dr. Heinz K. Meier, Dean of the School of Arts and Letters, helped with funding for research time and manuscript preparation.

I am grateful too for the quotations which add richness to the text, giving a sample of what the reader can find by going to the more complete works. The Revised Standard Version of the *Holy Bible* copyrighted 1946, 1952, †1971, 1973, has been quoted extensively with permission of the Division of Education and Ministry, National Council of Churches of Christ in the U.S.A. Some interesting documents of the Church are quoted from Henry Bettenson, *Documents of the Christian Church* by permission of the publishers, Oxford University Press. Quotes from the Quran are taken from M. M. Pickthall, *The Meaning of the Glorious Koran.* The author is grateful to the publisher, George Allen and Unwin Ltd. for permission to quote these representative passages.

PREFACE

A significant event of recent times was the meeting at Camp David in Maryland, U.S.A., in 1978 of Mr. Begin of Israel, Mr. Sadat of Egypt, and Mr. Carter of the United States. The purpose of the meeting was to work out a plan to reach a permanent peace of the world; it pivoted on the progress of that meeting. The economic success of industrialized countries rested upon a settlement that could be accepted by oil-producing Arabs.

Most of the world regarded the meeting at Camp David as a great success, although Palestinians and Arab states other than Egypt were cool or hostile to it. Meetings were to continue between Israel and Egypt until terms of a lasting peace could be found. The heads of these two countries were awarded the Nobel Peace Prize. Mr. Carter, whose leadership had been rated as weak a few days before the meeting, emerged with new recognition as a man of strength and ability.

Something worked toward the success of this meeting besides the need for peace and economic stability. Each leader came from a different faith, proponents of all three of which had fought with each other for centuries. Mr. Begin spoke out of the experience of the Jews, once slaves of the Egyptians, and ever since persecuted by Muslims and Christians alike. Mr. Sadat spoke out of Muslim experience, aware that Christians have been at war with Muslims in the past and that Jews have despised them as enemies of "God's chosen people." Mr. Carter spoke out of a Southern Baptist Protestant Christian experience, and could recall that Christians have been persecuted by Jews and by Muslims. All of the men were aware of these facts, and Mr. Begin even mentioned them publicly on international television. Yet, in spite of that history of conflicts, there was a common foundation of beliefs that could contribute to cooperation.

During the conference it was reported that each leader took time for prayers. The prayers were not together, for each man had a separate time and custom of prayer. But it was believed by many that the God to whom they prayed was one God and that He was creator and Lord not only of Jews but also of Christians and Muslims. Each leader held a faith that could be traced back to a common ancestor, Abraham, whom each faith acknowledges as the father of its spiritual heritage. Each faith knows many of the same prophets of God and acknowledges that these prophets spoke truly of His will. Each man came from a tradition which shares with the other two faiths common concepts of law revealed through prophets as the will of God. In spite of their deep differences in practices of faith, of government, of economic and of geographical goals, there was a common ground of faith and belief in values that not only made discussion possible, but also made it possible to expect a treaty of peace.

Whether the inhabitants of all sides like it or not, the Near East and the West are locked together in the modern political and economic world. Their mutual welfare and progress are strongly intertwined. But they have a moral, natural, historical bond, in that they are children in faith of a common father. They have deep-seated sibling rivalry. But their "genes of faith" make them closer to each other than they are to peoples of Marxism, Buddhism, Confucianism, Hinduism, Shinto, or any of the native religions of Africa or South America. Their common heritage and beliefs are as strong as their differences. If they can develop an awareness of their common past, they may be able to develop a common future that will be rewarding to all alike.

TABLE OF CONTENTS

INTRODUCTION

A person who has lived in the United States for any length of time is already aware of religions from the Near East. Anywhere one goes in the United States one is reminded of Judaism and Christianity. Names of villages, towns, and cities, buildings designed for worship, symbols worn by citizens, coins used in trade, and even the pledge of allegiance to the flag recall the religious heritage of this people. Here and there also one encounters symbols of the Muslims: another religion of the Near East is making its impact in the lives of Americans too.

Yet, a more systematic introduction is in order. Few citizens now have deep religious training in their own faith, if they have any, and even fewer have much knowledge of the two other faiths from the Near East. One cannot know everything, but there are some practical benefits to knowing enough about these three religious to get along socially and commercially, to understand some of the principles behind American ideas and idealism, and to appreciate the feelings held by peoples of the three faiths toward each other.

More of the pages below are devoted to Judaism than to Christianity and Islam: not only is that the oldest faith, but the other two are in large part outgrowths of it. The nature of God, the concept of law, the duties of worship, and a community of faith are set forth in the historical development of Judaism.

A detailed treatment of these three great religions is not attempted here. Rather the author seeks to highlight personalities who have presented great ideas, established customs, or made significant political achievements; and to illuminate the sources of concepts which influence contemporary ethics and law. The stories which have influenced English literature, art, and music are sketched with some detail.

In Christianity, only the new or different ideas from Judaism are set forth, for Christianity has relied upon Judaism for much of its content. However, considerable attention is given to the relationships between Jews and Christians in the early centuries in order to explain the feelings which have persisted until modern times. The early ideas which led to divisions in Christendom are explored in some detail so that readers can understand the deep feelings associated with the divided groups of Christianity today.

Less space is devoted to Islam, not because it is inherently less important, but because even at the present time it is a smaller factor in the traditions and lives of people of the United States. Many of its concepts are explored under Judaism and Christianity. American students, encountering Islam's names, concepts, places, and dates, find that they can be quickly overwhelmed by them. The writer has tried to be selective in order to give a faithful presentation of Islam without discouraging American students with terms that seem irrelevant to their lives. The author believes he has given enough material so that the reader will be able to appreciate Islam and to understand Muslims and their attitudes today in dealing with Christians and Jews.

The following pages are only an introduction. It is hoped that the reader will be stimulated to do some additional reading, which is suggested in the notes for each chapter. At the very least one needs to read from the sacred books of the three religions. To pursue their thoughts and to read from the secondary sources mentioned should reward one with a deeper appreciation of the great heritage of the children of Abraham. If with that appreciation can come some greater understanding among the peoples of the three faiths, all will be the richer for it.

SUGGESTIONS FOR ADDITIONAL READING

General Resources for Study

The Bible. Any translation one finds readable that is recognized as authoritative by some major religious group. Quotations in this book are from the Revised Standard Version, New York: Thomas Nelson and Sons, 1952.

The Koran (Qur'an). Translations or paraphrases are available. Those by A. J. Arberry, M. M. Pickthall, and J. M. Rodwell are acceptable.

Encyclopedias

Gibb, H. A. R. and others, editors. *The Encyclopedia of Islam.* 3 volumes. London: Luzac and Company, 1960.

Gibb, H. A. R. and Kramers, J. H. *Shorter Encyclopedia of Islam.* Ithaca, New York: Cornell University Press (no date)

Hastings, James, editor. *Encyclopedia of Religion and Ethics.* 12 volumes. New York: Charles Scribner's Sons, 1924.

Roth, Cecil, editor. *Encyclopedia Judaica,* 16 volumes. Jerusalem: The MacMillan Company, 1972.

Singer, Isador, managing editor. *The Jewish Encyclopedia.* 12 volumes. New York: Funk and Wagnalls Company.

Spellman, Francis Cardinal, editor. *The Catholic Encyclopedia for School and Home.* 12 volumes. New York: McGraw-Hill Book Company, 1965.

Commentaries on the Bible

Albright, W. F. and Freedman, D. N., editors. *The Anchor Bible.* 38 volumes, plus supplements. Garden City, New York: Doubleday, 1964 ff.

Buttrick, G. A., editor. *The Interpreter's Bible.* 12 volumes. New York/Nashville: Abingdon Press, 1952 ff.

Dictionaries of the Bible

Buttrick, G. A. *The Interpreter's Dictionary of the Bible.* 4 volumes. New York: Abingdon Press, 1962. *Supplementary Volume,* 1976.

Miller, M. S. and Miller, J. L. *Harper's Bible Dictionary.* New York: Harper and Row Publishers, 1973.

CHAPTER 1

ABRAHAM

Abraham was the father of the major religions from the Near East which have come to dominate the cultures of the western world. Abraham means "father of a multitude." Today the descendants who trace their lives of faith back to him number, according to the *World Almanac and Book of Facts,* 1980, 14,383,100 Jews, 546,025,000 Muslims, and 968,184,100 Christians.

While the origins of Judaism, Christianity and Islam were in the Near East, the three might also be referred to as *the* religions of the West. They have dominated the formation of the cultures in Europe, Africa, and North and South America. They are present in some form in most other areas of the world as well. But just as Hinduism, Buddhism, Taoism and Confucianism represent the spirit of religions of the East, so do Judaism, Christianity and Islam stand in contrast as representatives of the spirit of religions of the Near East and of the West.

If one would understand the hopes, fears, beliefs, and practices of the people of the West and of the Near East, one should know the faiths which have developed among the spiritual children of Abraham. The laws, institutions, morals, arts and educational systems of these peoples grew from roots which were grounded in the rich soil tilled by the children of Abraham through the centuries. A more interesting father could hardly be found.

The pride that the children of Abraham have in their father is well deserved, for he stands tall among other men of history, meriting the profound respect not only of his contemporaries but also of generations through the centuries. A case could be made that he has been a prototype for the ideal man in the near eastern world and in the western world. From a culture rich in civilization he ventured forth into strange lands, encountering potentially hostile natives whom he came to understand and from whom he won a deep respect not only for his character but also for his ability to create wealth and political allies. He successfully weathered natural disasters such as drought and earthquakes, human conflicts such as serious disputes over water rights, and warfare with those who would exact excess taxes and furnish no benefits. Everywhere he went men great and small wanted his friendship and were eager to make him presents of considerable value.

Abraham was a man of generosity and understanding. His tent and his hand were open to passing strangers; he insisted on providing food for those who approached his encampment. He was generous, almost to a fault, with his nephew Lot. When Abraham died, not only his legal son Isaac but also his natural son, Ishmael, together laid him to rest with his beloved wife Sarah. In death, as well as in life, he was honored as an outstanding man among men.

How does one explain the greatness of Abraham? What molded the character that makes him revered by Jews, Christians and Muslims? The Bible leaves no doubt about the answer. God chose Abraham, and he formed, guided and blessed him so that he could become the father of many nations. The patriarch was neither an accident nor a self-made man. He was the direct result of God's presence in human history inviting a human being to choose freely to become a partner with God in a grand plan for forming great nations loyal to His kingdom. Yet the presence of the divine dimension does not eliminate the dynamics of human factors. Abraham was never a marionette created and dropped on the stage to dance without resistance when his strings were pulled. At all times he was a genuinely free human being who had to agonize over choices and run the risks of committing himself on the basis of unknown or uncertain outcomes. Above all things, Abraham, a free man, chose to live by faith.

The Bible clearly describes the human family to which Abraham belonged.[1] They were inhabitants of the city of Ur in the country of the Chaldeans. Abraham's name, given him by his father Terah, was Abram. His wife's name was Sarai. Terah, Abram, Sarai, and Lot (Abram's nephew and the son of his dead brother Haran) began a journey designed

---

[1]Genesis 11:10-32.

to take them finally to the land of Canaan, the territory at the eastern end of the Mediterranean Sea lying between the Sea of Galilee and the Dead Sea. On that journey Terah died in a place called Haran.

Abram was in Haran when, according to the story, he was approached by God and instructed to leave his home and journey to a land to be shown him by God.[2] The promise extended by God with the challenge was that He would make of Abram a great nation, blessing him with a name that would bless all the families of the earth. At the ripe age of seventy-five, then, Abram, together with Sarai and Lot, responded to the challenge and promise of God and departed from Haran.

Journeying with all their possessions from Haran, the pilgrims made their way to the land of Canaan, to a place called Shechem. And there, according to the story, in the midst of the Canaanites who occupied the land, God promised Abram that He would give the land to Abram and his descendants. In response, Abram built on that place an altar to the Lord. That was beginning of the claim which Jews make on that land today.

Lot, although a beloved nephew, was not an adequate substitute for a son. How could Abram truly be an "exalted father" when he had no children of his own? Not only was he growing old—approaching the mid-eighties—but Sarai was only ten years younger and supposedly barren. In a moment of magnanimity (which did not last indefinitely) Sarai decided that Abram should have a son, though it be by another woman. Therefore she presented her Egyptian maid, Hagar, to Abram for the purpose of his having intercourse with her. That part of the plan worked well. Hagar conceived by Abram and was quite pleased with herself. Unfortunately, Sarai developed feelings of inferiority, convinced that her maid was laughing at her infertility. Sarai took revenge by speaking so harshly to Hagar that she ran away. According to the story, however, God had great plans for the baby Hagar was carrying, so he convinced her to return to Abram and have her child born in his camp. In due time Hagar gave birth to a son who was named Ishmael, a significant person in Islamic tradition.

Again God appeared to Abram to make a promise that he would become a leader of many peoples. This time he made a contract, or covenant, with Abram. He asked Abram always to walk before God blameless. On his part, God instituted an outward sign as witness of the covenant. Every male in Abram's household, whether born or brought there, was to be circumcised. From that day on the operation would be the

---

[2]Genesis 12:1.

mark of every male descendant from Abraham (the new name for Abram) who was covered by the covenant of God. It is still required of Jews, although Christians do not require it as a part of their religion. God also changed the name of Sarai to "Sarah," and promised that nations would come from her.

Both Abraham and Sarah, on separate occasions, responded in a most natural way to the divine message that they would produce a son who would be the means of their becoming the parents of many peoples. Abraham was almost a hundred years old and Sarah was ninety. Moreover all physical signs associated with the child-bearing years had long ceased with Sarah. Laughter seemed to be the only appropriate response to the promise of a son to be born the next spring. But true to the promise, a son was born. And by the instructions of God he was named, for the doubting response of his parents, "Isaac" or "he who laughs."

The developing Isaac was a source of joy for Abraham, who gave a feast to celebrate the weaning of his son. Sarah had another concern. When she saw Ishmael and Isaac playing together, she was aware that they should not be equal in their father's house. Perhaps also remembering the humiliation she had felt during the time of Hagar's fertility and her own barrenness, she began prodding Abraham to cast Hagar and Ishmael out of the house. The children were no problem for Abraham and he was reluctant to take such a harsh action, for there was no place for the maid and her son to go. But Sarah would not be placated and eventually Abraham prepared to send away Hagar with Ishmael who was still a child. His most generous gesture was to start her out in the morning with a loaf of bread and a skin bag full of water.

The water did not last long in the desert and soon Hagar and Ishmael were at the point of death. Faced with the futility of struggle Hagar placed Ishmael under a bush and then moved some distance away, unable to bear the pathetic sight of her dying son. It appeared to be a dreadful end to a sad story. But again, according to the story, God had other plans and intervened to inform Hagar of them. God opened the eyes of Hagar and showed her a well of water. She managed to fill the water skin from the well and give her crying son a drink. They survived, living in the wilderness of Paran. In that setting Ishmael became an expert with the bow and arrow. When he was grown his mother found a wife for him from her own nation, the Egyptians. God had mighty plans for his son of Abraham for it was through him that the Arabs in Muhammed's time traced their lineage to Abraham. The Bible of the Jews recognized that role of leadership for Ishmael.

The heart-tugging story of Hagar and Ishmael is, in some ways perhaps, exceeded by an episode involving Abraham and Isaac. God came to Abraham and directed him to take his son Isaac to the land of Moriah and offer him as a burnt offering on a mountain which God would choose. As the Danish philosopher Kierkegaard pointed out so dramatically in his book *Fear and Trembling*, this experience must have been excruciatingly painful for the patriarch.[3] Since the death of his father Haran, Abraham had followed the directions of God with an exemplary measure of faith, trusting him alone in nearly all major decisions of his life. Now he had a son who could make it possible for him to become, literally, the father of many nations. For the God who gave him Isaac to direct him to offer the child back as a sacrifice burned on a mountain altar must have torn at the heart and mind of Abraham as he plodded three days to the site chosen by God. Yet, even in this circumstance Abraham trusted God and had the lad carry the wood for the sacrifice on his back as father and son made their way to the mountain top. There Abraham bound Isaac and placed him on a stone altar, surrounding his body with wood, and raised the sacrificial knife to end the life of his son. At that moment something totally unexpected happened. God told him to halt. God then knew that Abraham was faithful to him in all things, for he had passed the test of faith. God allowed Abraham to substitute for Isaac a ram which had been caught by his horns in a thicket. Isaac was freed, and God again renewed his blessings to Abraham, promising him descendants as numerous as the stars of the heavens and as the sand of the shore. Moreover, he promised that Abraham's descendants would possess the gates of their enemies. The drama ended with Abraham and Isaac returning to dwell in Beersheba.

When Sarah died at the age of a hundred-and-twenty-seven, Abraham thought that he did not have much more time himself, and there were two things yet to be done. The first was to acquire for all time a permanent burial ground for his deceased wife and, eventually, for himself. He was careful not to accept from the Hittites a gift of the plot he wanted, the cave of Machpelah owned by Ephron son of Zohar. He insisted on paying its fair market value, in weight four hundred shekels of silver, to Ephron in front of Hittite witnesses. The story is explicit that it was a binding legal contract and not a temporary loan of convenience among friends. The second thing was to find a proper wife for Isaac, to carry on his lineage.

---

[3]Soren Kierkegaard, *Fear and Trembling and Sickness Unto Death*, translated by Walter Lowrie (Princeton: Princeton University Press), 1954.

Abraham did not leave the important matter of choosing a wife to Isaac. Instead, he commissioned one of his servants to carry out the search and commitment. Above all things, the servant had to promise not to take a bride for Isaac from the Canaanites. Instead, he was to go to the land of the Chaldeans in order to find, if at all possible, among Abraham's people, a daughter who would make a suitable bride. In a beautiful romance the story relates how the servant came to choose the industrious and beneficent daughter of Bethuel, the son of Abraham's brother Nahor. Thus the bride carefully chosen for Isaac, with the help of divine guidance, was the grand niece of Abraham, the second cousin of Isaac. Rebekah, the favored one, returned with Abraham's servant to the land where Isaac was dwelling. He took her to his tent, and she became his wife, giving him comfort after the death of his mother.

Abraham, it turned out, was a long way from being dead, and he married another wife after the death of Sarah. Keturah bore him six sons. But in no way did they share in the inheritance of Abraham. Abraham left everything to Isaac. When Abraham did die at the age of a hundred and seventy-five Isaac and Ishmael came together and buried their father with Sarah in Machpelah. The life of the patriarch whom the three major religions of the Western world regard as their father was closed.

What had Abraham accomplished? Perhaps most important of all he had established a covenant relationship with a particular God. He traveled through the land of Canaan stopping at Shechem and at Bethel, receiving promises from his God that He would give Abraham and his descendants the land. He produced two sons, one to carry on the family line of Jews and the other to be regarded by the Arabs as their ancestor. (Ishmael will be met again in the story of the Arabs.) Abraham lived by faith in God long before Moses was given the Ten Commandments, a fact which centuries later endeared him to the Christian, Paul.

The story of the Jews continued through Isaac and Rebekah who produced twin sons, Jacob and Esau. Esau was a carefree, athletic boy whose outdoors life won the approval of his father. Jacob led a more cerebral life, remaining close to the tent and carefully calculating the future with the help of Rebekah, who conspired with him against his father and his brother. The story makes clear that Esau set very little value on the birthright which would have given him his father's worldly goods and position of leadership in the family, for in a moment of hunger he lightly traded it to his brother for a bowl of stew. Jacob then only had to find a way to get his father to award the birthright to him. With the alliance of his mother, he fastened hairy skins to his arms so that Isaac, who was blind in his old age, would think that he was touching his elder, robust son. The trick worked; Isaac bestowed his blessing on Jacob, leaving nothing for Esau. So Jacob, the man with a clever mind, ascended to a key place in the family tree of the Jews.

Jacob also took his wife, or wives, not from the land of the Canaanites, but from Paddan-aram, the land of Laban, Rebekah's brother. The quest proved to be a long one, however, for in Laban Jacob met a man almost as clever as himself. He first had to serve Laban seven years for the daughter he loved, Rachel. But at the end of the seven years he was tricked into consummating marriage with Leah, the more homely elder daughter. Laban then let him have Rachel, the pretty one, but Jacob had to serve seven more years for her. Jacob next had to serve six years in order to obtain his own flocks with which to support his wives and children.

Jacob was a rich man when he finally escaped Laban. Not only was he wealthy in flocks, but also he was abounding in wives and children. He had Rachel and Leah as wives, and he had a maid of each of them, Zilpah from Leah and Bilhah from Rachel. Among the four women he produced the twelve sons who were regarded as the twelve patriarchs of the twelve tribes of Israel, another name for Jacob. The sons of Leah were Reuben, Simeon, Levi, Judah, Issachar, and Zebulun. The sons of Rachel were Joseph and Benjamin. The sons of Bilhah, Rachel's maid, were Dan and Naphtali. The sons of Zilpah, Leah's maid, were Gad and Asher. All of these sons were born to Jacob in the land of Paddan-aram.

His final escape from Laban closed a chapter in Jacob's life, but he was filled with anxiety as he opened a new chapter in returning to Canaan. Esau was there. Not knowing what Esau had in store for him and taking no chances, Jacob placed his flocks, his wives, and his children ahead of himself and his favorite wife, Rachel, as the entourage moved into Canaan. However, Jacob had nothing to fear, for Esau ran to meet Jacob and welcomed him as a recovered brother. In time Jacob came also to Isaac at Mamre. When the old man died at age 180, both his sons together buried him before they went their separate ways to graze their flocks. As God had changed the name of Abram to "Abraham" to signify a covenant relationship, so he changed the name of Jacob to "Israel." It was a name that would later be applied to his descendants.

The geographical location which was sacred to Jacob was Bethel: God had appeared to him there to extend him a blessing while he was fleeing from his brother Esau. Now God called him there again and renewed the covenant relationship which had begun with Abraham. Jacob made everyone in his household get rid of all foreign gods and earrings, which he hid at Shechem. He set up a stone pillar at Bethel as a memorial to God's speaking to him, promising him that he would become a great nation and receive the land in which they dwelled. Who was this special God? Throughout history in Judaism and Christianity he has been referred to as *the God of Abraham, Isaac, and Jacob.*

The remainder of the story of Jacob centers around one of his sons, Joseph, a young man who dreamed dreams and lived to see them come true.[4] Sold into slavery in Egypt by his jealous brothers, Joseph became manager of the household of Potiphar. Accused of rape by Potiphar's wife, Joseph endured prison until he was reprieved for interpreting a dream of the pharaoh predicting famine. Joseph was placed in the powerful position at the head of Egyptian agriculture and stored tremendous amounts of food for emergency use. The famine which did arrive also brought his hungry brothers from their land to Egypt. Joseph gave them food and eventually revealed himself as their brother. Israel and his children moved to Egypt with the pharaoh's blessing and established their people in the land of Goshen. They were to remain as honored guests until the overthrow of that group of pharaohs and the coming to power of people who knew not Joseph and his great works for Egypt.

What of the promises of God to Abraham to give him and his descendants the land of Canaan? Establishing a people in Egypt under the protection of the Egyptian monarch may seem to some an unwelcome digression. To the Hebrews, however, it was an essential part of the preparation of the children of Israel which would be furthered under another great leader, Moses.

One might readily admit that Genesis relates an interesting story, full of entertaining episodes. Yet there are questions that come to mind. Is it true? In what sense is it true? How does one know? Is there any way of verifying the story outside of the account itself?

One theory simplifies matters considerably. It holds that God dictated to Moses (who will be presented in the next chapter) the books of Genesis, Exodus, Leviticus, Numbers, and Deuteronomy. For that reason they are completely true and accurate even though some of the events occurred prior to the birth of Moses, such as the creation of the world, and some occurred after his death, such as the description of his death and the period of mourning which appears in Deuteronomy.[5] The world was created in six days and God literally rested on the seventh. Adam ate the forbidden fruit and was cast out of a geographical garden of Eden. The

---

[4]Genesis 37-50.

[5]Deuteronomy 34.

whole earth was flooded for 150 days, the only survivors being those in the Ark with Noah. A human woman, the wife of Lot, turned to a pillar of salt at the destruction of Sodom and Gomorrah. The "worldly" events are just as described, and so are the "heavenly" events, or those portraying the interaction of the divine with humans. The whole thing was dictated by God, who would not lie nor allow an error to creep into the account. That is one theory which has been long and widely held.

Another type of theory is considerably more difficult to live with even in its most simple forms. Yet even the reader who settles on the first view should be aware of the alternative. This theory is that the first five books of the Bible were completed in their present form around 400 B.C. by an editor (or editors) who was a priest of Israel. While he made necessary comments and interpretations to tell the story as he thought it should be told, he relied on at least three documents which previous editors had prepared.

Perhaps the oldest document used by the priestly editor was that of the Yahwist who used JHVH as the symbol for God in his account of the beginnings of things and the history of the Hebrews. The theoretical source of this line of stories is the "J" document, supposedly the edited work of a man who collected all sorts of legends about Israel and composed from them a history of epic proportions. It begins in Genesis 12:1 and continues through the call of Abraham and the story of Moses. It is the story of how God brought to fruition the promise to Abraham through the journey to the land of Canaan. His heroes are stately and strong, the way patriarchs should be thought of in a period of pastoral idealism.[6]

Some of the same history was available to the priestly editor from another document, known as the "E" document. In it the name used for God is "Elohim." It also begins with Abraham and continues through Moses. The author emphasizes the history of his people more than he does the guidance of God. Perhaps he has more priestly concerns, and uses a more classical form of Hebrew. One writer finds "E" characters more moved to outbursts of joy and sorrow than are the same characters in "J."

The "D" document is assumed by liberal scholars to have been composed in the seventh century B.C. and to have contained in legal code the insights of the eighth century prophets. It is the source of most of the

---

[6]Robert H. Pfeiffer, *Introduction to the Old Testament* (New York: Harper Brothers Publishers, 1948), chapter 2.

law codes which are contained in the first five books of the Bible, according to the scholars of the liberal tradition.

The weaving of "J," "E," and "D" into the present form was done by a priestly editor who inserted his own interpretations as well, according to those who hold to literary-historical criticism. This material they refer to as the "P" document. It brings together "J," "E," and "D" in a setting which establishes correct dates, periods of time, proper order, cataloging of details, persons, and definitions. It contains the careful codification of a priestly mind who places everything within the context of theology. Presumably this material was composed after the Babylonian captivity.

According to followers of literary-historical criticism, this theory of editing several documents explains several problems one sometimes meets in reading the Bible. One example is that there appear to be two stories of the creation. Elsewhere there seem to be duplications with slightly different versions of the same events. For those who know the ancient languages, there is the evidence of more than one name for God. For some it also seems to be the proper explanation of why the laws of Exodus and Deuteronomy are more appropriate to a settled, urban society rather than to that of the nomads in the time of Moses.

However, there has been some return to conservatism in recent years even by people who in general hold the literary-historical criticism approach to the development of the Pentateuch. Essentially their position is that some of the early scholars went too far in identifying ever more documents on rather self-fulfilling hypotheses. They are also inclined to assign more historical value to the stories than did some of the earlier scholars, who definitely doubted that there was an historical Abraham. Some had doubted that there was a figure in history such as Moses.

In the extreme, nothing was regarded as being reliable history until the time of King David, when there was a contemporary written record of events. Some who hold the general theory of literary-historical criticism now believe that the Abraham and Moses stories are portraits of real men of history, no more distorted than other people's accounts of their own national heroes and forefathers—although they are probably no more accurate either. They believe that the writings were done for religious purposes and thus were under the inspiration of belief in the God they describe. They further believe that outside documents and archeological evidence support some of the account as it stands and that in absence of strong evidence to the contrary, the material should be accepted as representing truth as the writers were best able to know it.

Which theory the reader prefers to hold makes little difference so far as the rest of the work in this introduction is concerned. The writer attempts to present the literature of the religions as it stands in present form, for one must know it in that form before one can do anything about applying either theory of its origin. Regardless of its origin the literature does exist, it has been believed to have extraordinary merit, and it has had profound influence in developing the literature, art, music, values, laws, governments and vocations of the peoples of the West.

SUGGESTIONS FOR ADDITIONAL READING

Albright, W. F. *Archeology and the Religion of Israel*. Baltimore: The John Hopkins Press, 1968.

Albright, W. F. *Archeology, Historical Analogy, and Early Biblical Tradition*. Baton Rouge: Louisiana State University Press, 1966.

Anderson, Bernard W. *Understanding the Old Testament*. Englewood Cliffs, N. J.: Prentice Hall, Inc., 1957; pp. 1-26.

Anderson, G. W. *A Critical Introduction to the Old Testament*. London: Gerald Duckworth and Co., Ltd., 1959.

Burrows, Millar. *What Mean These Stones?* London: Meridian Books, 1957.

Delury, G. E. *The World Almanac and Book of Facts, 1980*. New York: Newspaper Enterprise Association, Inc., 1979.

Eichrodt, Walter. *Theology of the Old Testament*. Translated by J. A. Baker. Philadelphia: Westminster Press, 1967.

Finegan, Jack. *Light from the Ancient Past*. Princeton: Princeton University Press, 1946.

Kierkegaard, Sören. *Fear and Trembling and Sickness Unto Death*. Translated by Walter Lowrie. Princeton: Princeton University Press, 1954.

Noth, Martin. *The Old Testament World*. Translated by Victor Gruhn. Philadelphia: Fortress Press, 1966.

Oesterley, W. O. E. and Robinson, T. H. *Hebrew Religion*. London: S. P. C. K., 1955.

Pfeiffer, Robert H. *Introduction to the Old Testament*. New York: Harper and Brothers, 1948.

Rowley, H. H. *From Joseph to Joshua*. London: Oxford University Press, 1950.

Rowley, H. H. *The Old Testament in Modern Study*. Oxford: The Clarendon Press, 1951.

Van Seters, John. *Abraham in History and Tradition*. New Haven: Yale University Press, 1975.

Wright, G. Ernest, editor. *The Bible and the Ancient Near East*. New York: Doubleday and Company, Inc., 1961.

CHAPTER 2

MOSES

In order to appreciate the love and hate relationship between Egypt and Israel in modern times, one should know not only the life of Joseph but also the life of his desendants. For a sharp turn of events in Egypt left an indelible impression on Judaism down to the present day.

The beautiful life of the children of Israel during the time of Joseph was dependent upon the favor of a beneficent Pharaoh who looked upon them as allies in the land of Goshen. With the passing of that line of pharaohs, probably with the expulsion of the Hyksos, the fortunes of the Israelites changed dramatically. An Egyptian who had expelled the foreign rulers quite naturally looked with suspicion upon other foreigners within his borders, and that was especially true of the Israelites who had enjoyed favor under the foreign pharaohs. Besides a normal dislike for friends of former enemies, the Egyptians saw the possibility that should a conflict arise with foreign powers the Israelites, living within their borders, could turn on the Egyptians and join their enemies. Moreover, the Israelites were multiplying rapidly and requiring more territory.[1]

They were manpower, nevertheless, and properly harnessed they could provide labor which would strengthen Egypt. Of course slave labor was the cheapest of all. So it was easy for the Egyptians to solve their security problem and their economic problem by making the Israelites

---

[1] Exodus 1.

their slaves. The public work to which they were assigned was the building of the store cities of Pithom and Ramses. The new life was a great shock to the Israelites who found servitude extremely bitter. Indeed, the pharaoh and his taskmakers saw to it that labor was not the bitterest part of their lives.

Population control was also instituted, according to the story. Midwives who served the Israelites were instructed by the Egyptians to destroy all male infants of the Israelites upon birth. Females of the Israelite infants were to be saved. The purpose of the program is not made clear but the way seemed open to produce a body of slaves of mixed ancestry. Nevertheless the program was of limited success since the Israelite mothers learned to manage without midwives. The directive to destroy male children remained in force, however, and once a male was discovered his life was in danger.

Moses, an infant of three months, was in peril of losing his life. He was born the son of a father and mother belonging to the tribe of Levi, parents who cared for him but who could no longer hide him among his people with any hope of saving his life. So his mother took a great step of faith with hope that some way to spare her infant son would occur. She made a basket, waterproofed it, placed the infant in it, and then put the basket in the river amongst the reeds. The fate of the child was to be observed by his sister, who hid by the river.

The future of Israel hinged on who would find the baby and how soon. The results could not have been better, for it was the pharaoh's own daughter who found the child while she was bathing in the river. Hearing his cries, she took pity on the Hebrew boy and decided to save him. His sister was right on the scene offering to find a Hebrew woman to nurse the child. Pharaoh's daughter agreed and the mother of Moses was brought to nurse him. Not only was he safe, raised as the child of Pharaoh's daughter, but also he was under the love and guidance of his own mother who kept him aware of his Hebrew heritage.

It was his consciousness of his Hebrew roots which cost Moses his place of safety before Pharaoh. When he was grown, Moses saw an Egyptian beating a Hebrew. Checking quickly to see whether there were other witnesses, Moses stepped in and killed the Egyptian. However, either there was a witness he did not see or the rescued Hebrew described the way he was delivered, for on the next day when Moses tried to referee a fight between two Hebrews, one of them asked Moses whether he intended to kill him as he had killed the Egyptian. Moses realized that his deed was known and that the pharaoh sought his life. Moses had to flee the country to remain alive. He was an outlaw, wanted in Egypt for the murder of the Egyptian.

In the desert of Midian there was safety and, in time, comfort. At the customary meeting place, a well where flocks were watered, Moses came to the defense of the seven daughters of Reuel, a priest, and helped them water their flock without their having to wait until last after all the men had watered their animals. When the story was related to Reuel, Moses was invited into his home to stay. One thing led to another and in time Moses married Zipporah, one of the seven daughters. They had a son whom he named Gershom. Moses had established a comfortable life which he could have continued until the end of his days.

God, the story relates, had other ideas. One day as Moses was keeping the flocks of his father-in-law he came to Horeb, the mountain of God. There he saw a bush that appeared to be burning, yet it was not consumed.[2] God addressed him and asked him to come closer. In the dramatic conversation which followed God revealed himself as "I Am," the same deity who was known to Abraham as El Shaddai. He asked Moses to return to Egypt and lead the Hebrews out of captivity and into His service in a land that had been promised to them. Moses, of course, thought of several good reasons why he should not comply. But God established the brother of Moses, Aaron, as his spokesman to assist him in his efforts to convince the pharaoh to free the Hebrew slaves. Finally, Moses accepted the challenge, and leaving his father-in-law, he took his wife and son and returned to Egypt. The pharaoh who had sought his life had died, so the risk of immediate punishment was lessened.

The story is clear: the whole drama which led up the release of the Hebrews from Egypt was written by God and merely played out by Moses and the pharaoh. It took a series of ten plagues and battles of magic between the God of Moses and the priests of the pharaoh before the point was driven home that Pharaoh also was under the power of God and had to free the Hebrews because that was the will of God.

The last of the ten plagues is of great importance for it has become a perpetual memorial for the Jews everywhere and in all times. It was the forerunning event of the Feast of Passover, when the angel of the lord killed all first-born sons and cattle of the Egyptians but passed over the houses of the Hebrews whose doorposts and lintels had been marked with the blood of a carefully selected lamb. On that night the Hebrews ate roasted flesh and unleavened bread with bitter herbs. They memorialized their bitter service in Egypt and their sudden and miraculous deliverance by their God. They were ready to leave in the morning, taking not only

---

[2]Exodus 3.

[3]Exodus 7-13.

their own possessions but also rich presents which they had requested of the Egyptians. The Egyptians wanted them to leave in a hurry and were eager to give them whatever it took to get them moving out of their country.

The journey of the Hebrews was continuously led and defended by their God who went before them in a pillar of cloud by day and a pillar of fire by night. But no other incident has captured the imaginations of other peoples as the story of the crossing of the Red Sea.[4] Whether it was really the Sea of Reeds and the original episode was a natural phenomenon of winds and tides not understood by Hebrews seems of little importance, for the story is told to magnify the power of God who manifested himself in delivering the Hebrews and destroying the Egyptians. The Egyptians drove the Hebrews to the very edge of the sea, where God directed Moses to stretch out his hand over the sea. He did and a strong east wind blew back the waters until the Hebrews who numbered , according to the story, six hundred thousand men plus women and children could cross safely on dry ground. Then, the Hebrews having crossed safely, the waters flowed together over the pursuing Egyptian chariots and soldiers. The sea consumed the horses and the riders. The victory scene was captured in a song attributed to Miriam, the sister of Moses and Aaron, as she danced, beating a timbrel and reciting:

Sing to the Lord, for he has triumphed
gloriously; the horse and his rider he
has thrown into the sea. (Exodus 15:21)

The logistics of caring for so many men, women, and children could have broken most men standing alone, for the Hebrews in the wilderness were like travelers of most ages: they exercised their rights to criticize the accommodations which their travel guide had arranged for them. Moses was able to endure because, according to the story, God gave him help with food and drink. God told him where and how to obtain water and provided a bread substitute, manna, which could be gathered on the prior day. He also provided meat in the form of quail. The scholars who take a natural view of things explain that the manna still occurs in the desert, produced by insects on plant life at night. The quail are exhausted from flying across the desert and are easily caught. A person who has lived in the desert for some time, as Moses did, would know where to find water. But the story that comes in the Bible makes it plain that the provisions were from God.

---

[4]Exodus 14.

It was in the season of the third new moon after leaving Egypt that Moses and the Hebrews came to the wilderness and mountain of Sinai. The time had come for the Hebrews to meet the God of Moses for the purpose of establishing a covenant relationship with him. It took them three days to wash their clothes and to prepare themselves to come to the foot of the mountain which, even then, they could not touch, upon pain of death.

Not that many people would have wanted to venture upon the mountain, for on the third day the top of the mountain was covered with a thick cloud. There was thundering, lightning, and the blasting of a very loud trumpet. God appeared on the mountain in the form of fire and smoke. Moses spoke to God and God answered in thunder. Even the priests were not allowed to come upon the mountain, except for Aaron whom God invited to ascend with Moses.

According to the story the legal foundation for the Jewish people was given by God to Moses when he and Aaron ascended Mount Sinai. Since the whole relationship of God to Israel from that time on has been based on the law and since it has endured into modern times in countries of Jews and Christians, it is worthwhile to see what has been reported as the requirements of God for his people. In Exodus 20 one finds the Ten Commandments, respected by Christians as well as Jews. Other laws which are not so fundamental as the ten commandments but which played an important part in the life of the Hebrews and have influenced the making of laws in Christian lands as well, were also given. Many of the laws in predominantly Christian countries show the influence of the Law of Moses.

Slavery was practiced by the Hebrews, even upon their own kind. Nevertheless, it had limits. A Hebrew could keep another Hebrew as a slave only six years; the seventh year he had to be set free. A female Hebrew sold to a male Hebrew had to be treated fairly as a concubine or set free. Should one destroy an eye or tooth of a slave, the slave should be set free. The poor also were protected by a provision that if they gave their garment in pledge for a loan, the garment had to be returned to them at night, prior to sundown, for how else would a poor person sleep on a cold night?

The penalties for certain crimes were severe. Capital punishment was called for in murder by one who had killed after lying in wait for his victim, for anyone guilty of kidnapping, for anyone cursing either of his parents, for anyone blaspheming God, for anyone having sex with a beast, or for anyone sacrificing to another God, or for anyone practicing sorcery.

In other cases, one was to make restitution for any damage caused by himself, or by his acts, or by his possessions, such as oxen. The restitution was usually equal to the amount of the loss. The limiting and guiding principle was "an eye for an eye and a tooth for a tooth." In another circumstance it was a life for a life. Payment had to be made but unlimited revenge was prohibited. Thieves, however, were to pay four or five times for the value stolen and if they could not pay they were to be sold into servitude to pay the debt.

Compassion was to be shown because God is compassionate. The poor, strangers, widows and orphans, lost animals, even those belonging to one's enemy, and seduced virgins were all singled out by name as those to whom Hebrews were expected to show mercy. The same concept can be found in Christianity and in Islam.

Instructions for the worship of God were presented as essential for establishing the people of God. God was interested in ritual as well as in law and ethics. Since the Hebrews were nomads traveling in the wilderness, the instructions for ritual life had to take that mobile life into consideration. Everything was to be portable, including the tabernacle or tent for God.

At some time the nomads would have to leave Sinai in order to enter Canaan, the promised land. How, then, would conversations with God be arranged? The answer was that a wooden box, covered with gold and appropriately carved, known as the ark, would become the symbol for the presence of God with his people. Although it did not contain a graven image of God it may have been received as a throne upon which he was invisibly present. It was, according to the directions of God in the story, to be made with lifting rings and carrying poles so that it could be carried in processions.

The ark and other furniture, such as table, lampstand, laver, and altar were designed to go with a portable house of God, the tabernacle. It was to serve the Hebrews until the reign of King Solomon when they would succeed in building a permanent temple. Perhaps other Semites had similar tents, but this one became a symbol of Israel's God tenting with his people both when they traveled and when they rested. Its size, while not large enough to assemble 600,000 men, was adequate to accommodate Aaron and the priests of Israel. Its quality of materials and work of artisans was as high as one could well imagine for a people migrating from slavery to a permanent home.

Moses realized some time before his death that God would not allow him to enter the land across the Jordan river. It was his duty to prepare and dedicate to God his associate, Joshua. God then commissioned Joshua as the successor of Moses when the two met with him in the tent of meeting. In spite of the fact that he still had a strong voice and a clear vision, Moses prepared to die in his 120th year. Although God would not permit him to enter Canaan, because Moses had failed to follow God's instructions in the wilderness of Zin at the waters of Meribathkadesh, Moses was allowed to reach the land of Moab and Mount Nebo. From the top of the mountain he could look across the Jordan into Jericho and see the land of Canaan, which his people would finally possess under Joshua. Moses died and was buried in Moab, but the story says that no man knows the place of his burial.

One can generally accept the story of Moses as illustrative of what later Hebrews thought was important about their development as a nation. There is no major problem in regarding Moses as a very good human leader of a group migrating from Egypt to Canaan. Nor is there a major problem in accepting that he led his people into the land of Midian where he introduced them to a god who was to be their particular champion. One can accept that a particular law code was imposed on the Israelites during that period; however, there is no problem in saying that not all the law reported as coming from that period was enforced at that time. The difficulty is that some of the laws reported at that period of nomadic wandering actually reflect, according to many scholars, the life of a people settled in a country and engaged in agriculture. Since such a style of life came to the Israelites only after they had invaded and established themselves in Canaan, the laws make more sense if they are interpreted as coming from that period. A more conservative position might argue that the laws were given in the nomadic period with the understanding that they would be applied once the Israelites had settled into farm life in Canaan.

The story of Moses, as it stands, is written to show the power of God working in history through individuals and through a congregation of people in order to fulfill his purposes in history. The mighty works of the plagues and the crossing of the sea ahead of the Egyptians are described so as to give vivid support to the idea of God entering history and nature to accomplish his purposes. This was the purpose of the priestly editor, and attempts to get back to the events behind the oral tradition, earlier written accounts, and J or E documents can only lead to speculation. What one can be sure of is that one has an account of what some priests of the Jews thought to be important around the fifth century B.C. Both liberals and conservatives can agree on that conclusion.

SUGGESTIONS FOR ADDITIONAL READING

Commentaries on the Books of Exodus, Leviticus, and
Numbers

Auerbach, Elias. *Moses*. Detroit: Wayne State University Press,
1975.

Buber, Martin. *Moses: The Revelation and the Covenant.* New York:
Harper Torch Books, 1958.

Daiches, David. *Moses: The Man and His Vision.* New York:
Praeger Publishers, 1975.

Pearlman, Moshe. *Moses*. New York: Abelard-Scheman, 1974.

Roshwald, Mordecai and Miriam. *Moses: Leader, Prophet, Man.*
New York: Thomas Yoseloff, 1969.

CHAPTER 3

JOSHUA

The Children of Israel believed that the land before them was the land promised to them by the covenant. Abraham had settled in it; God had freed them from the Egyptians so that they could repossess what he had already given them. To their way of thinking, the Canaanites who occupied the cities in the land were squatters who had to go. Something of the same idea was revived by Jews in the twentieth century when they faced Arabs in that land.

Joshua was less as a spiritual leader than Moses had been, and something more as a military leader. His outstanding success in conquering a foothold in the land of Canaan for his people comes from two sources, according to the book of Joshua. He was a capable military leader of strong fighting men, and the mighty power of God was with him in a special way. His role was to lead the Israelites across the Jordan river and to take the fortified city of Jericho. To do so, he utilized both his military and his religious leadership.[1]

Without diminishing the religious element in the capture of Jericho, it is worthwhile to note the very effective psychological warfare practiced by the Israelites against the besieged city. One can imagine the fear of the people of Jericho as they looked out over their city wall to see the fierce nomads from the desert who were encamped against them. How were they to explain the strange procession which occurred once every day for

---

[1]Joshua.

six days? First there was an armed guard. Then there were seven priests blowing seven rams' horns. Not another person in the procession spoke a word or made a sound. Then came the ark of the covenant, the symbol of the presence of the Israelite God. Then came a rear guard of warriors. The strange procession circled the walls once and then returned to the Israelite camp. What did it mean? What would come next?

The seventh day gave the answer to the question which had been building all week. The procession went around once, as it had for six days, but that was not the end. It went around a second time, a third, a fourth,and so on, until it had completed seven circuits. Then, with a mighty shout, the Israelites broke their silence and turned toward the walls. The walls of the city fell with a crash! The encircling army marched straight ahead, advancing every man toward the center of the circle. Nothing escaped their advance, except the apartment of Rahab. Every man, every woman, every child, and every animal was slaughtered. The warriors did not seize plunder for themselves but placed all valuables collected into a common treasury. Then the city was put to the torch. Nothing was left standing. With the exception of Rahab and her family, who were taken into the Israelite camp as a reward for helping Israelite spies, the city and everything in it was offered to the God of the Israelites.

Gradually the Israelites spread their camps northward through the highlands of Canaan. Some people became their servants; others became their enemies. After the death of Joshua the centralized leadership weakened and the various tribes became almost self-governing units. When they were of equal strength with their Canaanite neighbors, interchange of ideas became normal, and Israelite nomads learned from their more settled neighbors how to farm. They also learned how to call upon the Canaanite deities who were credited with making the crops grow. It was difficult to maintain the purity of Israelite worship according to the teachings of Moses under those circumstances.

Where the Israelites were weaker than their neighbors they suffered periodic raids upon their livestock and their fields. Any comforts they developed were usually short-lived for incidents of humiliation were all too common. The later historians writing about the period had a formula they used to describe the cycles of pleasure and the cycles of oppression. When the Israelites did what was evil in the sight of God by worshipping the Canaanite gods, or Baals, God allowed them to be chastened by foreign oppressors. Then when the people had enough and cried unto God for deliverance, he would raise up a strong man or woman to champion a band of warriors and deliver the Israelites from their oppressors. Safe again, the Israelites would once more sink into Baal worship. The cycle was repeated over and over.

The deliverers, known as judges, were a varied lot of individuals with assorted talents and limitations. None was of the stature of a Moses or a Joshua, yet each was a folk hero around whom grew up tales which extolled virtues prized not only by the early settlers in Canaan, but also by their succeeding generations. They had to make do until a stronger central government could be formed. One might compare them to the frontier heroes who settled the American West.

In passing we note the following: Deborah, a woman judge, used a male general Barak to defeat Sisera and his iron chariots. Sisera in turn was killed in his sleep by another woman, Jael. Gideon, by carefully selecting his troops and applying psychology, routed the Midianites in their own camp with a daring night raid. Samson, the strong man, went through a long series of physical and mental contests with the Philistines, and in his dying act "brought down the house."[2]

In theory the government of the tribes of Israel was a theocracy, that is, a kingdom ruled directly by God. It was the model later preferred by Calvin and by Calvinists in America and it has recently interested some Shiite Muslims of Iran. While theocracy made theological sense in Israel, politically it left something to be desired in visible leadership. God had ruled in the past through a Moses or a Joshua and the unity was visible. In the period of the judges such strong spiritual personalities were not found. It continued after a fashion in the person of Eli at Shiloh although he was not a particularly strong character and his sons, Hophni and Phinehas, who were the priests of the sanctuary, were morally corrupt.

The next strong religious leader was Samuel. The story of how he was born late in the life of a childless woman, Hannah, and subsequently dedicated to service in the sanctuary at Shiloh soon after he was weaned is one which has often been a favorite with mothers and their children. Samuel was well seasoned by the time Eli died, after learning of the tragic loss of the ark of the covenant to the Philistines during a battle with them and after learning of the death of his two sons. Samuel judged Israel all of his life, circuit-riding between Bethel, Gilgal, Mizpah and his home in Ramah. Under his leadership, the Philistines were removed from the land and the ark of the covenant, which had caused plagues among the Philistines during its captivity among them, was returned to Israel. But as was his predecessor, Eli, Samuel was cursed with sons who were immoral, in this instance taking bribes.[3]

---

[2]Judges.

[3]I Samuel.

The people of Israel had not found the theocracy satisfactory for the human representatives of God had not measured up to the standards they felt necessary in order for them to hold their own against other nations who had strong kings to lead them. There was mounting pressure upon Samuel to make a king for Israel. It was an idea displeasing to Samuel and, the story says, also to God, for it was a sign of lack of faith in God. But with God's permission Samuel relented and selected a king for Israel, sure that the people would soon discover that a human king could make life miserable for them.

The candidate Samuel chose to be the first king of Israel certainly had the physical appearance for the role. It was said that there was not a man in Israel more handsome than he and from the shoulders up he was taller than other men. Moreover, he was the son of a wealthy Benjaminite named Kish. But the story plainly reports that God brought Saul and Samuel together. So Samuel anointed Saul king.

Saul was a stern and practical leader of his troops, pushing them to their limits and rewarding them in times of victory. His son, however, was just as successful in battle and so beloved by the troops that on at least one occasion they defended him against his father for disobeying orders. The stern side of Saul gradually deepened into a depression which decreased his effectiveness as a king. He failed to keep the religious directives of Samuel by doing his own sacrificing, by allowing men to eat blood with their meat, and by allowing them to take livestock of the Amalekites as booty for themselves when Samuel had told him that God commanded that every living thing be destroyed. While Saul looked for a way to soothe his troubled mind, Samuel looked for a king to replace Saul.

Saul found a skilled player of the lyre who was able to calm his mind with music when he was beset by depression. He was David, the son of Jesse, from the region of Bethlehem. The youngest of eight sons, he served as a shepherd for the flocks of his aged father. He immediately won the friendship and love of both Saul and Jonathan. As it turned out, David had another talent besides playing the harp and composing the poetry of the shepherd.

On one occasion when the Philistines and the Israelites faced off in opposing lines ready for battle, the Philistines issued a challenge to the Israelites. Why not have them choose a champion to represent their side and let him take on their champion, Goliath? Goliath, a giant of a man in heavy armor, stood out in front of his line and taunted the Israelites to send some men against him. None of the regular soldiers responded. According to a very popular story, David agreed to take on the Philistine giant, reasoning that he could not be any worse than the lion or the bear he had killed while protecting his father's sheep. When Saul's armor would not fit him well enough so that he could be confident in battle, David removed it and chose instead his customary instrument of destruction with the flock—a mere slingshot and some stones. Practically naked he stepped forth to face Goliath.

Goliath sneered at David for being a youth and coming at him with implements for chasing dogs, not fighting a Philistine champion. David said that he came with the blessings of the Lord to demonstrate that there is a God in Israel. David needed only one shot. His sling sent the stone deep into the forehead of Goliath, and the giant fell to the ground. David ran forward, took Goliath's sword, and chopped off the head of the Philistine. The fall of the Philistine champion marked the beginning of a fabulous rise to success for David.

David, who could have become the third person of a powerful troika to lead the armies of Israel, was in the eyes of the ailing king Saul a threat to be destroyed. But Saul's son Jonathan could not do enough for his friend David. The troops also regarded him as their champion. The women at home mentioned the exploits of Saul but they sang the praises of David even higher. Saul became sicker by the day and wasted his energies in pursuing David over the countryside, seeking to kill him. David, with respect for Saul, tried to stay out of his way. The last thing he wanted to do was to defeat Saul.

At last the Philistines ended Saul's problem for him. In a battle which ranged to Mount Gilboa the Israelite soldiers were in full retreat before the Philistine. Jonathan and two of his brothers were killed. Archers so wounded Saul that he committed suicide. The Philistines beheaded Saul and hanged his body on the city wall of Bethshan along with the bodies of his three sons.

David's persecutor was dead and he survived as the most popular leader of Israel. But there was no joy in David. He had not desired any harm for Saul. In the death of Jonathan he had lost his closest friend. He was in deep grief. One of the finest pieces of poetry in the Bible is David's lament over Saul and Jonathan which begins "Thy glory, O Israel, is slain upon thy high places!" and ends "How are the mighty fallen, and the weapons of war perished."[4]

Israel was ready for a second king.

---

[4]II Samuel 1:19-27.

SUGGESTIONS FOR ADDITIONAL READING

Commentaries on the Books of Joshua, Judges,
I and II Samuel.

Deen, Edith. *All of the Women of the Bible.* New York: Harper Brothers, 1955.

Morton, H. V. *Women of the Bible.* New York: Dodd, Mead, and Company, 1943.

CHAPTER 4

DAVID

"David" is a name greatly honored in Judaism and in Christianity. David is a model of a layman who devotes his talents to the service of his God and the people of God. For many generations he has been a symbol of the strong deliverer blessed by God to free his people from unjust oppression.

David eventually became the next king of the Hebrews. Upon the death of Saul the commander of Saul's army, Abner, had Saul's son Ishbosheth declared king.[1] But the men of Judah anointed David as king and thus divided the kingdom of Saul. David and Ishbosheth did not contend person to person for control, but the struggle waged back and forth between Abner and Joab, the commanders of their armies. These commanders were politically powerful: the kings themselves could scarcely overrule their decisions. David's opposition was eliminated by Abner's joining David when Ishbosheth made the mistake of reprimanding Abner for taking one of Saul's concubines as a lover. David promised Abner safety. But Joab, David's commander, had not been a party to the agreement, so without David's knowledge Joab killed Abner. David reigned at Hebron seven-and-a-half years and over all of Israel and Judah at Jerusalem for thirty-three years.

Gradually David established security in the land of Israel and Judah. He engaged the Philistines and pushed them back so that they were no

---

[1]II Samuel 2.

longer the scourge of Israel as they had been in the days of the judges. With the help of carpenters and cedar trees provided by Hiram, king of Tyre, David built a house in Jerusalem. He gathered more concubines and wives so that he could enlarge his family. He had the ark of the covenant brought into Jerusalem and he personally danced in the procession to the accompaniment of music and the praise of the women of Jerusalem. An orderly kingdom seemed to be in hand.

David exercised a privilege of the king in such a way as to draw wrath upon himself from his respected prophet, Nathan. David was entranced by Bathsheba, the wife of a soldier in his army, so he had her brought to the palace for an afternoon of pleasure. In due time, she informed David that she was going to have a child. To conceal what he had done from Bathsheba's husband, Uriah the Hittite, David gave Uriah a pass home from the army so that he could spend a night with Bathsheba. Uriah, however, was a dedicated soldier and refused to stay with his wife when his friends were in battle. After several attempts to persuade Uriah to visit his wife, David gave up and sent him back to the army with a message to Joab. The secret message instructed Joab to place Uriah at the front of the battle and then suddenly withdraw, leaving him alone and exposed to the enemy. The plan worked and Uriah the Hittite was killed. Bathsheba went into the proper period of mourning for her slain husband. When that duty was over, David sent for Bathsheba and made her his wife.

The marriage, however, was far from the end of the matter. Nathan the prophet went in to the king and told him a story about a poor man who had a pet lamb which lived with his family. A certain rich man, when he needed to prepare a meal for a traveler, did not take from his own vast flocks but forceably took the ewe lamb from the poor man and served it as food. David immediately saw the injustice in the story and pronounced judgment, "As the Lord lives,the man who has done this deserves to die; and he shall restore the lamb fourfold, because he did this thing, and because he had no pity."[2] The stature of Nathan in the eyes of the king is attested to by his courage in saying to David, "You are the man. . . ."[3] Not only that, but Nathan continued to declare the curse that God would send on the house of David for taking Uriah's wife and for having Uriah killed. In conclusion he announced that the child conceived of the adultery would die.

---

[2] II Samuel 12:5, 6.

[3] II Samuel 12:7.

A series of tragedies then came upon the house of David. The child born of his relationship with Bathsheba did indeed die, although David spent almost a week in fasting and prayer in hopes that the child would be spared. For consolation he gave Bathsheba another son, who grew up to become the famous "Solomon." David's son, Amnon, raped David's daughter, Tamar, born of the same mother as Absalom. Absalom bided his time for two years and then had Amnon killed. Then Absalom fled to the king of Geshur and hid for three years even though David sorely wanted him to return home. Joab interceded with David and finally Absalom was brought back to live in Jerusalem. However, he did not go into the presence of David. Then, after two years, he was restored to his father and made his peace with him.

Once back in the good graces of the king Absalom immediately sought a way to dethrone him. A handsome young man with long hair, the father of three sons and a daughter, Absalom wheeled around town in a chariot and also placed himself in conspicuous public places in order to act as a judge over disputes of the people. All the while he proclaimed how much better things would be for the people if he were in power. After four years of building a following Absalom requested permission to go to Hebron in order to pay a vow to God. David let him go. Once he was there, Absalom proclaimed himself king. He had enough following that David and his supporters decided that they had better flee Jerusalem and hide out beyond the river Jordan.

In time, David regrouped his forces and prepared to do battle with the men who had joined Absalom. However, David instructed his army to deal gently with Absalom. In the battle which ensued the servants of David defeated the servants of Absalom. Absalom fled on a mule only to be caught and killed by Joab. Joab was dismayed and disgusted when the king responded to the end of this great threat to his life by lamenting, "O my son Absalom. . . . Would I had died instead of you. . . ."[4]

When David was an old man, cared for by a young nurse named Abishag the Shunammite, the plots against his throne continued, this time over who would succeed him.[5] On one side Bathsheba and Nathan the prophet supported Solomon; on the other Joab and Abiathar the priest supported another son of David named Adonijah. Although Adonijah was older than Solomon the special relationship between David and Bathsheba made it easy for the old king to listen to her request.

---

[4]II Samuel 18:33.

[5]I Kings.

He directed that Zadok the priest and Nathan the prophet take Solomon down to Gihon and anoint him king over Israel. They were then to blow the trumpet and announce that Solomon was king instead of David while the king was still alive. The act was done and fear ran through Adonijah, Joab and Abiathar. Solomon did not kill them at once, but in due time he killed Adonijah and Joab. Dismissing Abiathar as priest, he sent him from Jerusalem to the land of his people to dwell in obscurity.

According to the writer of Kings, Solomon was renowned for his wisdom, not only among his own people but also among other nations. It is reported that he uttered three thousand proverbs and a thousand and five songs. He knew well plants and animals and was especially wise in judging human beings. One case which impressed his people was one in which two prostitutes, living together and having given birth to infant sons about the same time, had a dispute as a result of the death of one son. Each woman claimed the surviving boy as hers.[6] Solomon requested that a sword be brought and ordered that the live son be cut in half and each woman be given a part. One woman loudly protested and urged him to go ahead and give the boy, alive, to the other woman. The other said to go ahead and cut the boy in half. Solomon awarded the live boy to the woman who was willing to give him away in order to spare his life for he knew that that one was his real mother. All of Israel, it is reported, stood in awe of the wisdom of the king for the wisdom of God was with him.

Generally speaking Solomon ruled without the fear of war which had occupied Saul and David so much of the time. He made peace with Egypt by marrying the daughter of Pharaoh. He accumulated seven hundred wives and three hundred concubines, many of them foreigners. It was said that he ruled from the Euphrates to the land of the Philistines and the borders of Egypt, collecting tribute. He did not make slaves of Israelites, but all of the people left of the Amorites, the Hittites, the Perizzites, the Hivites, and the Jebusites, he turned into slaves. He formed work parties which spent one month away from home and two months at home working in shifts to take care of his public works. He traded oil and grain to Hiram, king of Tyre, in exchange for cedar, cypress, and workmen. He opened stone quarries and shipyards. He built stables for horses and chariots. He had a steady stream of gold flowing into his coffers. So impressive was his wealth and wisdom that by the time the queen of Sheba visited him, she was overcome by him. She was generous to him and so was he with her. He gave her all that she desired

---

[6]I Kings 3:16-28.

and more besides. Never had the Israelites reached such strength and wealth before, and never have they since until the late twentieth century.

In all things, in his early years Solomon is reported to have been completely devoted to the God of his people. He was a man of prayer and devotion, setting an example for his people. He built the first permanent structure of worship to house the ark of the covenant in Jerusalem. The priestly historians recount each detail of its construction for it was their magnificent place of operation. It was constructed of stones shaped at the quarry so that no sound of stonecutting was heard at the temple. The wood in the building was cypress and cedar. Inside everything was overlaid with gold, and the furnishings and implements of the service were of gold. Considering that the building was about thirty by ninety by forty-five feet, it would have been impressive by almost anybody's standards.

Other things, however, disturbed the people and the priests. All of those forced labor levies weighed heavily on the subjects of Solomon, and the splendor of what they could see in results did not completely remove their resentment. Feeding all of his wives and horses and indulging his other expensive tastes required some heavy taxes. His subjects were approaching the threshhold of maximum tolerance of that kind of tax burden and were beginning to think of relief. The priests, getting used to their temple, gradually grew alarmed about all of the foreign gods to whom Solomon built places of worship for his wives. Moreover, in his old age Solomon appeared to the priests to grow a little lax himself, giving a little more loyalty to foreign deities and a little less devotion to the God of Israel. In their minds this was the beginning of the end for Solomon; the Lord withdrew some of his support from him. Although God would not snatch the kingdom from him during his lifetime his son would never inherit it whole.

When Rehoboam succeeded his father Solomon, Jeroboam, from the tribe of Ephraim, returned from hiding in Egypt and went with men of Israel to see the new king to inquire about his policies on forced labor. Rehoboam requested three days for consultation with his advisors. Although the old men advised him to ease up and win the loyalty of Israel, the young companions of Rehoboam advised him to announce that Israel hadn't seen anything compared to what he had in store for them in terms of service to the king. Unfortunately Rehoboam announced the advice of the young men of Judah as his own position. With that harsh promise, Jeroboam and the men of Israel, the ten northern tribes, withdrew and left Judah to go its own way.

Rehoboam did not have the exclusive right to make bad judgments, although in the eyes of Jewish historians he made his share. Israel stoned Adoram, taskmaster of forced labor for Rehoboam, an act that sent Rehoboam fleeing back to Jerusalem. Jeroboam's real sin in the eyes of the Jewish historians who were in Judah was committed in his attempt to solidify his new kingdom. After all, how could he tolerate his people going down to Jerusalem to worship in Solomon's temple which now was in the stronghold of his enemy? They could not do without a place of worship of their own, so he decided that there should be two centers, one in Bethel and the other in Dan. He made a golden calf for each sanctuary and instructed that sacrifices be made to them on altars at each location. When the prophets learned what had happened they were quick to predict that Jeroboam's reign would come to a bad end.

Samaria became the symbol for the center of power in Israel. It was purchased by Omri and constructed as a fortified city. A long description was not wasted on him but the summary gives a pointed opinion. "Omri did what was evil in the sight of the Lord, and did more evil than all who were before him" (I Kings 16:25). It would have been hard, however, for Omri to outdo the evil of his son, Ahab and Ahab's wife Jezebel. Ahab and his wife were champions of the worship of Baal and Asherah and his description reads, "Ahab did more to provoke the Lord, the God of Israel, to anger than all the kings of Israel who were before him" (I Kings 16:33).

Ahab and Jezebel did not have their own way, however, either in their private lives or in their support of the priests of Baal, without sharp cirticism and opposition from representatives of God. One opponent was Elijah the Tishbite, a prophet or spokesman for God. While he did many things remembered with vivid impression by the historians of Israel, two things stand out as particular acts of courage in his resistance of the king and his wife.

Jezebel overshadowed her husband in evil. In one deed she framed Naboth, a neighbor, with the charge of blasphemy which cost him his life.[7] She was merely interested in acquiring Naboth's vineyard for Ahab. Elijah condemned this injustice. Jezebel also supported priests of Baal. They suffered a setback when 450 of them could not call down fire from heaven, a feat which Elijah accomplished. The 450 priests of Baal were killed. Nor was Jezebel successful in charming her way into the good graces of Jehu, the fast driver, who had her killed and then arranged to entrap Baal priests and worshippers in their temple and slaughter them.

---

[7] I Kings 21:5-16.

Her end and that of excessive Baal worship occurred about the same time. Jehu wiped out Baal from Israel.[8]

The story of the kings continued, but the religious leadership definitely shifted from the kings to individuals who were more like Elijah and his successor, Elisha. They were the prophets.

SUGGESTIONS FOR ADDITIONAL READING

Books of Samuel and Kings and related Commentaries

Corvin, R. O. *David and His Mighty Men.* Freeport, New York: 1970.

Landay, Jerry M. *The House of David.* New York: E. P. Dutton, Co., Inc., 1973.

---

[8]II Kings 10:28.

CHAPTER 5

AMOS, HOSEA, ISAIAH, AND MICAH

Judaism, Christianity and Islam agree at many points in their concepts of God. Major insights into the nature of God were first given by Hebrew prophets who lived over seven hundred years before Christ. Generally they are respected by Jews, Christians and Muslims alike.

The prophets of the eighth century B.C. were in the tradition of the strong, independent individual such as Elijah, rather than in the tradition of the members of the groups who were popularly known as prophets or as "sons of the prophets." While there were individuals such as Nathan who confronted King David on his murder of Uriah the Hittite and Elijah who confronted Ahab upon the murder of Naboth, the general population of Israel and Judah seems to have been more familiar with the wandering groups known as "sons of the prophets." They often used music and dancing to prepare themselves so that the spirit of God would fall on them and they could prophesy. Their efforts seemed to be effective and contagious, for when Saul fell in with them back in the days of Samuel, Saul stripped off his clothes and lay naked for a day and a night. They were usually nomads and seem to have had distinctive clothing and, perhaps, distinctive markings on their bodies and hands. They seem to have lived by gifts and contributions from people who sought their prophecies. Amos made it clear that he was not one of them.

Tekoa near Jerusalem was the home of Amos who prophesied about the middle of the eighth century B.C. in the city of Bethel in the northern kingdom (Israel).[1] Amos was not seeking a profession for himself and he cursed Amaziah the priest of Bethel for listing him among the professional prophets or seers. He said that God took him from his regular work (a shepherd of sheep and a dresser of Sycamore trees) and sent him to Israel to deliver a message in God's name.

The short book of Amos opens with an act which must have gained attention as it went along until the hearers were ready to cheer the prophet for his curses of the enemies of Israel. He forecast doom from God for Damascus, for Gaza, for Tyre, for Edom, for the Ammonites, for Moab, and for Judah. But just when he had gained complete attention and enthusiasm from Israel, he slipped in a shocking punch:

> Thus says the Lord:
> "For three transgressions of Israel,
> and for four, I will not revoke the
> punishment. . . ."[2]

What had Israel done to justify being lumped with those marked for destruction or punishment by God?

Amos hammered at the wrongs of social life in Israel with ringing blows that must have pricked the ears of those who had been deaf in social conscience. To them righteousness counted for little as compared to silver; for a pair of shoes a person could be sold into slavery. The poor and the afflicted were trampled into the dust. Immorality was rampant, with father and son having intercourse with the same woman. Garments taken in pledge for debts of the poor were used to sit upon even in the presence of an altar for the worship of God. Their house of God was a place where they drank wine forced from the people in fines.

There was a startling contrast between the lives of the rich and the poor. Consider the wives of rich men, whom Amos referred to as "cows" of Bashan, living in Samaria, who crushed the poor and summoned their husbands to bring more wine for them to drink. Or consider the rich in general who stretched out on couches or beds made of ivory and ate tender lambs or stall-fed calves. They amused themselves playing on their harps and making up idle songs as if they were another King David. They had no concern for the failures of their people and could see no farther than drinking bowls of wine and anointing themselves with fine

---

[1] J. M. Powis Smith, *The Prophets and their Times* (Chicago: University of Chicago Press, 1941).

[2] Amos 2:6.

lotions. Amos had no doubts about their future. God would punish them severely.

The sanctuaries of Israel were an abomination in the eyes of God, proclaimed Amos. Bethel, Gilgal and Beersheba had become places of worship in Israel to compensate for the loss of the temple in Jerusalem when Jeroboam and Rehoboam parted ways after the death of Solomon. Jeroboam had made two golden calves and installed one at Dan and the other at Bethel. By the time of Amos it is likely that Gilgal and Beersheba had a similar type of worship, one condemned by Moses with vigor when Aaron molded a golden calf at the foot of Mount Sinai. But there was something even more wrong in the eyes of Amos. Worship had nothing to do with correcting ills of social life. For Amos, worship of the real God may have begun in the sanctuary, but it must always proceed into the relationships between human beings in everyday life—such as in the market place. The merchants had no concern for the poor or for religion. They wanted the holidays to end quickly so that they could open shop again—business as usual, which, according to Amos, meant selling wheat chaff with the wheat in short measure, for the highest price, using dishonest scales. It meant buying the poor for silver or for sandals. In light of these deficiencies, proclaimed Amos, their practices of worship angered God. God hated their feasts, solemn assemblies, cereal offerings, meat offerings, their songs and instrumental music. He wanted something else instead, proclaimed Amos:

> But let justice roll down like waters,
> and righteousness like an overflowing
> stream.[3]

The people of Israel, of course, thought their life was good but that it could be better. As did other Hebrews they claimed to desire the coming of the day of the Lord. But Amos told them that a "day of justice" would be a day of condemnation for Israel. God was standing by Israel as by a wall, holding a plumb line to see whether it was straight and true. When he found that it was not, he declared that destruction was at hand. Of course there is in Amos a plea for repentance and a hope that reform would turn aside the wrath of God. However, Amos seems to have seen the resistance to change so deeply imbedded that destruction would almost surely come from God. Whether relief would come was not clear. One thing was certain: if it were to come, it would be the direct result of Israel's change to ethical conduct.

---

[3] Amos 5:24.

Another prophet proclaiming the word of God to Israel was Hosea, a man captivated by images taken from family life.[4] His essential message was that Israel, having vowed to be faithful to God, had been unfaithful. In addition to keeping his promise in justice, however, God is also merciful and forgiving, willing to restore the relationship of faithfulness he had once enjoyed with Israel. It was how Hosea proclaimed that message that added dimension to his stature.

Hosea's concept of Israel's relationship to God was based upon his wife's relationship to him. The traditional view is that Hosea married Gomer, who was a good woman, and that after their marriage she became unfaithful and ran off with strange lovers. Hosea kept going after her and bringing her back home, trying to reform her. Out of his experiences with his wife Hosea came to see that Israel had been unfaithful in her covenant with God and that in a similar way God had gone after Israel, trying repeatedly but unsuccessfully to restore her to the original relationship of loyalty. A view by J. M. Powis Smith is somewhat more dramatic. According to him, Hosea already understood the nature of God, and in order to make the lesson clear to Israel, he went to the temple and married a temple prostitute, taking her home with him and trying to reform her.[5]

Under either interpretation, the children of the marriage were given names that stood for a message of doom. The first son was named "Jezreel" to announce the punishment that would come to the house of Jehu for his destruction at Jezreel. The second child was a daughter named "Not Pitied" for the Lord would no longer have pity for the house of Israel. A third child, a son, was to be called "Not My People" to say that Israel was not God's people and he was not their God.

If the object lessons were not enough, the words of Hosea were also a sharp warning. Israel was pictured as an unfaithful wife who had run away from her first love and his care and compassion in order to follow lovers who had since abandoned her. Her first love would take his presents from her and leave her to her enemies. Israel had been chasing after Baals instead of God. Chastisement would be severe and public.

Or again Israel was pictured as a child in Egypt chosen and called by God his father. Yet from the beginning he was rebellious. God was a devoted parent all the same:

---

[4]Hosea 1, 2, 3, and 11.

[5]Smith, *ibid.*

Yet it was I who taught Ephraim to walk,
I took them up in my arms;
but they did not know that I healed them.
I led them with cords of compassion, with
the bands of love, and I became to them
as one who eases the yoke on their jaws,
and I bent down to them and fed them.[6]

In spite of the rebellions of the son, how could God give him up to harsh punishment?

My heart recoils within me,
my compassion grows warm and tender.
I will not execute my fierce anger,
I will not again destroy Ephraim;
For I am God and not man,
the Holy One in your midst,
and I will not come to destroy.[7]

The message seems clear. God had always loved Israel tenderly. In spite of rebellion or unfaithfulness, God's love endures. Discipline may be used, and will be used in an attempt to bring about reform of behavior. Nevertheless, the punishment is not for the purpose of destruction but in order to restore a relationship that God highly prizes. In spite of all the rebellions of Israel, God does not give up on the relationship.

For Hosea, the trouble with Israel which would lead to punishment was Baal worship. The Canaanite deity was probably similar to the dying and rising gods of Egypt, Isis and Osiris. Their story explained the seasonal changes and the fertility of the fields exhibited in Canaanite agriculture. Union with the Baals was through the symbol of uniting with a temple prostitute at sacred places such as Bethel, where Baal worship was probably carried on alongside the worship of Yahweh. This type of disloyalty to exclusive Yahweh worship was seen by Hosea as the misconduct which would be the downfall of Israel.

A third prophet of the eighth century was not only from the southern kingdom but was also called by God to prophesy in the city of Jerusalem. One learns little about the early personal life of Isaiah, but a clear date of his call to be a prophet of God is given. "In the year that King Uzziah died

---

[6]Hosea 11:3, 4.

[7]Hosea 11:8, 9.

I saw the Lord. . . ."[8] The only problem is in dating the year referred to, which is still around 750 B.C., with J. M. Powis Smith saying the year was 751 B.C. and Theodore H. Robinson placing it at 744 B.C.[9]

The vision of Isaiah has become a classic account, a kind of model of what Jewish or Christian worship is expected to be. Isaiah was entering the temple in Jerusalem when a vision of God came to him. It utilized the earthly furnishings of the temple but it had divine dimensions which overshadowed them. (1) Isaiah saw the Lord sitting on the throne, his presence filling the temple. Above the Lord seraphim called in adoration, "Holy, Holy, Holy is the Lord of hosts; the whole earth is full of his glory." This symbolized the recognition of the holiness of God and the worshipper's adoration of him. (2) With the shaking of the foundations of the thresholds the prophet cried, "Woe is me! For I am lost; for I am a man of unclean lips, and I dwell in the midst of a people of unclean lips, for mine eyes have seen the King, the Lord of hosts!" In the presence of the great and awesome God, Isaiah was painfully aware of his own uncleanness and his own unworthiness. The glory of God by contrast reveals the sinfulness of man. (3) In the vision of Isaiah one of the seraphim flew to him bearing a hot coal from the temple altar and touched Isaiah's tongue with it, saying, "Behold, this has touched your lips; your guilt is taken away, and your sin forgiven." In worship man's confession of his sin is followed by God's forgiveness and declaration that God has made him clean, whereas in his own right he was not clean. (4) Then the prophet heard the voice of the Lord saying, "Whom shall I send, and who will go for us?" To the worshiper who has been made clean by God the Lord then speaks words of challenge and exhortation. Will one do something in return for what God has already done for him? (5) Then Isaiah answered God, "Here I am! Send me." The challenge stands until it is accepted. Once the worshipper is committed to act in his life for God, the worship experience is essentially completed. God made clear that Isaiah was to go to his people and speak the words of warning from God until there was no longer any hope that they would respond and avoid destruction.

What was the essential message from God that Isaiah was to deliver? It was that for a number of injustices and sinful acts Israel was about to

---

[8]Isaiah 6:1.

[9]Theodore H. Robinson, *A History of Israel*, vol. 1. (Oxford, Clarendon Press, 1955).

suffer at the hands of God. But deliverance was possible through reform and trusting only in God rather than in turning to human allies in hopes of deliverance.

One of the first oracles of Isaiah was given when Rezin, king of Damascus in Syria, and Pekah, king of Samaria in Israel, joined forces against Judah and came to seize Jerusalem. In Isaiah 7 one reads that Isaiah was sent by God to go out with his son Shearjashub (meaning either "a remnant shall remain" or "a remnant shall return") to meet king Ahaz of Jerusalem in Judah. The message of the prophet was that Ahaz should not be afraid and run to seek an alliance, for the two kings to the north would soon fail. All Ahaz had to do was to trust in God.

> If you will not believe,
> surely you shall not be established.[10]

Isaiah asked Ahaz to seek a sign of prophecy, but the king refused. So Isaiah announced a sign. A virgin, or young woman, would give birth to a child whose name would be called "Immanuel" (God is with us) and before he was old enough to choose between good and evil, the alliance of Rezin and Pekah would be dissolved.

In a third oracle on the same alliance Isaiah took a tablet and wrote on it in large letters "Mahershalalhashbaz" and had it witnessed by Uriah the priest, with Zechariah to attest for him. The words meant "the spoil speeds, the prey hastes." Then he fathered a child through the prophetess and gave the child the name "Mahershalalhashbaz," for before the child could learn to call his parents the wealth of Samaria and Damascus would be carried away by the king of Assyria.[11]

Isaiah's point seems simple now, although it must have seemed an impossible strategy to Ahaz. The prophet knew that seeking alliances with other nations betrayed a distrust of God. More than that, it meant an alliance with the gods of Egypt or of Assyria, a corrupting of Yahweh worship. In addition, it meant paying tribute to a foreign power by stripping the temple of God of its gold. In practical terms, which may not have been known to Isaiah, or certainly that was not the basis for his prophecy, Egypt was useless before Assyria so no alliance should be sought with that weak reed. Besides, Assyria, in the person of Tiglath Pileser, would look after her own interest and come to put down the revolt by Syria and Israel. Judah did not need to do anything but wait for

---

[10]Isaiah 7:9b.

[11]Isaiah 8:1-5.

Assyria to act. If she were not called on for help by Judah they would not owe any tribute.

Once he was under siege in Jerusalem by Rezin and Pekah—according to II Kings—Ahaz lost his nerve and sent to Tiglath Pileser in Assyria asking for military assistance. He sent along a valuable gift with the request. It was answered, and Assyria took Damascus. When Ahaz met with Tiglath Pileser in Damascus, he studied the way the Assyrians worshiped their god and sent back to Jerusalem the plans for a new altar so that Assyrian gods could be worshiped in a manner to which they were accustomed. The fears of Isaiah were realized.

According to II Kings, all did not go well with Israel after the Assyrians had taken charge. Hoshea, king in Samaria, was supposed to be paying tribute to Assyria on a regular basis. However, seeking to escape that burden, he tried to make a deal with So, king of Egypt, to rebel against Assyria. The plot failed, and Shalmaneser of Assyria came to collect what was due from his vassal; he not only imprisoned Hoshea but also laid siege to Samaria. When the Assyrians captured it, they took all the Israelites away to Assyria and replaced them with foreigners. The fall of Israel was in 721 B.C.

Why Jerusalem did not fall at that time or shortly thereafter is a mystery that still has not been explained conclusively by purely rational means. Around 713-711 B.C. Judah joined Philistia, Egypt, Moab, and Edom in a revolt against Sargon. Isaiah had gone naked for three years trying to persuade Judah not to join Egypt. He pictured Egypt being led stripped naked as prisoners to Assyria (20:1-6). Instead of being led and protected by priests of clear vision who should have opposed an alliance with Egypt in order to preserve purity of Yahweh worship, Judah was led, said Isaiah, by priests whose vision was clouded and whose walk was unsteady with wine (28:7-22). But Judah did join with Egypt against Assyria and Sennacherib came down to straighten out matters. As Isaiah had prophesied, Sennacherib defeated the Egyptians at Altaku. Then the Assyrians laid siege to Jerusalem. Sennacherib recorded that he shut up Hezekiah "like a caged bird."[12]

Hezekiah thought the end was at hand and went to the temple of God to pray (II Kings 19). God then sent Isaiah to him to condemn the behavior of Judah against God and to tell of the suffering they must endure. At the same time, however, Isaiah prophesied that the city would

---

[12]Jack Finegan, *Light from the Ancient Past*, (Princeton: Princeton University Press, 1946), p. 177.

not fall to Sennacherib at that time for God would deliver it. Then, according to the account in Kings, the angel of the Lord went forth that night and killed 185,000 in the Assyrian camp. In light of that catastrophe, Sennacherib took the remnants of his army and went home. The historian for Judah than adds that after the king of Assyria was at home worshiping his god Nisroch, two of his sons killed him with the sword and fled into the land of Ararat. His son Esarhaddon succeeded him on the throne.

The results of prophecy in Israel and in Judah were somewhat condensed in the short work of the prophet Micah. A product of the countryside rather than the city, he also was concerned with the social wrongs which had stirred the wrath of Yahweh. The leaders of Israel were pictured as having skinned and chopped up the common people of Israel in order to eat them as meat in a chaldron. The prophets promised peace to anyone who gave them food and promised war to those who did not feed them. The people who spoke of the future in order to gain their bread would be brought low, for they told what pleased the payers, not the truth of God. Prophets, seers, and diviners would all come to shame for their unfaithfulness to God (Micah 3:1-12). Corrupt officials who did not care for justice or equity but who depended on bribes, filling Jerusalem with blood, were responsible for Zion becoming a wasteland and Jerusalem a heap of ruins (3:9-12).

One of the great insights of Micah (as Isaiah before him) was in the realm of worship. In Micah 6 he asked the pointed question, "How shall one worship God?" What has the highest value in pleasing the Lord? What about burnt offerings of yearling calves? What about a thousand rams? What about ten thousand rivers of oil? Even more, what about offering up one's first-born son, the fruit of one's body for the sin of one's soul? Micah's answer was in the great tradition of the other eighth century prophets—Amos, Hosea, and Isaiah:

He has showed you, O man, what is good;
and what does the Lord require of you
But to do justice, and to love kindness,
and to walk humbly with your God? (6:8)

What then were the results of the work of the eighth century prophets? After all, their call for reform was not effective in saving Israel, for ten of the twelve tribes of Israel disappeared from history. Judah was spared for a century, but it does not appear to have been as a direct result of reform according to the recommendations of the prophets. The prophets, nonetheless, did make some lasting contributions in the eighth century. For one thing they clearly separated the role of the prophet from that of the priest. The prophet was one who spoke the words of the Lord regardless of the consequences to himself due to the unpopularity of the words with political or religious powers. The priest, on the other hand, was one who identified with the political establishment, reenforcing its views with assurances that God would aid in their fulfillment. The priests were accused by the prophets of being more concerned about their food and their safety than about the common people of the land or of the welfare of the nation. Second, the eighth century prophets reevaluated worship from an exclusive interest in ritual and sacrifice to an emphasis upon moral living. Justice was more important than wealth, mercy more important than donations to the temple, and humble obedience to God more important than strength bought by compromising purity of worship for the alliance of Egypt or any other foreign country with foreign gods. And third, God was recognized as requiring justice in the dealings of one human being with another and one nation with another. But his exacting standard of justice is tempered with a love which makes provision for forgiveness when there is repentance. Sometimes penalty is exacted to bring about reform, and sometimes loving care is repeatedly used to win a responding love. But in all things God works for the good of his people to accomplish his will for them.

The insights of the Hebrew prophets on the nature of God can be found reflected in both Christianity and in Islam. God is just and requires justice among human beings; God is merciful and requires mercy among human beings. Humility before God is also expected in both Christianity and Islam. Islam stresses the compassion of God, however, while Christianity prefers to stress the love of God.

SUGGESTIONS FOR ADDITIONAL READING

Amos, Hosea, Isaiah, and Micah and related
Commentaries.

Kaiser, Otto. *Isaiah*. 1-12, 1976. 13-39, 1974. Philadelphia: The Westminster Press.

Leslie, E. A. *Isaiah* and *Hosea*. New York: Abingdon Press, c. 1963.

Mauchline, John. *Prophets of Israel*. New York: Abingdon Press, 1964.

Mays, J. L. *Amos*. Philadelphia: The Westminster Press, 1969.

Mays, J. L. *Hosea*. London: S. C. M. Press, Ltd., 1969.

Mays, J. L. *Micah*. Philadelphia: The Westminster Press, 1976.

Smith, J. M. Powis. *The Prophets and Their Times*. Chicago: University of Chicago Press, 1941.

Wolff, *Amos the Prophet*. Translated by F. R. McCurley. Philadelphia: Fortress Press, 1973.

CHAPTER 6

JEREMIAH AND EZEKIEL

If the Jews were given the promised land by God how did it happen that they were ever driven from it? Why were they first reduced from twelve tribes to only one? How did they fall under domination of foreign powers? Were they mistaken about God's promises to them or was there another explanation? Two other prophets give answers.

The two great prophets came a little over a century after Amos and directed their messages to the people of Jerusalem. Their work (as Isaiah's) spread over a number of years, speaking to situations very threatening for the survival of the faith of the children of Abraham.

Jeremiah was the son of Hilkiah, a priest in the land of Benjamin, from the town of Anathoth.[1] Although he began to prophesy first during the reign of Josiah, king of Judah, Jeremiah was convinced that God had called him to be a prophet even before he was formed in his mother's womb. Moreover he was called upon to begin prophesying while he was still a youth, with only a promise from God that he would be delivered from harm so that he could continue the work of God.

In chapters two through four of the book bearing his name, Jeremiah spoke for God, using the kinds of analogies found in Hosea. Israel was pictured as a young bride eagerly following in the steps of her husband, as Israel followed God when the people were in the desert after they left Egypt. But after she was settled in the promised land she turned from her

---

[1]Jeremiah 1:1.

loving husband and went after other lovers, committing harlotry under every green tree in the land—an analogy for Israel's turning to Baals. For those sins Jeremiah saw destruction coming from the north aimed at the city of Jerusalem.

It was during the reign of King Josiah that a general reform of religion took place in Jerusalem. While the temple was being repaired the high priest Hilkiah found a book in the building which appeared to be quite old.[2] Josiah was told of the discovery and heard the book read. He had it taken to the prophetess Huldah for her opinion. She predicted that destruction was coming to Jerusalem but that for reform which Josiah was about to execute the evil would not occur in his lifetime. The book is believed to be contained in the present book of Deuteronomy, the second law, and it has been regarded as a book of Moses.

On the basis of the book, Josiah took systematic steps to remove all signs of worship of Baals and foreign gods from the temple of Jerusalem, gods which had been placed there from the time of Solomon. Furthermore, he went into the countryside and tore down all signs of Baal worship and killed the priests of the country shrines. From that time on all legal worship was centered in the Jerusalem temple where corruption by Baal worship could be eliminated. The priesthood was limited to Levites, and a sharp distinction was made between clergy and laity. The humanitarian problems referred to by Jeremiah were addressed in the book of the law. With the stream of worshippers coming to Jerusalem there came economic prosperity. The deuteronoic reform during the time of Josiah eradicated many of the evils which the prophets had cried against since the time of Ahab. However, as Huldah pointed out, the sin had already been done and the seeds of destruction had already been sown.

Judah was caught between trying to remain neutral and swinging either behind Egypt or behind Assyria. Pharaoh Necho went up against Assyria in 608 B.C. Josiah went to meet him and was killed at Megiddo as soon as Necho saw him. The Egyptians enthroned Josiah's son Jehoahaz, twenty-three years old in order to rule through him. They found him unsatisfactory so he was imprisoned and replaced by Eliakim, another son of Josiah, whose name the Egyptians changed to Jehoiakim. His job was to tax the people of Judah and send the money to his master in Egypt. His reign must have been more satisfactory for he managed to survive on the throne for eleven years.

---

[2]II Kings 22.

Although the people of Jerusalem should have realized that their position was weak, they did not want to hear any discouraging word from a prophet. They wanted to think as positively as possible, while on the other side Jeremiah was under orders from God to point out every weakness. The people of Jerusalem seemed to think that their temple was indestructible; Jeremiah kept predicting its destruction. On one occasion the common people revolted and would have killed Jeremiah had the nobles not intervened on his behalf. On another occasion Pashur, chief of the temple police, angered over Jeremiah's prophecy, had him arrested and placed in stocks. Of course Jeremiah predicted captivity in Babylon for Pashur. He was also plotted against by the men of Anathoth, his home town, because they hated his prophecy. In return Jeremiah predicted their utter destruction by God.

Jehoiakim did not last long for in 600 B.C. he revolted against Nebuchadrezzar of Babylon. Jehoiakim died and was succeeded by his son Jehoiachin. After a long siege Jerusalem surrendered to Nebuchadrezzar in 597 B.C. Nebuchadrezzar sought to avert future revolts by deporting to Babylon some of the leading citizens of Jerusalem. Jeremiah saw the remnants of the Jerusalem population as a basket of bad figs, good for nothing. The future, he believed, lay with the quality people in exile; nevertheless, he did not see a speedy return for them. He counseled them to settle down in Babylon, realizing that Yahweh is God in Babylon as well as in Jerusalem. But his words of encouragement were not welcomed by the exiles, and they petitioned the people in Jerusalem to silence the troublesome prophet.

Jeremiah was strong in his belief in the future of Jerusalem. The days were coming with certainty when God would watch over Judah to build up and plant, just as he had come to tear down and destroy. No longer would children suffer for the sins of their fathers, but each individual would answer for his own sins.[3] Moreover, no longer would the law be something outside of an individual, something foreign taught him by his neighbor. The new covenant would be written directly on the hearts of individuals, and each person would know the Lord directly. The Lord would forgive their iniquities and forget their sins. He would be their God, and they would be his people.

The future may have been bright for Jerusalem in the plans of God, but the immediate future of Jeremiah was a continuation of his past. Some subjects of Jerusalem did not see any future for themselves in that

---

[3]Jeremiah 31.

city and made plans to escape and take refuge in Egypt. In spite of his resistance, Jeremiah was forced to accompany them. As was his custom, he soundly denounced them and their actions. What became of them or of Jeremiah is not known to us today, but it is likely that the prophet died either on the journey or during exile in Egypt. He went to his death loyal to his unpopular and unsought role as a spokesman of Yahweh whose will was consistently contrary to the desires and beliefs of Jeremiah's contemporaries.

The main development of the children of Abraham who had been in Jerusalem continued, after 597 B.C., as Jeremiah had projected, in Babylon rather than in Judah. The captives, who numbered several thousand, were given what the Babylonians apparently considered to be a somewhat permanent settlement. Babylonian records indicate that food was given to the captives and a king Yaukin (Jehoiachin?), king of Yahud (Judah?).[4] And from Jeremiah's scroll it appears that they had materials with which to build houses. Some of them entered the commercial life of the country, and, perhaps surprising to the modern reader, frequent communication seems to have been maintained with the people who remained behind in Judah.

Babylon was an impressive city at that time as can be shown through archeological studies of its walls, its buildings and its magnificent Ishtar gate.[5] It is little wonder that some of the Jews reached the conclusion that Marduk, god of the Babylonians, was greater than Yahweh. Just as Yahweh worship had been threatened by Baals of Canaan, so now it was threatened by the success and prosperity of the Babylonians. As the Psalms of the Jews indicate, at first there was deep sorrow and homesickness among the captives. They were tormented with the requests of their captors to sing them songs of Zion. But over a period of time there were Jews who thought less and less about Jerusalem and made a satisfactory life for themselves among the Babylonians. After the destruction of the city and the temple accompanying the downfall of Zedekiah and the desolation which settled as Jeremiah had foretold, there was even less reason to leave the leading civilization of the world to return to a wilderness.

But before the second fall of Jerusalem under Zedekiah, there was an attempt by another prophet beside Jeremiah to try to avert disaster. This

---

[4]Jack Finegan, *Light from the Ancient Past* (Princeton: Princeton University Press, 1946), p. 188, 189.

[5]*Ibid.*

unusual seer and prophet arose among the captives of the first group to be taken to Babylon. He was the son of a priest named Buzi, perhaps a Zadokite. His name was Ezekiel. He was in Tel-Abib, by the canal Chebar, in Babylon, in the fifth year of Jehoichin's captivity when his call came to be a prophet of Yahweh.[6] His main goal seems to have been to prevent the second revolt under Zedekiah and, consequently, the destruction of Jerusalem. While he was no more successful than Jeremiah in that appointed task, the attempts he made are as fascinating as those of Jeremiah.

The first chapter of Ezekiel's scroll is almost filled with his attempted description of his vision of the glory of the Lord which preceded his call to be a prophet. The imagery is a combination of Jewish and Babylonian figures which would be most difficult to paint or sculpt in their dynamic form. But one can easily get the point that something very impressive happened to Ezekiel which his powers of language were inadequate to convey to the reader.

In subsequent chapters his mission to the house of Israel is made clearer. His responsibility was to proclaim to a rebellious house the words of God exactly as they were given to him. His faithful delivery of the words of Yahweh would relieve him of responsibility of any failure on the part of hearers to repent and follow the directions of their God. But if he failed to deliver the message accurately from God then any failure to respond by the people would be laid to his account with God.

Besides carrying out his unpleasant duty of declaring the coming fall of Jerusalem, Ezekiel also had to proclaim a message of God's ways of working with human beings which was a break with the widespread conceptions of his day. He also broke with the concept that the sins of a father would be visited upon his children to the third and fourth generation. On the contrary, proclaimed Ezekiel in chapter 18, the new principle to be understood by Judah about the working of God could be couched in the words, "Behold, all souls are mine; the soul of the father as well as the soul of the son is mine: the soul that sins shall die."[7] If a father is righteous, that is, if he keeps the laws of God and deals justly with his neighbors, he shall surely live. If that righteous father has a son who violates the law of God and deals unjustly with his neighbors, then that son shall surely die and the blood be upon himself alone. On the other

---

[6]Ezekiel 1:1.

[7]Ezekiel 18:4.

hand, the son of a sinful father can choose to follow a different route from his father and live in justice under the law of God and thus live, in spite of the fate of his father.

Ezekiel went even farther. If a wicked man turns away from his sinful ways and starts to live by the laws of God and in harmony with his neighbors, his past deeds and transgressions will be forgotten.[8] He shall live. This is just as reasonable as the provision that if a righteous man turns to doing evil he shall surely die. The ways of the Lord are just, in spite of the thinking of Israel that such an arrangement is not just. The conclusion of Ezekiel was that God would judge each one in Israel according to that person's own deeds.

If Ezekiel carried a message of sure destruction, the book also carried a message of sure forgiveness under certain conditions. Even more clear is a belief that God would restore Judah. In chapter thirty-four Ezekiel placed much of the blame for the disastrous state of Judah upon the leaders of the nation, the "shepherds" of the "sheep." The "shepherds" had "fleeced" the sheep instead of caring for their needs and protecting them from wild beasts bent upon their destruction. They allowed them to suffer illness without attempting to cure them. They made themselves fat off the flock without doing anything to minister to the needs of the flock. Therefore, they would be dismissed and God would become the shepherd. He would search out his scattered sheep, bind up their wounds, judge between one sheep and another, make them secure in the midst of threatening beasts, and watch over them as their devoted shepherd. The beauty of the promise could not have been escaped in a people so familiar with the sight of shepherds and sheep.

Of a similar theme is the vision by Ezekiel of the valley of dry bones, celebrated in Black spiritual music of the United States. God showed Ezekiel a valley of very dry bones and asked the question, "Son of man, can these bones live?". To which the prophet responded, "O Lord God, thou knowest."[9] The prophet announced that God would place flesh upon the reassembled bones of Israel and again breathe life into a dead people. As he prophesied, the bones assembled and flesh and skin grew upon them, breath was blown into them, and they lived again. The vision continued with the promise that God would restore Ephraim (Israel) and Judah, make them one people again, and rebuild the temple in their

---

[8]Ezekiel 18:21-23.

[9]Ezekiel 37:1-3.

midst. Moreover, God would reestablish a covenant with them, an everlasting covenant.

> My dwelling place shall be with them;
> and I will be their God and they shall
> be my people. Then the nations will
> know that I the Lord sanctify Israel,
> when my sanctuary is in the midst of
> them for evermore. (37:27, 28)

The vision of restoration was not to be fulfilled in any form for many years after Ezekiel's first vision in Babylon. Meanwhile, some important developments were to take place in Babylon among the Exiles.

To scholars who engaged in "higher" literary-historical criticism, the most significant activity of the exiled Jews in Babylon was the compiling of their history from the beginning of the world. They generally assigned that task to certain priests who assembled oral and written accounts of events which are now described in the Pentateuch and subsequent books describing events down to the first fall of Jerusalem. The liberal scholars see that as the main period when the accounts they have labeled "J," "E," "D," "P" and oral tradition were woven into the account of Jewish history and laws in the present Bible.

Many scholars also look upon the exile period as a time when a major development in worship experiences occurred, giving an alternative to temple worship which would be invaluable to the Jews when they would be separated from the temple of Jerusalem for many centuries. That alternative was in the synagogue, which means "an assembly," from Greek words meaning "to come together." The minimum needed for an assembly was ten Jewish men. Almost any large city could produce enough men for a synagogue for the purpose of worshiping God.

The written and spoken words took the place of sacrifice of animals in the new form of worship. The call of Isaiah seems to have been either kept in mind or else paralleled in the gradual development of the typical service. Prayers to God for praise, thanksgiving, confession of sins, and assurance of pardon were accompanied by reading from the law of God and by commentary upon it with the purpose of challenging the worshipers to devote their lives to keeping Torah. Neither elaborate building nor equipment was required; only ten men, the law and almost any home were enough. The institution continued after the exiles returned to Jerusalem, and it existed not only alongside temple worship, but continued alone to the present day after the destruction of the temple by the Romans.

The insights of Jeremiah and Ezekiel emphasizing individual responsibility in keeping Torah seem to have been shared by the exiles. Each person was to know the law, and each person was responsible for keeping it in his life. That is not to say that corporate responsibility was ended for all time, for it was not, as one comes to see in the period of restoration in the sixth century B.C. Scribes and priests would still have their positions of leadership, but in the exile their power was severely curtailed and the individual Jew and the particular synagogue had to bear much more responsibility for the direction that Judaism would take for the present and in the future.

The traditional concept of Yahweh, which was severely challenged by the victory of the Babylonians under their deity Marduk, did not escape change. But while some exiles may have abandoned Yahweh altogether, the mainstream of religious people adjusted their concept to make it more in keeping with the historical events through which they had lived. The insights of the prophets were of some help in their task. They recognized God as still powerful over the people in exile in Babylon—he was now beyond the confines of an ark of the covenant or a tabernacle or a temple. He was international in his influence. Moreover, he was not limited in his activities to those events which involved Jews alone. God used Babylon to accomplish his purposes with Judah even as he had used Assyria to accomplish his purposes with Israel. That did not mean that Assyria and Babylon were more free from sin than Israel and Judah. In time, God would deal with those nations for their sins even as he had dealt with Israel and Judah. But those nations were used as a rod by God to chastise his beloved people to restore them to a rightful relationship with their own God.

The God of the returning exiles would be, in time, greater in concept than the God of the people who were first taken in Babylon. He was not limited to a single territory or people. He was now God of international influence ruling over history in the interaction of many peoples to bring about his purpose over a period of time, in spite of the freedom he allowed each individual and each nation. The punishment of his chosen people was not for their ultimate destruction but for their healing and for restoring them to a community in covenant whereby they would receive blessings upon themselves and be a blessing to the nations of the world. These concepts would not remain in Judaism alone; they would eventually be received by the Christians and incorporated as a part of their faith.

SUGGESTIONS FOR ADDITIONAL READING

Ezekiel, Jeremiah and related Commentaries

Ackroyd, P. R. *Israel Under Babylon and Persia.* Oxford: University Press, 1970.

Calkins, Raymond. *Jeremiah the Prophet.* New York: Macmillan, 1930.

Carmichael, Calvin M. *The Laws of Deuteronomy.* Ithaca, New York: Cornell University Press, c. 1974.

Cheyne, T. K. *Jeremiah.* New York: Fleming H. Revell Company, 1888.

Eichrodt, Walther, *Ezekiel.* Philadelphia: The Westminster Press, 1970.

Levenson, J. D. *Theology of the Program of Restoration of Ezekiel,* 40-48. Missoula, Montana: Scholars Press, c. 1976.

Nicholson, E. W. *Deuteronomy and Tradition.* Philadelphia: Fortress Press, 1967.

Van Zeller, H. *Jeremias: Man of Tears.* London: The Catholic Book Club, 1941.

Weinfeld, Moshe. *Deuteronomy and the Deuteronomic School.* Oxford: Clarendon Press, 1972.

Welch, A. C. *Jeremiah.* Oxford: Basil Blackwell, 1955.

CHAPTER 7

EZRA AND NEHEMIAH

The people of Israel have had three occasions in history when they have had to reclaim the land which they believe was given to them through God's promise to Abraham. The first time was the invasion under Joshua and the third time was the settlement after World War II. The second time was after the exile in Babylon, in the sixth century B.C. In this account one learns why Jews have had a warmer regard for Persians than for some of the other people of the Near East.

A person reading through the scroll of Isaiah without any prior introduction to the material might be taken aback by two references in chapters 44 to 45 to Cyrus, who was a king of Persia rather than a king of the Jewish people. The Lord says of Cyrus, "He is my shepherd and shall fulfill all my purpose. . . ." Again it is written, "Thus says the Lord to his anointed, to Cyrus, whose right hand I have grasped to subdue nations before him. . . ."[1] But that is how the writer on the latter part of the scroll of Isaiah saw Cyrus, and so did many other Jews after that time. For as Monarch of the Persians, Cyrus destroyed the Babylonians who had exiled the Jews. Moreover, he almost immediately initiated a policy to allow those exiled Jews who wished to do so to return to their home in Jerusalem and reestablish their particular kind of worship.

Cyrus was an instrument in the hand of God, as had been

---

[1]Isaiah 45:1.

Nebuchadrezzar. God had used one to chastise his people for their sins; he used the other to build them up again. Although both were regarded as tools of God there is no doubt that Jews hated Nebuchadrezzar and loved Cyrus, whose enlightened policies are clearly visible to the present time. According to the account in Ezra, Cyrus acknowledged that he had been commissioned by God to rebuild his temple in Jerusalem.[2] However, the work was in part dependent upon the Jews in exile who were willing to leave the civilization in Babylon and return to the ruins of Jerusalem. They needed some encouragement.

The liberal scholars of the Bible see the section composed of Isaiah 40-66 as the product of a prophet of the restoration period whose mission was to inspire the settled exiles to pull up roots and return to Jerusalem. Thus they explained the words in chapter 40 as extending comfort and encouragement to the people of God. The way back home was to be made a "highway" in the desert, and God himself would be the shepherd leading them. Conservative Christian scholars, on the other hand, regard these words as prophecy from the eighth century and as predicting the coming age of the Messiah.

By the middle of the fifth century B.C., the city of Jerusalem was still in a vulnerable position, unable to take any independent stand against the outside tribes and aliens in the surrounding community. Nehemiah, a cupbearer to Artaxerxes I, sought and received from the king an appointment as the royal governor of Jerusalem.[3] His specific goal, also made possible by letters of passage and letters of requisition, was to return to Jerusalem and rebuild the city wall which still lay in ruin. When Nehemiah arrived in Jerusalem he was well received by the Jews and settled down as their governor. After three days he went out by night and made an inspection of the ruined wall and the destroyed gates. His inspection led him to announce openly his intention to rebuild the walls. As might be expected, Sanballat the Horonite, Tobiah the Ammonite, and Geshem the Arab heard of his plan and were displeased. In spite of their resistance, Nehemiah organized the work parties of Jews to rebuild the wall.

Each section of wall and each gate in the wall became the responsibilty of a tribe or a city or a family. Work went forward rather well until the wall reached about half of its planned height. At that point the outside critics became an open threat. It was necessary for the

---

[2]Ezra 1:2.

[3]Nehemiah 2:1.

building to go forward under guards with swords and spears at the ready. The workers could not relax day or night, but even had to sleep with their clothes on, ready to fight. It was an ordeal, but they completed the wall in fifty-two days.

The governor also faced the problem of the impurity of the families of the chosen community. The people who had returned from exile definitely assumed that they were superior to the people who had been left behind in Judah. It was necessary to preserve their names and their families distinct from the more common people of the area. Moreover, some families had intermarried with the aliens. As in the days of Solomon, the foreign marriage partners often brought along their own deities and forms of worship, all of which weakened the purity of Yahweh worship. The next step was to consolidate the community.

Leaders called a gigantic assembly before the Water Gate and Ezra the scribe read the law of Moses to the assembled children of Israel. Systematically and deliberately the law was read so that it could be heard and understood. The assembled Jews wept.

Nevertheless, Nehemiah, Ezra, and the Levites told the people to cheer up and rejoice without weeping, for it was a holy day to God. They were to eat the fat and drink sweet wine and share with those who had nothing prepared. The restored community of Israel was almost a reality. The only thing remaining to be done, however, was not something easy for everyone to accept. The leaders commanded Jews to agree not to intermarry with the people of the land from that time forward, and they also asked them to put out of the community any foreigner, even though one might already be a member of the family. This act was not an option. Leaders separated families by threats and by force as a part of the program to reconsecrate a pure community of Yahweh.

Jerusalem, in the eyes of Nehemiah, was to be a holy city. He brought an end to trading in the city on the Sabbath. In addition he threatened and drove away the merchants who had camped outside the walls of Jerusalem on the Sabbath offering goods for sale. To make sure the ban on trade was effective the gates of the city were ordered closed for the Sabbath and observance of the day was obtained whether everyone wanted it or not. The secular governor and Ezra scribe saw their era as a time of rebirth of the people of God, perhaps comparable to the time in the desert near Sinai when Moses consecrated the children of Israel as the people of God. They were determined to wash away the mistakes of the past and to begin again, laying a solid foundation for the people of the community as they had established the foundations of the temple and the wall of Jerusalem.

The reforms of Nehemiah and Ezra were thorough and effective. However, they not only caused hardships on some families, but also they were contrary to a philosophy which had run through the fabric of Hebrew life from early days. There was always a tension between those who wanted racial and religious purity and men such as Solomon who found strength by cultivating diversity of races within the community. And, according to scholars of literary-historical criticism, there was a mild protest made during this period of reform which took the seeemingly innocuous form of a novel. It is the book of Ruth.

In the delightful story one usually identifies with an attractive Moabite widow named Ruth, who was devoted to her Hebrew mother-in-law, Naomi, expressing her loyalty in the memorable words:

> Entreat me not to leave you or to return from following you; for where you go I will go, and where you lodge I will lodge; your people shall be my people and your God my God; where you die I will die, and there will I be buried. May the Lord do so to me and more also if even death parts me from you.[4]

In due time Ruth married Boaz, a kinsman of Naomi. From that union of a Hebrew and a Moabite widow issued a son named Obed. From Obed came Jesse, and from Jesse came David. David, the great king of Israel, was descended from a foreign woman married to a Hebrew.

One can find an amount of Babylonian imagery in Ezekiel, and the exile had some influence on the concept of God as a god of international relations. The question naturally arises whether the Persians left any similar influence on the Jews. It is difficult to prove that any idea or practice was derived directly from the Persians and only from them. One could argue that Jews developed these concepts entirely on their own or that the concepts gradually entered Jewish thought by their general circulation in the ancient world. However, for liberal scholars there seem to be several concepts found in Jewish literature which have such a strong similarity to Persian thought that they assume some Persian influence was present, for the ideas do not appear in the literature prior to the exile in the same way they do after the exile.

A few influences from Persia are found in literature after the exile. One change seems to be that the concepts of demons were more clear and organized and there is even an appearance of a figure of evil, Satan, who operates in open rebellion against God. To balance against the demons,

---

[4]Ruth 1:16, 17.

angels are also conceived as being in a hierarchy, with seven archangels. The shadowy experience of Sheol as the destination of the dead changes to a more vivid concept of the resurrection of the dead and an afterlife in another realm with a pronounced theme of either reward or punishment for one's earthly life. There is a concept that God's agent would come in the clouds to deliver his people at the end of the world. The Zoroastrian concept of a last judgment, as contrasted with the specific times of judgment within a life of a nation as in Amos, became gradually more pronounced until it had a strong grasp on the minds of Jews of certain religious parties. There seems also to have been a recognition that Persia, as well as Egypt, was a land of scholars and wise men.

While new institutions were brought home from the exile, namely the synagogue and services of worship led by the laymen, the old institutions of worship were revived and purified. The priests and scribes were well established and in control of Jerusalem with the support of Nehemiah. The temple was rebuilt and refurnished. There is no doubt that it had precedence over the synagogues and that priests were more important in worship than were lay people. While the institutions of the exile would survive the destruction of Jerusalem under the Romans and help maintain Judaism during its worldwide dispersion, their presence immediately after the exile led to a dual system of worship and politics which remained in tension through the next few centuries.

The literature assembled during the exile formed a common basis for the life of the Jews in Judah. Nevertheless, the rather rigorous interpretation given to the law by Nehemiah and by Ezra did not go without challenge, as one might find in the book of Ruth. There were also people who remembered the great prophets of the eighth century B.C. and of the seventh and sixth centuries. Their dynamic view of life and God's continual interaction with his people remained alive in the minds of some people. The interaction of the spirit of God with individuals and with the nation was somewhat in tension with the rigid concept that the complete relationship of God and Judah was spelled out once and for all in the law of Moses.

Although the Jews in the time of Ezra and Nehemiah had not known the great kings of the children of Israel, they knew about them. If anything, the kings had grown in stature across the years. It was easy enough to see that aside from the Persian rulers, no one else known to the Jews had the stature of their former kings, David and Solomon. They looked back at those good old days with reverence; but they also began to think of the possibility that such a king might arise again among their own people.

A marked class consciousness was emphasized by Ezra and Nehemiah that had not been present in such a strong way during the time of Moses and Joshua. Wealth was not the dividing line; purity and ancestry was. The people who returned from the exile were the good, old, first families of Jerusalem. Those who had remained behind in Judah and kept themselves from foreigners were next down the pyramid, and those of Judah who had married foreigners were below them. But alas, the Jews of Samaria who had intermarried with foreigners and those who had been brought in by Assyria to populate the land of the ten northern tribes were looked upon as even lower than the pure foreigners. Each class developed its own beliefs, practices, and heroes. Their hopes and aspirations for the future were different, and those differences increased until the destruction of Jerusalem.

In the prophet Zechariah, one finds exhibited a desire for a new anointed one, a messiah, who would provide civil and religious leadership for the nation. Zechariah picked a poor candidate in Zerubbabel, as other people came to realize. The absence of a suitable candidate at any given time in history did not dissuade people from the process of expanding the concept that a mighty leader of some sort would arise among them to restore the former glory of their people. Such hope almost guaranteed a following of sorts for any self-proclaimed leader who might emerge to deal with a grievance of any sizable group of people. The kind of independence from foreign rulers which had allowed the kingdom of David and Solomon to enjoy prosperity and creative strength was not to return in the few centuries, and the hope of some kind of super-historical solution gained ground among Jews who were not satisfied with their life under those conditions.

The expectation that God would send a messiah to deliver his people from oppression was a concept which would have profound influence on the beginnings of Christianity.

SUGGESTIONS FOR ADDITIONAL READING

Ezra, Nehemiah, Ruth, Haggai and Zechariah,
and related Commentaries

Fuerst, Wesley J. *The Books of Ruth, Esther, Ecclesiastes, Song of Songs, and Lamentations.* Cambridge: Cambridge University Press, 1975.

Hals, Ronald M. *The Theology of the Book of Ruth.* Philadelphia: Fortress Press, 1952.

CHAPTER 8

GREEKS, MACCABEANS, AND ROMANS

The modern state of Israel has found it almost impossible to establish borders which are recognized and respected by its neighbors. That condition has existed at almost every period when Jews have attempted to have a state on that location. The people who have threatened their sovereignty in the past have changed, but one will recognize that Syria was an ancient enemy for them.

The location of Judah on the highways running between Egypt and Asia and between Egypt and Europe meant that any major changes in the world power were sure to have some effect on Judah. The powers of Assyria and Babylon had worked against the Jews. The power of Egypt had sometimes worked in their favor and sometimes against them. The Persian influence was the only one that the Jews regarded as completely positive, probably because it corrected a situation that had been intolerable to them. The Greeks and the Romans who came after the earlier invaders each made contributions to Judaism, but their final assessment by the Jews was very much on the negative side.

The Greeks entered the lives of the Jews during the lifetime of Alexander the Great, the son of Philip of Macedon, whose rule lasted from 336 to 323 B.C. With an ambition to bring Greek culture to the whole world, this former pupil of the Greek philosopher Aristotle was well on his way, having reached the Indus river in Pakistan by the year

326. Had he not died in the thirty-third year of his life, he may have succeeded in his dream. Upon his death, however, his kingdom was divided so that Egypt went to Ptolemy and Mesopotamia and Syria went to the Seleucids. In both realms Hellenism, a culture of Greek thought and customs fostered by the successors of Alexander, kept the influence of the former leader alive. The great Hellenic city of Egypt, Alexandria, had a library that was renowned in the ancient world.

While the long interchange between Greek thought and Jewish thought was to accomplish changes on both sides, the two thought systems could never be resolved without tension if one tried to remain true to both of them. The ground of Jewish thought was the God of Abraham, Isaac, and Jacob; all truth came down from God above to human persons and entered through them into history. On the other hand, the ground of Greek philosophical thought was the human mind, which could, through its exercise of reason, know all that is worth knowing about the world and arrive at new truths by the application of logic. The life based on reason and self-examination was to be prized far above any life based on tradition and authority. A certain amount of tension between these two systems was inevitable.

There is disagreement among scholars as to whether there was direct influence of Greek thought in Jewish scriptures. Both sides have to admit that the Septuagint, a Greek translation of the Jewish scriptures prepared under Ptolemy II (285-246 B.C.), was a product of Hellenist influence. Beyond that, liberal scholars often hold that until the Hellenistic influence took hold after the life of Alexander there was almost no trace of a "wisdom" literature among Jews such as appeared after the time of Alexander. Scholars who line up on the side of little Greek influence in Jewish thought argue that the Jews had a separate tradition of their own wisdom which developed independently of Greek influence. A possible third position seems to be that while there was Greek influence upon Jewish thought and literature, the particular form it took in Judaism was, in the final analysis, Jewish rather than Greek.

The literature is referred to as "wisdom" literature because rather than being concerned so much with Jewish history, the cult of worship, or with experience of God, it is concerned with a quest for wisdom in its own right. As one example, one might consider the book of Proverbs, usually attributed in Jewish tradition to King Solomon himself.[1] The book is a collection of short sayings to be memorized and applied to life:

---

[1] Proverbs.

The fear of the Lord is the beginning of knowledge;
    fools despise wisdom and instruction (1:7).

My son, be attentive to my wisdom,
    incline your ear to my understanding;
that you may keep discretion,
    and your lips may guard knowledge (5:1).

Go to the ant, O sluggard;
    consider her ways and be wise (6:6).

Wisdom builds her house,
    but folly with her own hands tears it down.
He who walks in uprightness fears the Lord,
    but he who is devious in his ways despises him (14:1, 2).

One who has read the Greek philosophers (lovers of wisdom) recognizes how different such ready-made and applicable sayings are from the searching inquiries of Plato's dialogues or the treatises of Aristotle.

The book of Ecclesiastes, which introduces itself as a product prepared by the son of David who ruled in Jerusalem, is anything but a writing prepared by the outgoing and optimistic Solomon presented in the book of Kings. The theme of the book is announced immediately in the first line:

Vanity of vanities, says the Preacher,
    vanity of vanities! All is vanity.[2]

The sense of progress of history developed in Isaiah, Jeremiah, and Ezekiel has given way to a conviction that there is nothing new under the sun!

What has been is what will be,
    and what has been done is what will be done;
and there is nothing new under the sun (1:9).

He recites how he attempted to gain satisfaction in life through acquiring possessions and pursuing pleasures and discovered in the end that such a course is folly. Turning aside from this life, he decided to pursue wisdom. It is true that wisdom is better than folly as light is better than darkness. However, it then became obvious that the wise man will die the same as the fool. So wisdom too, in the end, is vanity and striving after the wind.

In time, everything happens according to its season. If one does not

---

[2]Ecclesiastes.

like what is happening now, just wait, it will change. For everything there is a season, and a time for every matter under heaven:

> a time to be born, and a time to die;
> at time to plant, and a time to pluck up what is planted;
> a time to kill, and a time to heal;
> a time to break down, and a time to build up;
> a time to weep and a time to laugh
> a time to mourn and a time to dance. . . (3:2-4).

Man has eternity placed in his mind by God, yet he cannot find out what God has done from the beginning to the end. He knows and he does not know. To die is better than to be born, but never to have been born at all is better than either. One is not awarded according to one's merits and death comes suddenly without one having knowledge when it will be.

There is a certain cynicism in Ecclesiastes. There is also a sense that man is in the hands of fate, *Moira*. Nothing that one does can really change the life that has already been recorded for one. A person cannot escape fate, which seems either to be equivalent with God, or perhaps even above him! Fate and God are past finding out.

Another fascinating piece of literature is the book of Job.[3] Whether one places it in this particular period depends to a great extent on whether one classifies the prose opening, chapters one and two, and the prose closing, chapter 42, as an integral part of the original work, which is in poetry rather than prose. As the book stands today it is the story of a pious man, Job, who feared God and was blameless in every way. God had made him prosperous with children and many possessions. Satan argued to God that Job did not love God as God but only for the possessions. To prove otherwise, God turned Job over to Satan to be tested. Not only did Job lose his children and his possessions, but also he became painfully afflicted himself and had to suffer the indignities of "friends" who told him that his punishment was because he had sinned against God. Job, nevertheless, remained faithful to God, much to the disgust of Satan, and God restored double Job's wealth to his faithful servant.

But take away the prose setting of the poem and one has an earnest set of dialogues, reminiscent of the dialogues of Socrates, which wrestle with the perennial human question, "Why do the righteous suffer?" Eliphaz, Bildad, and Zophar, who come to comfort Job, represent the traditional pious people who believe that good conduct is rewarded with

---

[3]Job.

health and wealth and that financial loss and human suffering are a sure sign that one has displeased the almighty by sinning, even though one may not be fully aware of what one has done, at least in the beginning. "The patience of Job," which in myth seems to have been endless, is certainly not found by one who really reads what Job says. He is impatient not only with his wife and his visitors, but also he is ready to go to court with God to seek an impartial decision in his case. He can find no reason at all why he should suffer when he has been a completely righteous man according to Jewish law.

The trial was really no contest at all. For the questions God asked Job were unanswerable, at least by him:

> Then the Lord answered Job out of the whirlwind:
> "Who is this that darkens counsel
>   by words without knowledge?
> Gird up your loins like a man,
>   I will question you, and you shall declare to me."

> "Where were you when I laid the
>   foundations of the earth?
> Tell me if you have understanding.
> Who determined its measurements
>   —surely you know!
> Or who stretched the line upon it?
> On what were its bases sunk,
>   or who laid its cornerstone,
> when the morning stars sang together,
>   and all the sons of God shouted for joy?" (38:1-7).

After many verses of questions on the inscrutable power and wisdom of God, Job could only answer:

> I know that thou canst do all things,
>   and that no purpose of thine can be thwarted.
> Who is this that hides counsel without knowledge:
> Therefore I have uttered what I did not understand,
>   things too wonderful for me, which I did not know.
> Hear, and I will speak;
>   I will question you, and you declare to me.
> I had heard of thee by the hearing of the ear,
>   but now my eye sees thee;
> therefore I despise myself,
>   and repent in dust and ashes (42:2-6).

What is the answer to why the righteous suffer? There is none for man to know. Some things are past finding out and must be left by human beings in the hands of God. This answer is essentially a Jewish answer rather than an answer of Greek philosophers, who wanted to settle all questions by reason rather than by relying on faith in gods. About the closest the Greeks came to the position of Job was in the philosophy of the Stoics who counseled a rational, dispassionate approach to the inevitable changes one must encounter in any life.

Hellenism affected Jewish life in ways far more serious than literature and games. The Seleucids of Syria and the Ptolemies of Egypt were under constant tension and political struggle, which could not help but have influence on the little country of Judah, caught between them. Antiochus IV (175-163 B.C.), was better known as Antiochus Epiphanes because he claimed to be Zeus manifested in the world.

It was a squabble between the two high bidders for the office of high priest that brought Judah under the unwelcomed attention of Antiochus. Two Jews, both Hellenizers with Greek names, Jason and Menelaus, had each placed a bid of office with Antiochus and each assumed that he had won the office. They began to fight each other and Menelaus appealed to Antiochus to come to his aid in securing the office he had bought with the higher bid. Antiochus was glad to oblige. With his army Antiochus established Menelaus as high priest and then plundered the temple as a lesson to the Jews, one which spilt Jewish blood. He was not through with the stubborn and rebellious Jews, however. He erected a statue of Zeus in their Jerusalem temple and sacrificed a pig—the most unclean of animals according to Jewish thinking—on the altar. Nor did he stop with that pointed insult. He made three acts essential to Judaism punishable by death: possessing a copy of Torah, observing the Sabbath, or practicing circumcision. Since Judaism could not survive under those conditions, it was only a matter of time and circumstances for open rebellion to occur.

The explosion came in an out-of-the-way place, Modin, a small village northwest of Jerusalem, where a priest named Mattathias refused to make the pagan sacrifice demanded by the Syrian officer in charge. The order was obeyed by another Jew. Enraged, Mattathias killed the Jew and the Syrian officer. He had to flee for his life then, and he went to the hills, taking his five sons with him. They were not alone in their struggle, for other Jews came out with them to join in their fierce guerilla warfare against the occupying troops from Syria. Upon the death of Mattathias in 166 B.C., leadership passed to his oldest son, Judas, who was known as "the hammer," Maccabeus. Judas was victorious over the Syrian army and negotiated a peace which permitted him, in December of 165 B.C., to restore the service of Jewish worship in the Jerusalem temple. Hanukkah or the Feast of Lights celebrated by Jews in the month of Kislev marks the occasion of this mighty victory by the Maccabees. The wars continued under the leadership of three brothers, and over a period of time the Jews attained a measure of independence which lasted almost a century.[4]

Such a powerful struggle for survival of the Jewish faith may not have been without its effects upon the literature of the Jews. Although the book of Daniel purports to describe events during the fall of Jerusalem and the subsequent captivity in Babylon, it contains so many historical inaccuracies that some scholars of literary-historical criticism think it belongs in a period much later.[5] And since it predicts the future in terms more accurate than the period which it ostensibly describes, it is thought to have been a product of the period of Antiochus Epiphanes.

The book of Daniel represents a new kind of prophetic literature. It deals with a current problem facing the Jews and it talks about the intervention of God as a judge, as did other literature of the prophets. The difference is that it presents a hero who stands firm for his faith no matter what the threat from the enemies of his faith. Moreover, it presents a time of judgment which, rather than punishing the Jews for their unfaithfulness to God, rewards those Jews who have been faithful to him. Those punished are the enemies of the Jews who have tried to force them to abandon their law and customs. There is also a vision of a kingdom of God which is not of this world in which persons whom God has raised from the dead will live in victory and peace. The whole message is couched in symbols that would be readily interpreted by Jews of the period of the author but would be confusing to outsiders who might read the scroll. Such literature came to be known as apocalyptic, that is, revelation.

Daniel is described as a captive taken to Babylon. He has an amazing amount of contact with the king, considering that he is a captive. He turns out to be wiser than all the wise men of Babylon, and healthier than the Babylonians by rejecting their food and remaining true to the diet of the Hasidim. He informs the king that it is his God who makes him superior, and according to the story, Nebuchadnezzar also acknowledges the power of Daniel's God.

Several stories in Daniel have been popular in western literature. One concerns Shadrach, Meshach, and Abednego, three friends of Daniel who

---

[4]Apocrypha, Maccabees.

[5]Daniel.

survived their attempted execution in a fiery furnace. Another concerns Daniel's miraculous survival after having been confined in a den of hungry lions. A third story involves cryptic writing by a human hand at the feast of Balshazzar.

The message of the book of Daniel is parallel to the teaching of the Hasidim in the time of the Maccabees. In spite of the worst kind of persecution imaginable, a Jew who is faithful to his God will be saved by God and vindicated before the enemies of his faith.

Another book with a setting in the Persian period, in the reign of Xerxes I (486-465 B.C.), designated Ahasuerus in the account, is the story of Esther. It is essentially the story of a heroine who risked her own life to save her Jewish people from a massacre which arose through anti-Semitism.[6]

Displeased with his queen, Vashti, because she refused to yield to his command invitation to show her beauty to his dinner guests in the winter palace, Ahasuerus ran a beauty contest to find a new queen. The position was easily won by a Jewish girl, Hadassah, or Esther. Unfortunately, the new queen had a cousin who failed to give proper courtesies to Haman, the grand vizier of Xerxes. Haman persuaded the king to schedule a massacre of all Jews on the thirteenth day of the month of Adar because they insisted on keeping their own laws and refused to be assimilated with the Persians. At the peril of her life, Esther approached the king to intercede for her cousin and her people. As things worked out, Haman was hanged on the very gallows he had constructed for Esther's cousin Mordecai and Haman's ten sons were also executed so that his family line came to an end. On the thirteenth and fourteenth of Adar the Jews were allowed by the king to kill their persecutors in Susa and throughout the kingdom. This story, although not religious in the sense of talking about God, was closely associated with the festival of Purim, giving an explanation why the celebration, which was so popular in Maccabean times, was held annually.

Whether the book of Esther was written at the close of the Persian period or during the Hellenist age, perhaps during the Maccabean struggles, is not of monumental importance. What is important is that in a time when the Jews were being persecuted for their faith they were given a model of beauty and courage to consider and a hope that as they had weathered adversity in the past, so would they be able to overcome it in new situations.

---

[6]Esther.

The measure of independence which the Jews achieved after the Maccabean wars, enduring almost a century, was, in light of their past history, too unusual to last much longer. Unfortunately it was the Jews themselves who brought about a condition which led them to invite intervention by an outside force. The line of the Maccabean sons came to an end with Simon and his sons John Hyrcanus and Alexander Jannaeus. Alexander's widow ruled about nine years, holding on to a stable period of government, but conflict developed between her sons after her death. Each of them sought support for his side by going to the Roman leader Pompey, who was in Syria. In fact, a third faction also went to him asking for an abolition of the monarchy altogether. Pompey was willing to go to Jerusalem to restore order and in 63 B.C. Roman rule began in Judea, although it was nominally through Jewish officials. A son of Alexandra, Hyrcanus II, was appointed High Priest by Pompey. Much to the resentment of the Jews, an Idumean by the name of Antipater was his minister to carry out Roman policy.

The rule of the house of Herod began in 40 B.C. with the appointment of Herod as king of Judea and Samaria, a position he held until his death in 4 B.C. In many ways he was a ruthless ruler, murdering members of his own family when he doubted their loyalty to him. On the other hand he tried, without much success, to overcome the Jews' resentment of his Idumean ancestry by constructing a new temple in Jerusalem. Although the work began in 20 B.C. it was not completed until after the death of Herod during the succession of his three sons. In spite of strong Jewish feelings for the house of Herod by some and bitter opposition from others, the Romans found the house satisfactory for their purposes as long as its members could keep order and pay their taxes.

The Jews were not always buffered from the Romans themselves. From 6 to 66 A.D. Judea experienced the administration of 14 procurators. In part they ruled through the High Priest and the Sanhedrin by allowing them to handle matters which were primarily Jewish. However, the procurators had difficulty understanding why the Jews were so obstinate about the worship of one God and so touchy about their holy days and daily customs. Partly they were not in office long enough to learn very much and partly they did not care enough to make the effort to understand what to them was a perverse people. They seemed to be concerned, however, to maintain order and were largely successful in doing so down to the time of Felix (51 A.D.) when assassinations became rather commonplace.

Several political and religious parties sprang up during the Roman period for the Jews could not agree among themselves either about religion or about politics. In some ways the political parties were the easiest to describe. The Herodians were partial to the house of Herod and wanted rulers from that family to have power. Zealots were Jews who could not stand Roman rule and who pledged themselves to work for open rebellion. The religious parties had different ideas not only about religion but also about politics.

Sadducees were cultured Hellenizers and were willing to compromise with Rome. They were wealthy, aristocratic, and willing to go along politically in order to maintain their high status. Religiously they were conservative, following the position of the Zadokites in worship and accepting only the Torah as their guide to life. The new doctrine of the resurrection of the dead was rejected by them.

Pharisees, on the other hand, were conservative politically and liberal in religion. They were middle and lower class with little to gain by maintaining the status quo. They resisted Hellenism in order to keep their ceremonial purity, and in the same way they resisted the Romans politically. In religion they were more a phenomenon of the synagogue than of the temple, looking to the authority of the scribes and the rabbis or teachers. They also accepted Torah, as did the Sadducees, but the Pharisees reserved the right to interpret it and to include in their beliefs and practices the contents of oral tradition. They definitely believed and taught the doctrine of the bodily resurrection of the dead.

A third group was the Essenes who withdrew from society more than did the other groups, seeking the kind of purity of the Hasidim. They resisted Hellenism and avoided interaction with Romans. They tried to live by Torah and other sacred writings and kept themselves ceremonially pure, often using ritual washings and burial of body wastes. They kept strict observance of the Sabbath and generally avoided marriage, depending on recruiting of converts to keep their communities going. They were interesting enough to attract the historians Philo and Flavius of the first century. Later studies of the Dead Sea Scrolls and the site of the Qumran community have shed even more light on that type of holy community withdrawn from the Roman world to protect its Jewish purity.

With all that tension within the Jewish community and between Jews and Romans, it was only a matter of time until Jewish ways would clash with the efficiency of Roman administration and the strength of the Roman law. By the late sixties of the first century, the conflict was open and serious. But before that conflagration began for Jews a new faith, Christianity, was born within the ancient faith of Judaism.

SUGGESTIONS FOR ADDITIONAL READING

Proverbs, Ecclesiastes, Job, Maccabees, Daniel,
Esther and related Commentaries

Burrows, Millar. *More Light on the Dead Sea Scrolls*. New York: Viking Press, 1958.

Charles, R. H. *The Apocrypha and Pseudepigrapha*, 2 volumes. Oxford: Clarendon Press, 1973.

Collins, J. J. *The Apocalyptic Vision of the Book of Daniel*. Missoula, Montana: Scholars Press, 1977.

Enslin, M. S. *Christian Beginnings*. New York: Harper and Row, 1938.

Fuerst, W. J. *The Books of Ruth, Esther, The Song of Songs, Lamentations*. Cambridge: Cambridge University Press, 1975.

Goodspeed, Edgar J. *The Story of the Apocrypha*. Chicago: The University of Chicago Press, 1967.

Gordis, Robert. *The Book of Job*. New York: The Jewish Theological Seminary of America, 1978.

Gordis, Robert. *Koheleth, The Man and His World: A Study of Ecclesiastes*. New York: Schocken Books, 1973.

Hereford, R. T. *The Pharisees*. New York: The Macmillan Co., 1924.

Jastrow, Morris. *A Gentle Cynic* (Ecclesiastes). Philadelphia: J. B. Lippencott Company, 1919.

Kallen, Horace M. *The Book of Job as a Greek Tragedy*. New York: Hill and Wang, 1959.

McKane, William. *Proverbs*. Philadelphia: The Westminster Press, 1977.

Metzger, Bruce M. *An Introduction to the Apocrypha*. Chicago: The University of Chicago Press, 1967.

Oesterley, W. O. E. *Jews and Judaism During the Greek Period*. Port Washington, New York: Kennikat Press, 1941.

Pfeiffer, Robert H. *History of New Testament Times with an Introduction to the Apocrypha*. New York: Harper and Row, 1949.

Rosenberg, David. *Job Speaks*. New York: Harper and Row, 1977.

Schubert, Kurt. *The Dead Sea Community.* Westport, Conn: Greenwood Press, 1959.

Singer, R. E. *Job's Encounter.* New York: Bookman Associates, 1963.

Snaith, N. H. *The Book of Job.* London: S. C. M. Press, Ltd., 1968.

Stendahl, Krister, ed. *The Scrolls and the New Testament.* New York: Harper and Brothers, 1957.

Van der Ploeg, J. Translated by Kevin Smyth. *The Excavations at Qumran.* London: Longmans, Green, and Co., 1958.

Von Rad, Gerhard. *Wisdom in Israel.* New York: Abingdon Press, 1974.

Whybray, R. N. *Wisdom in Proverbs.* Naperville, Illinois: Alec R. Allenson, Inc., 1965.

Wilson, Edmund. *The Dead Sea Scrolls, 1947-1969.* New York: Oxford University Press, 1969.

CHAPTER 9

A SEARCH FOR DELIVERANCE:

Judas, John and Jesus

While the Sadducees were at least satisfied to accept Roman rule with as much grace as possible and to enjoy the fruits of this world coming to them in their privileged position, the Zealots were pledged to do something to rid the country of the imperial intruders. When Quirinius, the governor of Syria, ordered a census, to the Jews always a sign that inescapable tax increases were to follow, some Zealots and Pharisees decided that enough was enough. So in 6 A.D. Zadok the Pharisee and Judas the Galilean tried the road of the Maccabeans, the way of open revolt. Their platform was simple and solid, easily understood by all Jews, and sure to arouse moral support:

No God but Yahweh.
No tax but to the temple.
No friend but the Zealot.

However, more than enthusiasm was needed by the Zealots when the Roman general Varus entered the fray with two of his legions. The Romans were much stronger than the Syrians who had been faced by the Maccabees and the rebellion ended with the burning of Sepphoris and the crucifixion of thousands of Zealots. Killing prisoners on a cross of wood was a normal form of capital punishment used by the Romans, as surely painful as it was surely permanent in ending their problem with a particular individual.

The object lesson was effective with other Jews for better than sixty years and serious, open revolt was held in check. Resentment continued under a tense surface of civility, occasionally violated by individuals and small bands of Jews whom the Romans chose to label "robbers." Dreams and hopes of the future in which some deliverer would provide a way out of oppression glowed warmly in most of the Jews except the Sadducees. Even the people of the land, those without particular party affiliation, had their own hopes, which were as diverse as the people who made up the masses of Jews. The major prophets of the Hebrews had painted some glowing visions of what life could be under God's rule, when he restored his people to their chosen place and destroyed all of their enemies. For many of the masses there was a feeling that the time of God's intervention was near at hand.

The people were not without their ideas of how the deliverance might come. For some there was hope that a descendant of the great king David would seize a throne and establish again the kingdom which initiated a golden age for the Hebrews of the past. According to the prophecies they favored, a direct descendant would appear to accomplish this crucial task. Others seemed to think more of a wise and wealthy ruler like king Solomon, whose reign was, if more restrictive, more golden, in the physical sense of the term. Of more recent and vivid memory was that other Judas, the successful son of Mattathias whose exploits against the Syrians earned him a place alongside Joshua, Saul, and David in military leadership. The Zealots and the Pharisees could concur with the common people who envisioned that kind of leadership.

People whose temperaments led them more in the ways of the Essenes or the community of Qumran on the Dead Sea thought more in non-military terms. They sought a humble and holy servant, a man of righteousness and peace who would bind and heal the wounds of his people. In a sense, his kingdom would not be of the worldly type, but a kind of servant of the Lord type, where the real ruler would be God himself. The direct reign of God was the only way that people could see to overcome both the strength of Rome and the corruptibility of human leaders.

The Jewish feeling that God would soon intervene to establish his kingdom was given a boost among the common people by the preaching of a man called John, known popularly as "the baptist." John, the son of a priest, had turned his back on the formal worship to be found in the temple of Jerusalem or in any village house which served as a synagogue.[1] As did the Essenes, he preferred to live apart from the centers of population. However, John was a lonely figure by comparison. It is true that he attracted disciples, but there is little evidence that he tried to form an ordered community of like-minded individuals. Instead, he lived in lonely places beyond the Jordan, surviving on a restricted diet of wild honey and locusts. His coarse cloak was woven of camel hair; it was gathered around his waist with a wide leather belt.[2] His stark figure and his ascetic life heightened the effect of the compelling and austere message which he proclaimed to the crowds who came out to the Jordan river to seek him.

"Repent, for the kingdom of heaven is at hand!" (Matthew 3:2) was his short but startling theme. For those who did want to repent and turn around in their thinking and practices, John had an outward way of symbolizing their birth into a new life. He took them into the Jordan River and used its water to wash away their sins. That was not the end of the matter, however. When they asked what they were to do, John's ethical message was sharp and clear. Do you have two coats? Give one to him who has none! Do you have extra food? Give some to those who have none! When tax collectors wanted to straighten out their lives with God, John told them, "Collect no more than is appointed you!"[3] To the soldiers who asked what they could do, he responded, "Rob no one by violence or by false accusation, and be content with your wages!"[4]

Such a celebrity attracted the curious as well as the contrite. Among those who came from Jerusalem were the Pharisees and the Sadducees, both representing the staid approach of well-established religious institutions. John's confrontation with them was so clear that even the lowliest peasant could not escape his opinion of the religious leaders of Israel. "You brood of vipers, who warned you to flee from the wrath to come?"[5] was not a greeting calculated to win friends in the establishment. Their claim that they had Abraham as their father was of no value in the judgment to come. After all, God could turn stones into descendants of Abraham if he wanted to. The question is simply whether one bears fruits

---

[1]Luke 1.

[2]Mark 1.

[3]Luke 3:13.

[4]Luke 3:14.

[5]Luke 3:7.

that speak of repentance, for already the ax has been swung at the roots of the trees, and anyone that does not bear fruit will be cut down and cast into the fire! There was no doubt that John was an awesome prophet in the tradition of the major prophets of Israel and Judah; he was also like them in arousing anger in persons strong enough to plot his silence.

John did not proclaim himself to be the deliverer the Jews had been hoping for; instead, he pictured himself as a forerunner, a preparer of the way of the Lord. Although he baptized with water for repentance, he proclaimed that there was one coming after him who would be greater than he was, so great that John was not worthy even to tie his sandals. That one's baptism of the Jews would be with the Holy Spirit and with fire; like a thresher he would stand on the threshing floor with his winnowing fork in his hand, separating out the wheat for the granary and the chaff to be burned with unquenchable fire. According to some accounts, John flatly denied being the messiah.[6]

Among those who came out to John at the Jordan was the son of Mary, a kinswoman of John's mother, Elizabeth. Jesus, a name based on that of the Hebrew leader Joshua, had been given to that kinsman born only a short time after John. Now he had come and presented himself to be baptized, to testify in public to his identification with the message, movement, and symbol of John. Apparently his character was already such that John had some question about his need for any repentance or about his own role as one who could purify Jesus. Nevertheless, Jesus insisted on the rite and received it from John in public. It was reported later, by his followers, that on coming out of the water Jesus received the Holy Spirit, which descended upon him as a dove, and heard the voice of God saying, "This is my beloved Son, with whom I am well pleased."

According to accounts prepared later by his followers, Jesus then went himself into the lonely places inhabited by John in order to fast and pray, seeking the guidance of God on the kind of fruit his own life would bear in relationship to the movement begun by John. The period of fasting was reported in the familiar terms of "forty days and forty nights," after which Jesus was hungry. In that weakened state he was confronted by the tempter (devil) who offered three routes he could go with his own work.[7]

The kind of fearless criticism John the Baptist made of the leading Jews was not long to be endured in a land given over to a climate of

---

[6]John 1:20.

[7]Matthew 4:1.

repression. John's personal preaching in public was brought to an abrupt end by Herod the tetrarch.[8] Herod had taken the wife of his brother Philip, Herodias, for his own wife. John had declared to Herod that the action was not lawful. Naturally Herodias was angry and so was Herod. He vented his wrath by having John bound and cast into prison. Yet at the same time he was a little afraid of John, either because he might be right or because masses of people looked to John as their leader. In time, however, Herodias forced Herod to go further in dealing with John than he had intended. Herod entrapped himself so that he had to behead John.

From the time that John was cast into prison, a cloud hung over the hopes people had for his movement of deliverance from the evils of the age. Yet, in spite of the gloom, a ray of hope began to shine in the region of Galilee, for the Jesus who had come to John for baptism had now begun his own work, apparently in the tradition of John. The message of Jesus was essentially that of John, "The time is fulfilled, and the kingdom of God is at hand; repent, and believe in the gospel."[9] Like John he gathered disciples around him, the first from Capernaum, a town on the Sea of Galilee. They were two sets of brothers who were commercial fishermen of the Sea; Simon and Andrew and James and John, the sons of a man named Zebedee whose operation was large enought to include hired workers in addition to his family.

Jesus was not as spectacular as John in his dress or in his place of habitation, but he immediately attracted attention. His appearance was ordinary, it seems, and he operated simply in the established synagogues of villages and towns, doing what any Jewish male might do on the Sabbath by reading the scrolls to the congregation and commenting upon what he had read. But according to his followers there were two things that made an indelible impression on people who saw him in action: his teaching and his healing.[10] It was not that he said anything that they had never heard before; it was the way he said it, for he did not give a list of opinions of rabbis but stated clearly what the passage meant as if he had the authority to give the true and final word on the matter. The second thing that impressed the people of the Capernaum synagogue was the way he dealt with a person who would be described today as mentally ill. In those days the man was described as being possessed by an unclean

---

[8]Matthew 14.

[9]Mark 1:15.

[10]Mark 1:21.

spirit. Jesus commanded the spirit to be silent and to come out of the man. The man went into a convulsion and cried with a loud voice, but then he was well. The witnesses had one question. Who was this man who had authority over the unclean spirits? As lightning, the word of this man's authority crackled through the community. What would he do next?

With his four disciples he left the synagogue and went to the home of Simon and Andrew. When he found Simon's mother-in-law ill with a fever he went in and took her by the hand and the fever not only left her but she was well enough to get up and serve the guests. In the small town the word of the second healing passed from house to house. When the sun went down and the Sabbath ended, the townspeople brought their ill to Simon's house, and it seemed that the whole town was gathered at Simon's door seeking healing from Jesus of Nazareth. It appeared that he had found a home and a base for his mission as far as the people of Capernaum were concerned. But the next morning he was up long before day, spending a period of time alone in prayer. His disciples found him and informed him that everyone was searching for him. He told them that he had to move on to the other towns of Galilee to do the same kind of work he had done in Capernaum.

The very number of people coming to Jesus attracted attention not only of the curious but also of the cautious. The first thing the people of Capernaum had noticed about Jesus was self-assurance, his authority. For those who were authorities in religion and in civil administration, Jesus' manner created a problem. Where did he think he obtained his authority and how much did he think that he had? What kinds of problems would he create for them with the people of the land? The scribes and the Pharisees were deeply disturbed almost at once and came to listen and observe for themselves. They did not have to wait long before they took exception to concrete examples in Jesus' behavior.

When he returned to Capernaum and it became well known that he was at home again, the house where he was teaching was filled to overflowing so that no one could get in the door. A lame man was carried on a bed roll by four of his friends, for they had hoped to have him healed by Jesus. When they found that they could not get into the house to gain the teacher's attention, they cleverly climbed the stairs to the flat roof above the room where Jesus was. Then they removed some of the roof tiles and while the inhabitants below looked up in surprise used lines tied to the bed roll to lower their crippled friend down to the floor immediately in front of Jesus. Naturally Jesus paused in his teaching and, impressed by the faith of the five men, said to the cripple on the pallet,

"My son, your sins are forgiven."[11]

The shock of the scribes in the room was visible. Who gave this man from Nazareth the authority to forgive sins? Jesus perceived their questions and responded,

"Which is easier, to say to the paralytic 'Your sins are forgiven,' or to say, 'Rise, take up your pallet and walk?' But that you may know that the Son of man has authority on earth to forgive sins," he said to the paralytic, "I say to you, rise, take up your pallet and go home." (Mark 2:9-11)

The paralytic got up, rolled up his bed and left. That healing had occurred was observed by all. But the fact that healing had occurred was lost on the scribes; they were obsessed with the belief that Jesus had committed blasphemy, a sin punishable by stoning, for, in their minds, God alone could forgive sins, and in claiming to forgive sins Jesus had equated himself with God.

Even with the great crowds of people who assembled by the sea to hear him teach Jesus ran some risks. For in addition to the fishermen from his fishing center of Capernaum he chose Levi, the son of Alphaeus, who was in the tax office—he was a collector of taxes, a profession despised by the common people of the Jews. Later when Jesus went to the home of Levi to eat a meal many of the guests were other tax collectors, people regarded as sinners by the Pharisees. Jesus was asked why he associated with such unclean people. Jesus responded, "Those who are well have no need for a physician, but those who are sick; I am not to call the righteous, but sinners."[12]

There seemed to be no end to the kinds of conflicts that could arise between Jesus and accepted practices of religion. John's disciples were fasting, perhaps because John had been arrested, and Jesus and his disciples were going to banquets. Why was Jesus enjoying himself with sinners? He grabbed a few grains of food from a grainfield he and his disciples were passing through on the Sabbath, and Pharisees who saw the act accused him of harvesting on the Sabbath. Again he healed a man in a synagogue on the Sabbath, for the man had a withered hand; the Pharisees accused him of violating the Sabbath by doing unlawful work.

---

[11]Mark 2:5.

[12]Mark 2:17.

While the Pharisees followed his actions in order to find fault the common people swarmed to him wherever he went. It was difficult for him ever to be alone with his disciples. He did slip away to the hills and take with him only those whom he invited. There he chose twelve of the disciples who were to have a special function, that is, to be sent out, apostles, to preach and do works in his name. According to the list in the gospel of Mark they were: Simon, whom Jesus called Peter; James and John, the sons of Zebedee whom he called Boanerges, that is, sons of thunder; Andrew; Philip; Bartholomew; Matthew; Thomas; James the son of Alphaeus; Thaddaeus; Simon the Cananaean; and Judas Iscariot, who betrayed him.

An ugly rumor developed which apparently concerned even some of his acquaintances, that is, that he was possessed by a demon himself, which accounted for the fact, supposedly, that he could cast out demons in others; the theory was that it took one to know one. Jesus did not abandon his crowds or his healing on this account, for he believed that healing occurred through the holy spirit of God and such remarks were a blasphemy against the Lord God. He calmed the waves of the Sea when he and his disciples were caught out on the Sea of Galilee at night in a storm. He healed a wild man thought to be demon possessed in the region of the Gerasenes. For his thanks the local hog farmers asked him to leave their country. A woman with a hemorrhage which had lasted for years touched his garment and was healed. He healed a twelve year old daughter of a ruler of a synagogue when it was reported to him that she was dead.

The success that Jesus had in the region of Capernaum was not repeated when he returned to his own country. The response in the synagogue of Nazareth was that they had never heard anyone speak with such authority, but who did he think that he was? They had known him for years and his family was there in their city. They refused to have faith in him and he could not do any of the great works there as he had done in Capernaum.

About that time he multiplied his own efforts through use of his apostles. He sent them through the countryside with strict instructions. They were to travel in pairs, to carry only a staff, no bread, no bag, no money, or extra tunics. They were to find a house and stay there until their work was done in that place; if they could not find people who would house them they were to mark openly and symbolically that those people had rejected the kingdom of God. He had instructed them to preach, and preach they did; he had given them authority over unclean spirits, and they cast out many demons and healed others who were sick.

The news of this great wave of preaching and healing swept the country.

The word reached even King Herod. People were saying that John the Baptist had been raised from the dead and was doing these things. Others said that Elijah the prophet had returned. Still others said that Jesus was his own man but like some of the prophets of old. Herod though, it was reported, thought that Jesus was John the Baptist, whom he had beheaded, returned to life.

SUGGESTIONS FOR ADDITIONAL READING

Abraham, I. *Studies in Pharisaism and the Gospels.* New York: K. T. A. V. Publishing House, Inc. 1967.

Beare, Francis W. *The Earliest Records of Jesus.* New York: Abingdon Press, 1962.

Beck, D. M. *Through the Gospels of Jesus.* New York: Harper and Row, 1954.

Burrows, Millar. *Jesus in the First Three Gospels.* Nashville: Abingdon, 1977.

Cadoux, A. T. *The Parables of Jesus.* New York: The Macmillan Company, 1931.

Carlston, Charles E. *The Parables of the Triple Tradition.* Philadelphia: Fortress Press, 1975.

Dodd, C. H. *The Parables of the Kingdom.* New York: Charles Scribner's Sons, 1961.

Duncan, G. S. *Jesus, Son of Man.* New York: The Macmillan Co., 1949.

Fredricksen, Anton. *The Problem of Miracle in Early Christianity.* Translated by Harrisville and Hanson. Minneapolis, Minn.: Augsburg Publishing House, 1972.

Goodspeed, Edgar J. *A Life of Jesus*. New York: Harper Brothers, 1950.

Grant, R. M. *Miracle and Natural Law*. Amsterdam: North-Holland Publishing Co., 1952.

Keller, Ernst and Keller, Marie-Luise. *Miracles in Dispute*. Translated by Margaret Kohl. Philadelphia: Fortress Press, 1969.

Laymon, Charles M. *The Life and Teachings of Jesus*. New York: Abingdon Press, 1962.

McArthur, Harvey K. *The Quest Through the Centuries*. Philadelphia: Fortress Press, 1966.

Montifiore, C. G. *Rabbinic Literature and Gospel Teachings*. New York: K. T. A. V. Publishing House, Inc., 1970.

Mowinckel, S. *He That Cometh*. Translated by G. W. Anderson. New York, Abingdon Press, 1954.

Rawlinson, A. E. J. *Christ in the Gospels*. Westport, Conn.: Greenwood Press, 1970.

Richardson, Alan. *The Miracle Stories of the Gospels*. London: S. C. M. Press, Ltd., 1975.

Russell, D. S. *The Method and Message of Jewish Apocalyptic*. Philadelphia: The Westminster Press, 1964.

Tennant, F. R. *Miracle and Its Philosophical Presuppositions*. Cambridge: University Press, 1925.

Via, Dan O. *The Parables*. Philadelphia: Fortress Press, 1967.

CHAPTER 10

THE KINGDOM OF GOD

Ceremonial purity, which clutched the minds of Pharisees but did not grasp Jesus, was one thing to stir discussion but it was not the thing that simmered a distrust in the political leaders. It was Jesus' talk about a kingdom which contributed to their anxiety. For to the politically attuned ear, kingdoms are of this world and are won, controlled, and defended by men of flesh and blood at the expense of other men's flesh and blood. So Jesus' teachings about a kingdom that was to come in connection with his work seemed to have certain similarities with other revolutionary movements which had taken their toll on political powers in the past. What kind of kingdom did Jesus envision?

Jesus thought that scribes could be included in it. A scribe who approached Jesus asked him which is the greatest commandment of all.[1] Jesus' response was completely in the tradition of Judaism, starting with the Shema, in his words, "Hear, O Israel: The Lord our God, the Lord is one; and you shall love the Lord your God with all your heart, and with all your soul, and with all your mind, and with all your strength." He continued, "The second is this, 'You shall love your neighbor as yourself.' "[2] In his opinion there were no commandments greater than these. The scribe agreed with him completely, saying that living by these

---

[1]Luke 10:25-28.

[2]Cf. Deuteronomy 6:5, Leviticus 19:18.

commandments was more important than all burnt offerings and sacrifices. The conclusion of their exchange was made in the words of Jesus, "You are not far from the kingdom of God."

If Jesus regarded these commandments as the foundation of the Kingdom of God then it could not be a radical departure from the foundations of Judaism, for those two teachings were a part of Deuteronomy and Leviticus spelled out in various ways in the law and in the prophets through the years. The concept had existed in the days prior to King Saul, when Samuel resisted the introduction of a human king, preferring a theocracy, an arrangement where God was king and ruled as such over his people, his kingdom. It was that kind of relationship, a personal one between God and his people, that Jesus seems to have had in mind rather than any radically new set of laws or any radically new political kingdom or even a restoration of a former kingdom such as that of David or Solomon.

Perhaps it would have been helpful to have a formal treatise on the Kingdom of God from Jesus in the way that one has a treatise on the Republic from Plato. But that was not the manner of Jesus' teaching. Most of his teachings about the Kingdom of God are variations on a theme given in small bits and pieces in a variety of circumstances over a period of time. Moreover many of his teachings were in the form of parables. (A parable was a short story with a single point stating not what the Kingdom of God is but what it is like.) If all of the parables are taken together and considered, some idea develops of how Jesus thought of the Kingdom of God. But the whole interpretation is not clear beyond question, and wisps of mystery are plentiful about the parapets.

One quality that seems to mark the presence of God's Kingdom for Jesus is trust. One must trust God in order to submit to his will, and it is in submitting to the will of God that one acknowledges God as his king. Obedience grows out of that trust, an obedience that fulfills the law but does more than that because it grows out of a personal relationship between the subject and the king. Another element in the Jewish concept of God is also utilized by Jesus. He called God "Father" and taught his disciples in praying to call upon "Our Father." Although Jesus did not reserve to himself alone the privilege of referring to God as "Father," he did not stress it so much in his public teaching. He did include his disciple in that Father-son relationship.

Perhaps the best collection of the teachings of Jesus on what life in the Kingdom of God would be like is found in the collection known as the Sermon on the Mount found in Matthew 5, 6 and 7. Jesus is pictured as teaching a vast crowd of followers as they have come to him on a mountain side, giving them an understanding of the contrast of how things have been done in their kingdom and how different life would be under the kingship of God.

In the opening words, concerning who shall be happy or blessed in the Kingdom of God, one immediately senses a reversed set of priorities. Blessed are: The poor in spirit, those who mourn, the meek, those who hunger and thirst for righteousness, the merciful, the pure in heart, the peacemakers, those persecuted for righteousness' sake, and those reviled and persecuted for their association with Jesus.[3] They are the salt of the earth, the light of the world.[4]

Would the Kingdom of God mean the overthrowing of the law and the teachings of the prophets? By no means, said Jesus. On the contrary his task was not to destroy the law but to fulfill it, for no part of the law would be allowed to pass away until it is accomplished.[5] One who relaxes the law will be called least in the Kingdom of Heaven and one who does the law and teaches others to do so will be called greatest. Indeed the righteousness of those who would enter the Kingdom of heaven must exceed that of the scribes and Pharisees, the people who regarded themselves as the most righteous of all.

The letter of the law allowed conduct which was, in the mind of Jesus, too lenient for the Kingdom of God. A person subject to the personal guidance of God in his life should live in a right spirit, a spirit which went beyond fulfilling the letter of the law by preventing those thoughts, attitudes and actions which would violate the letter of the law. The law says that one should not kill; Jesus said that one should not even be angry with his brother.[6] Reconciliation between men is to be initiated by one in the Kingdom of God, one should not wait to rely on the councils and the courts for judgment or redress. The law says do not commit adultery; Jesus said do not even look on a woman in a lustful way. The law said that anyone divorcing his wife should give her a writ of divorce; Jesus said that anyone who divorced his wife except for adultery made her an adultress and anyone who married a divorced woman committed adultery. Marriage was, for Jesus, for a lifetime and to be broken only by the death of one partner. Language in the Kingdom of God would mean exactly

---

[3]Matthew 5:1-12.

[4]Matthew 5:13-15.

[5]Matthew 5:17-20.

[6]Matthew 5:21-48.

what was said and a simple "yes" or "no" would carry as much weight as an elaborate oath does in the kingdom of man.

What about retribution and retaliation? The law of Moses had limited response to one eye for one eye and a tooth for one tooth. The tough teaching of Jesus goes even further. Do not resist one who is evil; if one strikes on the right cheek, turn to him the other also. If anyone forces you to go one mile, go with him two. Give to him who begs from you and do not refuse him who would borrow from you. The old teaching was love your friends and hate your enemies; Jesus said, love your enemies and pray for those who persecute you. What was the rationale for this seemingly impossible teaching? So that one could be a son of his Father in heaven, taking his character from him; for God makes the sun rise on the evil as well as the good and he sends his rain on the unjust as well as the just. The conclusion was that one who would live in the Kingdom of God must take his character from the example of the King; "You, therefore, must be perfect, as your heavenly Father is perfect" (Matthew 5:48).

Life in the Kingdom of God, according to Jesus, would be based on one's attitude of genuine love for God and for one's fellow man rather than upon appearances of piety and charity. Practicing piety before men in order to gain their praise might succeed in that purpose, but it would surely not bring any reward from God. A gift, on the other hand, given in secret will bring a secret reward from God. Prayer in private rather than in public is more likely to bring a reward from God. Prayer need not be elaborate or full of empty phrases; the simpler the prayer the better. The outline of prayer Jesus gave his disciples was extremely simple:

> Our Father who art in heaven,
> Hallowed be thy name.
> Thy kingdom come,
> Thy will be done,
>   On earth as it is in heaven.
> Give us this day our daily bread;
> And forgive us our debts,
>   As we also have forgiven our debtors;
> And lead us not into temptation,
>   But deliver us from evil.[7]

Forgiveness from God would be directly related to one's forgiveness of one's fellow man. Fasting, when done, should be done without outward

---

[7]Matthew 6:9-13.

signs of misery and suffering, for the point is to establish one's relationship with God, who knows what is happening without outward signs, and not to cultivate the praise of human beings through one's reputation for piety.

No one can serve two masters.[8] That was Jesus' pointed way of saying that in the Kingdom of God there can be only one king and one must be entirely devoted to him and entirely trusting of him. If one really believed in God's goodness, mercy, and providence then certain lifestyles would be characteristic of a subject in the Kingdom of God. One's treasure would not be on earth where moth and rust corrupt and thieves break in and steal, but one's heart and one's treasure would be together in heaven. Moreover one would not spend one's life in anxiety, asking, "What shall we eat? What shall we drink? What shall we wear?" Can one add any height to one's stature by worrying about it? The birds of the air are provided for by God and so are the flowers of the field, and certainly human beings are more valuable in the sight of God than are flowers and birds, as beautiful as they are. The first concern of every human being should be the Kingdom of God and God should be trusted to provide daily needs, not only for the day but also for the morrow.

Singleness of purpose in devotion of God and trust of him would keep one from falling into some serious errors. There would be no call to judge other people's behavior, for that could be left to God.[9] One would be concerned that his own behavior was right rather than with finding fault with others. One could receive from God simply by asking. As Jesus put it: "Ask, and it will be given you; seek and you will find; knock, and it will be opened to you. For every one who asks receives, and he who seeks finds, and to him who knocks it will be opened."[10] Human beings know how to give good gifts to their children; how much more should the heavenly father know how to care for his children. In dealing with people the secret is this: "Whatever you wish that men would do to you, so do to them; for this is the law and the prophets."[11]

Jesus was clear that finding life in the Kingdom was not the easiest thing in the world, for the way of destruction is much easier than the way that leads to life. The way that leads to life is hard, the gate is narrow, and

---

[8]Matthew 6:24.

[9]Matthew 7:1.

[10]Matthew 7:7, 8.

[11]Matthew 7:12, known as "The Golden Rule."

those who find it are few. Moreover there are false prophets who are wolves in sheep's clothing who can lead one astray; however, there is a sure test for people who are genuine. Just as one tells a good tree by its fruit so one can tell a person by his deeds—"by their fruits you can know them." It is not one's words of loyalty that count as much as one's deeds, doing the will of the father in heaven.

Jesus concluded his sermon on the mount with a vivid picture of the choice facing his hearers. Those who heard his words and lived by them would be like a wise man who built his house upon a rock foundation, which could withstand rain, wind and flood; those who rejected his words would be like a man building a house on the sand, which would be wiped out by the same kind of storm in life. Jesus spoke with that kind of authority.

Where was the Kingdom of God? Was it in heaven or on earth? When would it be available? There were always questions for Jesus. But his answers on time and place were somewhat evasive. He clearly stated that no person except God knew the day or the hour when it would come. Jesus said that it would come in the future. Since he said that some of his disciples would live to see it come in power, it was likely that he expected it to be established, at least in part, during the lifetime of some of his hearers. Its coming would be, as it was for the prophets, a time of accounting and judgment.

From the gospel of Matthew, in chapter 25, one can get some idea about the coming of the Kingdom of God. It would come suddenly, without prior announcement or warning. The time for preparation is now; at some point in the future it will not be opened again. It is also like a master returning from a long period of absence and demanding an accounting from his employees to whom he has entrusted certain sums of money. Those who have exercised a sound policy of investing the funds entrusted to them will be rewarded with more responsibility and praise. Anyone who has hidden his funds out of fear to invest will be shorn of his responsibility and his fund given to another. Moreover, he will be cast out into darkness where there is weeping and gnashing of teeth.

In the same chapter of Matthew the coming of the Kingdom is pictured in terms of a shepherd gathering his flocks (all the nations of the world), and separating them into sheep on his right and goats on his left. To the sheep he will say, "Come O blessed of my Father, inherit the kingdom prepared for you from the foundation of the world. . ." (Matthew 25:34). To the goats he will say, "Depart from me, you cursed, into the eternal fire prepared for the devil and his angels. . ." (Matthew 25:41).On what basis would the sharp, final division be made? Jesus indicates that even the persons judged may be surprised, for only God knows the value of what they have done. The choice will be made on several points of mercy: the Lord was hungry and they gave him food, he was thirsty and they gave him drink, he was a stranger and they welcomed him, he was naked and they clothed him, he was sick and they visited him, and he was in prison and they came to him. When did either the righteous or the unrighteous persons see the Son of Man in such conditions? The disturbing answer is that the Son of Man has identified himself with anyone in those circumstances of need—"Truly, I say to you, as you did it to one of the least of these my brethren, you did it to me."[12]

On the other hand, there is reason to believe that Jesus thought of the Kingdom of God as having already begun. His remark to the scribe that he was not far from the Kingdom of God could be interpreted in that light. So could his remark, "The Kingdom of God is in the midst of you." However, if it was present, it was only in the incipient stage; it was small compared to what it would be when it had fully arrived. It was, he said, like a man planting a seed and then waiting for it to reach the stage of harvest. He could not watch and understand every stage of the development, but when it was ripe he would put in his sickle and harvest it.[13] Again, he said it was like a grain of mustard seed, the smallest of all seeds, yet when it is grown, it is large enough to provide a home for birds.[14] Or it is like leavening a woman might place in three measures of meal; it works away until all of the meal is leavened. The Kingdom was indeed present in the work of Jesus; it would come in its fullness in God's own time.

Jesus organized his work to proclaim the coming Kingdom of God to thousands of people over a wide territory. He announced that its coming was good news. He asked people to repent. But in light of the quality of life in the Kingdom of God as he envisioned it, with almost a complete reversal of the priorities of the kingdom of men, how many people could enter it? It seems to have been possible for almost everyone who would ask, seek, and knock. Yet, the truth was that many would not find that narrow path and that narrow door. Nor would all who found it want to make the changes in their lifestyles required of subjects in the Kingdom of God. One can ponder for a long time Jesus' remark that "It is easier for

---

[12]Matthew 25:40.

[13]Mark 4:26-29.

[14]Mark 4:30-32.

a camel to go through the eye of a needle than for a rich man to enter the Kingdom of God."[15] Although there was sometimes lack of commitment among human beings, there is no lack of commitment on the part of God.

The gospel of Luke preserves three stories of Jesus to illustrate the eagerness of God to have even completely unworthy people seek to enter his kingdom. If a shepherd of a hundred sheep has lost one, he leaves the 99 that are safe in the fold and goes out searching for the one that is lost. When he has found it he comes home rejoicing more over finding the lost one than over the 99 he has which were already safe. There is more joy in heaven over one sinner who repents than over 99 who are already saved.[16] The same is true of a woman who had ten coins but lost one. For God is like a father of a prodigal son.[17] The boy wanted his share of the estate so that he could go live away from his father. He wasted his money and soon had no friends at all, reduced to earning his living by giving food to pigs and envying the pigs their husks. Remembering his father's house, he decided to repent and return home. But when his father saw him coming he ran to meet him, placed a new robe on him, and ordered a feast. Why such a celebration over a son who had made a fool of himself? "For this my son was dead, and is alive again; he was lost, and is found" (Matthew 15:24). According to Jesus, that is the way God deals with sinners, his prodigal sons and daughters. One does not first have to be worthy; one only has to turn toward his home and his father to be received and welcomed back where he belongs.

How important were the mighty works of Jesus, or miracles, in his program to proclaim the Kingdom of God? The gospel writers seem to have somewhat different ways of interpreting this part of the ministry of Jesus. In the synoptic gospels, Matthew, Mark, and Luke, who seem to see things in a similar way, the mighty works are almost incidental to Jesus' more important work; after all, in his temptation he had rejected any ministry of wonder working. On the other hand, Jesus does seem to be moved to have pity on individuals seeking help: a leper, a paralytic, a demoniac, a woman with a hemorrhage, and a member of a family he was visiting. These works of healing seem to have been the most common acts he did beside teaching, and it is obvious that for thousands of people they were signs of God's intervention in a merciful way in human life that could sometimes be too much to bear.

---

[15]Mark 10:25.

[16]Luke 15:1-10.

[17]Luke 15:11-32.

There were rarer works of even greater wonder. He was called upon to heal or raise from the dead the daughter of Jairus, and he was asked to heal the servant of a centurian who was at a distance. In both of these reported incidents he was successful, making a significant impression on those who knew of him. Two instances when he seemed to overcome nature were also significant to his disciples. When he was followed by five thousand people who had no food with them, he turned five loaves of bread and two fishes into enough food for the entire company. Again, when he was on the Sea of Galilee with his fishermen disciples a storm so severe that even they despaired for their lives caught him sleeping. When they awakened him at the point of sinking, he spoke to the sea and the waves ceased. He was seen as having power over nature as well as over demons and humans.

Inasmuch as the acts were seen by him as signs of God's mercy and power at work in human lives so much did he regard them as signs of the presence of God's Kingdom. Jesus claimed no power of his own apart from God; what he did was a manifestation of the power of God for which he was an instrument. The gospel of John makes the same point, with greater emphasis. However, in John's gospel the miracles are a definite part of Jesus' teaching. They are signs to cause belief in God. At a wedding feast he turned water into wine, in the temple the man who had been lame from birth was healed, he raised from the dead his friend Lazarus—in order that people might believe and believing have life. But in John, also, Jesus is emphatic that he does nothing of himself but only in concert with God. At the same time he who receives Jesus receives God, for the Son is in the Father and the Father is in the Son.[18]

In both the synoptic gospels and in the Gospel of John, Jesus is presented as more than a good man, a great teacher, or even another of the prophets. In his life God was present in a way different from his presence in other men; Jesus was completely under the will of God, and in that sense he was already in the Kingdom of God. He invited other persons to come, to submit themselves to the will of God, and so enter the Kingdom of God. In that sense the Kingdom was in the midst of the people of his day; many alive would recognize it, and many were not far from it. More than that, Jesus would go to the Father and dwell with him in heaven before the Kingdom would come in its fullness. At that time Jesus would return and with his Father establish the Kingdom which had been prepared for believers from the foundation of the world.

---

[18]John 14:11.

In his teachings, in his deeds, and in his claims, according to his followers, Jesus was a most unusual person. The Muslims, when they entered the scene of history, would list him as a true prophet of God. Some Jews of his own day violently disagreed.

SUGGESTIONS FOR ADDITIONAL READING

Branscomb, Harvie. *The Teachings of Jesus*. New York: Abingdon Press, 1931.

Bright, John. *The Kingdom of God*. New York: Abingdon Press, 1953.

Davies, W. D. *The Setting of the Sermon on the Mount*. Cambridge: Cambridge University Press, 1964.

Jeremias, Joachim. *The Parables of Jesus*. New York: Charles Scribner's Sons, 1962.

Ladd, George Eldon. *Jesus and the Kingdom*. New York: Harper and Row, 1952.

Manson, T. W. *The Teachings of Jesus*. Cambridge: Cambridge University Press, 1951.

Perrin, Norman. *Jesus and the Language of the Kingdom*. Philadelphia: Fortress Press, 1976.

Perrin, Norman. *The Kingdom of God in the Teaching of Jesus*. Philadelphia: The Westminster Press, 1963.

Sanford, J. A. *The Kingdom Within*. Philadelphia: J. B. Lippincott Company, 1970.

Schweitzer, Albert. *The Mystery of the Kingdom of God*. Translated by Walter Lawrie. New York: The Macmillan Company, 1960.

CHAPTER 11

PILATE

For the disciples of Jesus, a sharp turning point in their understanding of the role of their master took place during one of his rare journeys outside of Galilee. They had been seeking a rest from their strenuous ministry in Galilee and had journeyed north into the coastal region of Tyre and Sidon. When they reached Caesarea Philippi Jesus confronted them with a most disturbing question. Who do men say that I am? To that query they pondered and responded in broken guesses: John the Baptist? Elijah? One of the prophets? No doubt they had actually heard people make similar references. But the hard question of Jesus was more searching. "Who do you say that I am?" The astounding answer of Simon, called Peter, was, "You are the Christ."[1]

Jesus' response was pointed. Don't tell anyone what you have just said. Simon could not understand why not, but Jesus went on to explain that the Son of Man would be rejected by the Jewish religious leaders, and after suffering many things, be killed. At first Peter denied that estimate, but upon Jesus' reaffirmation of it, he acquiesced. Matthew reports, however, that Jesus indicated that Simon would be the cornerstone of the new church:

> Blessed are you, Simon Bar-Jonah! For flesh and blood has not revealed this to you, but my Father who is in heaven. And I tell

---

[1]Mark 8:29.

you you are Peter, on this rock I will build my church, and the powers of death shall not prevail against it. I will give you the keys of the kingdom of heaven, and whatever you bind on earth shall be bound in heaven, and whatever you loose on earth shall be loosed in heaven."[2]

In Christian tradition, one phase of the ministry of Jesus was ending and another was beginning.

Jesus understood how quickly severe opposition could rise to the surface. By that time the scribes and the Pharisees could be expected to raise questions wherever he went. Indeed, Jesus had not been well received in his home town, Nazareth.

He had gone there on the Sabbath, as was his custom, and when he was asked to read, he chose from the prophet Isaiah these words:

"The Spirit of the Lord is upon me, because he has anointed me to preach good news to the poor. He has sent me to proclaim release to the captives and recovering of sight to the blind, to set at liberty those who are oppressed, to proclaim the acceptable year of the Lord."[3]

He then remarked that the scripture had been fulfilled in their hearing that day. While some of them spoke well of him, there was doubt among others. He told them that he could not do for them what he had done in Capernaum because of their unbelief; they had been remembering his family and his growing up with them rather than recognizing what he had become. He continued, remarking that Elijah had helped many outside of Israel, not because there were not any in need in Israel, but because they lacked the faith that foreigners had. The people of Nazareth became so angry that they took Jesus out to a cliff to throw him off. He coolly walked through their midst and went away.

The conflict between Jesus and the Pharisees is well illustrated by the occasion when they came to him with a complaint that his disciples did not always wash their hands with the traditional ceremony before they ate. Jesus responded to them by quoting Isaiah 29:13:

This people honors me with their lips,
but their heart is far from me;
in vain do they worship me,
teaching as doctrines the precepts of men.

---

[2]Matthew 16:17-19.

[3]Isaiah 61:1-2, 58:6, Luke 4:16-30.

The Pharisees, according to Jesus, rejected the word of God in order to keep the traditions of men! By saying that they had set something aside for God, they tried to avoid doing their duty under God's law of honoring their fathers and their mothers. It is not what goes into a person that defiles him, said Jesus, but what comes out of a person, such as evil thoughts, fornication, theft, murder, adultery, coveting, wickedness, deceit, licentiousness, envy, slander, pride, and foolishness.

On his last visit to Jerusalem Jesus did more than teach by words; he openly challenged the established religious hierarchy in a way they could not possibly ignore. For he went into the temple and began to drive out those who sold animals for sacrifice and turned over the tables of the moneychangers, quoting from the prophets Isaiah and Jeremiah, "Is it not written, 'My house shall be called a house of prayer for all nations?' But you have made it a den of robbers."[4] The chief priests and the scribes were determined to destroy him, but they did not arrest him at once because they feared an uprising of the masses of people who supported him and his teaching.

On the following day they came to him and asked him by what authority he had acted the day before. And he responded with a question, "Was the baptism of John (the Baptist) from God or from man?" They were caught on a dilemma, for if they said from God, Jesus would condemn them for not supporting John; if they said from men, the people would rise up against them. So they declined to answer. Therefore, Jesus declined to answer their question about his own authority. He told them, instead, a parable.[5] A man built a beautiful vineyard and leased it to some tenants. Since he was traveling abroad, he sent a series of agents to collect the rent which was due him, but the tenants beat them, refusing to pay rent and even murdered some of the agents. Finally, the owner sent his beloved son to the tenants, thinking surely they would honor him. But they killed the son, arguing that now they would inherit the vineyard for themselves. Jesus' conclusion was that the owner would come and destroy the tenants and give the vineyard to others.

They correctly perceived that Jesus had told the parable against them and developed the tactic of trying to turn the masses against him so that they could arrest and try him. One question put to him by the Pharisees and Herodians, who were by now in league, "Is it lawful to pay taxes to

---

[4]Matthew 21:13; cf. verses 10-17.

[5]Matthew 21:33-46.

Caesar or not?"[6] Again this was a terrible dilemma they used to confront Jesus. If he said that they should pay taxes to Caesar, the crowds would turn against him. If he said that they should not pay taxes then the Romans would be after him for inciting a tax revolt. So Jesus escaped between the horns of dilemma with a question. "Whose image is on the coin?" They answered that the image was Caesar's. "Render therefore to Caesar the things that are Caesar's, and to God the things that are God's," concluded Jesus (Matthew 22:21).

On one occasion some Pharisees had come to him with the message that Herod wanted to kill him. Jesus replied,

> Go and tell that fox, 'Behold, I cast out demons and perform cures today and tomorrow, and the third day I finish my course. Nevertheless, I must go on my way today and tomorrow and the day following; for it cannot be that a prophet should perish away from Jerusalem.'[7]

Then Jesus lamented over the hardness of the people of Jerusalem who had a tradition of rejecting prophets when they were alive.

> O Jerusalem, Jerusalem, killing the prophets and stoning those who are sent to you! How often would I have gathered your children together as a hen gathers her brood under her wings, and you would not![8]

Jesus had a forboding that he would not leave Jerusalem alive. It was also clear to him that his disciples would be involved in any forceful strike against his work. He even told the multitudes, along with his disciples,

> If any man would come after me, let him deny himself and take up his cross and follow me. For whoever would save his life will lose it; and whoever loses his life for my sake and the gospel's will save it. For what does it profit a man, to gain the whole world and forfeit his life.[9]

Jesus was sharply aware of the decisions and divisions that were taking place in families on his account. To his twelve apostles he said,

> Do not think that I have come to bring peace on earth; I have

---

[6]Matthew 22:17; cf. verses 15-22.

[7]Luke 13:32.

[8]Matthew 23:37.

[9]Matthew 16:24-26.

not come to bring peace, but a sword. For I have come to set a man against his father, and a daughter against her mother, and a daughter-in-law against her mother-in-law; and a man's foes will be those of his own household. He who loves father or mother more than me is not worthy of me; and he who loves son or daughter more than me is not worthy of me; and he who does not take his cross and follow me is not worthy of me.[10]

On the surface the theme of judgment and destruction seems to be a sudden development when one recalls the conditions under which Jesus entered Jerusalem. He had sent his disciples to borrow an ass, a small beast of burden, and he rode the short distance from a suburban village into Jerusalem. Along the way, especially as he approached the Mount of Olives, many of the crowd ran into the road before him spreading their clothing on the ground or cutting branches from the fields and trees to place on the road for him to walk over. Among their shouts were the phrases, "Hosanna to the Son of David! Blessed be he who comes in the name of the Lord! Hosanna in the highest!" (Matthew 21:9).

But to one who knew the prophets, Jesus' entrance was not just the riding of a man during the last stages of a tiring journey. It was not simply a man of Galilee being greeted by the people from his home region. It was a mass demonstration in response to a proclamation made by Jesus about his own mission and personal role in it. As the gospel of Matthew makes clear, Jesus was identifying himself with the words in Isaiah and Zechariah:

Tell the daughter of Zion,
Behold your king is coming to you,
humble, and mounted on an ass,
and on a colt, the foal of an ass.[11]

That action, as much as Jesus' cleansing of the temple, could not have been ignored by the chief priests, the scribes, the Pharisees, and the Herodians. They were being confronted and bearded as lions in their den; they had to choose whether they were for Jesus and would support him or whether they were against him and would remove him from the scene. They had already decided how they must proceed; they needed only to choose the time and the place, preferably when his supporters had other

---

[10]Matthew 10:34-39.

[11]Matthew 21:5, Isaiah 62:11, Zechariah 9:9.

things on their minds. For assistance in their plot, they enlisted in their service one of Jesus' own apostles, who had apparently developed some serious doubts about Jesus. Judas Iscariot accepted thirty pieces of silver from the chief priests for his service of helping them find the right moment to seize Jesus.

According to the synoptic gospels, the enemies of Jesus did not have to wait long; the night when all good Jews would be indoors observing the sacred feast of the Passover would yield a perfect opportuniity for the purposes of the priests of the Jews. Jesus and his apostles obtained the use of an upper room in an establishment in Jerusalem so that they could eat the Passover meal together. It was a meal that the apostles would never forget, not only because it was the last supper that they would have together with Jesus, but also because Jesus used the bread and the wine of their meal in a way which departed from the traditional Passover recitations.

What were these unusual words and deeds of Jesus that his apostles seemed to remember always? Matthew and Mark agree rather closely in their accounts. In the words of Matthew:

> Now as they were eating, Jesus took bread, and blessed, and broke it, and gave it to the disciples and said, "Take, eat; this is my body." And he took a cup and when he had given thanks he gave it to them, saying, "Drink of it, all of you; for this is my blood of the covenant, which is poured out for many for the forgiveness of sins. I tell you I shall not drink again of this fruit of the vine until the day when I drink it new with you in my Father's kingdom."[12]

It was the beginning of an institution that would be incorporated into the life of Christians through the centuries even as the Feast of the Passover had been incorporated into the life of the Jews.

They sang a hymn and then Jesus and his disciples went out to the Mount of Olives to a place called the garden of Gethsemane. He desired to pray, for he sensed that he was about to be arrested. He asked his disciples to keep watch while he was in prayer but during periodic checks on three occasions he found them sleeping. It was there, away from other people, that Judas led the mob armed with swords and clubs, representing the chief priests, to Jesus. Judas went up to Jesus, and, calling him "Master," kissed him, giving the sign to the mob that this was the one to be taken captive. The men with Judas moved swiftly to capture Jesus who

---

[12]Matthew 26:26.

did not resist them. However, a man with Jesus drew one of two swords that were in the company and cut off the ear of a slave of the high priest. Jesus commanded that the sword be put away, saying, "Put your sword back in its place; for all who take the sword will perish by the sword."[13] To his captors Jesus expressed ridicule, "Have you come out as against a robber, with swords and clubs to capture me? Day after day I sat in the temple teaching, and you did not seize me."[14]

Jesus was taken to the home of Caiaphas, the high priest, where the scribes and the elders had gathered. The disciples of Jesus scattered to safety, except for Peter, who followed at what he thought to be a safe distance. Inside the house, in the hours of darkness, the priests conducted a trial of Jesus, producing witnesses as to what he said and did such as saying that he would destroy the temple and rebuild it in three days. But the essential question of the high priest was, "I adjure you by the living God, tell us if you are the Christ, the Son of God."[15] Jesus refused to affirm or to deny the question. He responded that they had so charged him. However, when Jesus made a statement to the effect that they would see the Son of Man seated at the right hand of power, the high priest tore his robe, the prescribed reaction of remorse to be taken in the presence of hearing blasphemy against God. Blasphemy against God was a crime among the Jews to be punished with death by stoning.

Under Roman occupation, however, the high priest could not carry out a death penalty. The Jewish officials would have to present a case to Roman Procurator, Pontius Pilate. This they prepared to do; however, it would not have mattered to Pilate that Jesus had referred to the Son of Man or even that he had not denied that he was the Christ. So Caiaphas cleverly translated the whole case against Jesus into terms by which Pilate would grasp the seriousness of it. He would say that Jesus claimed to be "King of the Jews." When it was morning the council bound Jesus and took him to Pilate.

Pilate listened to the charges against Jesus and then gave him a chance to answer them. But Jesus did not try to refute the charges by presenting his own case. Pilate came to the heart of the question when he asked Jesus, "Are you the King of Jews?" Jesus answered, "You have said so." Luke adds the account of how Pilate, learning that Jesus was from Galilee, sent him to Herod for trial. He was handled roughly by Herod

---

[13]Matthew 26:52.

[14]Matthew 26:55.

[15]Matthew 26:63.

and his soldiers, but according to Luke, Herod did not find Jesus guilty of anything serious, certainly not deserving of death. Herod sent Jesus back to Pilate for judgment.

The fate of Jesus rested with Pilate. The charges of treason against Rome had not been proven. Pilate could have dismissed the case. Instead, he tried to please the crowd that had assembled with the high priest and his associates. He raised the issue of their custom of releasing a prisoner at the feast and asked whether they would not like to have him release Jesus. Their response was noisy; they wanted a man by the name of Barabbas released. Without passing judgment himself, Pilate asked the crowd what he was to do with the man called Jesus. Their cry was definite: "Let him be crucified." Complying with the wishes of the crowd brought by the chief priests of the Jews, Pilate, without finding Jesus guilty, released Barabbas and delivered Jesus to be crucified. One can judge the tenseness of relations between Jews and Romans from this incident when a Roman judge, a representative of a nation whose strength was justice under law, without finding a prisoner guilty of breaking a Roman law, yielded to a very select and biased crowd and agreed to have Roman troops execute a Jewish prisoner.

The soldiers led him away to the praetorium, a kind of palace, and let a whole battalion have some fun with him. They clothed him in a purple garment, the color of royalty, plaited a crown of thorns and jammed it down his head, and then they beat his head and spat upon him while making elaborate bows and kneelings and calling out, "Hail, King of the Jews!" Jesus had already been scourged, a punishment which sometimes ended in death of the prisoner. He was very weak before they gave him the heavy cross beam which he was to carry to the place outside of Jerusalem where executions were held.

Jesus tried to carry the wooden beam, but the Romans had to enlist the aid of a passer-by, Simon of Cyrene, to carry it for him. When they came to Golgotha, the place of the skull, they crucified him, driving nails into his hands and feet to hold him to the completed cross. Two criminals were crucified with him. Jesus was probably naked on the cross, and his clothes were divided among the executioners who rolled dice for them. The Romans, over protest of the Jews who objected to the wording, nailed a sign to the cross of Jesus which said, "This is Jesus the King of the Jews." Of course, he was taunted by the friends of the high priest who challenged him to have God deliver him off the cross if he really was the king of the Jews.

There was darkness over the land from the sixth hour until the ninth. At about that time, Jesus cried out to quote Psalm 22 which begins, "My

God, my God, why hast thou forsaken me?" and not long after that he expired. Christian tradition preserves seven last "words" or more accurately, sayings of Jesus from the cross. The synoptic gospels quote the centurian who witnessed the death of Jesus as saying that Jesus was truly a son of a god. The execution was witnessed from afar by women who had been close to him and his followers during his lifetime.

Since the Jewish Sabbath was to begin at sundown, it was necessary by custom to speed the death of the prisoners and have the bodies covered by dark. It was a little surprising that Jesus was already dead, for some prisoners remained alive for much longer periods on a cross. John reports that just to make sure he was dead, one soldier pierced the side of Jesus with a spear. Joseph of Arimathea, a disciple of Jesus, requested from Pilate the body of Jesus. His request was granted, so that the body could be placed into a tomb owned by this same Joseph. The body was wrapped, spices being placed with it, but the burial or entombment was not completed. A stone was rolled over the door as a temporary covering. According to Matthew, the priests and the Pharisees had Pilate place guards on the tomb to prevent the disciples from stealing the body and then claiming that Jesus had risen from the dead.

After the Sabbath, on the first day of the week, near dawn, Mary Magdalene and Mary the mother of James and Salome went to the tomb with spices so that they could complete the preparation of the body of Jesus. When they came to the tomb, they discovered that the stone had been rolled away. When they went inside the body of Jesus was not there.

The meaning was not clear to the women. But the gospel writers report that the significance was explained to them by an angel of God. Jesus was not among the dead but among the living. He had been raised from the dead and was going to Galilee before them and there he would meet them.

It must have seemed to the chief priests, the scribes, the Pharisees, and the Herodians that they had averted one more trouble from among the Jews. Jesus was dead. One of his apostles had betrayed him. Simon, called Peter, had denied that he knew him when questioned even by a servant of the high priest. No one reported any apostles being present at the crucifixion except John. And what did anyone have to fear from the few women who prepared the body for entombment? Indeed it looked as if one more false alarm about a new king or a messiah had been exposed and ended before it could flare into either civil war or rebellion.

What had gone wrong with the movement of Jesus if there was such an expectation that something had to be done by God to deliver his people? There was a great variety in the expectations of deliverance. Various groups had different ideas of how it would be done, and each had its own vision of the kind of leader who could do the job. Perhaps Jesus could come close to meeting the expectations of the Essenes and people of that quiet spirit. But he must have been a disappointment to those who looked for a military leader such as a King David or a Judas Maccabeus. Nor did he exhibit the revolutionary disposition of Judas the Galilean. He was not aristocratic or conservative enough to gain support of the Sadducees. He undermined the priests and the scribes so they had to oppose him. He was always arguing with the legalism of the Pharisees and they had to oppose him. The Herodians had not cared for John the Baptist and Jesus seemed to carry on that tradition. The people who supported Jesus were the common people of the land. They responded to his compassion when he regarded them as sheep without a shepherd and fed them, taught them, healed them, and promised them a place in the Kingdom of God. But when it came to a conflict with the powers of the state they were of no help to him except in leading the authorities to be more cautious of the mobs.

Jesus appeared to be a complete failure, for there seemed to be no one for whom he filled the role of Messiah. One of the serious questions of history is what happened to revive a movement which could have died along with its leader.

SUGGESTIONS FOR ADDITIONAL READING

Bishop, Jim. *The Day Christ Died.* New York: Harper Brothers, 1957.

Cohn, Haim. *The Trial and Death of Jesus.* New York: Harper and Row, 1971.

Denney, James. *The Death of Christ.* London: The Tyndale Press, 1973.

Juel, Donald. *Messiah and Temple.* Missoula, Montana: Scholar's Press, 1977.

Sloyan, Gurard S. *Jesus on Trial.* Philadelphia: Fortress Press, 1973.

CHAPTER 12

PETER AND PAUL

The empty tomb was a surprise to the women who came to complete the burial of Jesus, but more astonishing experiences were ahead for them. They encountered a figure whom they recognized as Jesus, raised from the dead. Over the next few days he appeared to two disciples as they walked near Jerusalem to the village of Emmaus, and he appeared to the eleven as they met in a room in Jerusalem. He met with them continually for forty days, talking about the coming of the Kingdom of God. Matthew reports that they met with him on a mountain in Galilee and that he gave them a great commission saying:

All authority in heaven and on earth has been given to me. Go therefore and make disciples of all nations, baptizing them in the name of the Father and of the Son and of the Holy Spirit, teaching them to observe all that I have commanded you; and lo, I am with you always, to the close of the age.[1]

The Acts of the Apostles reports that he told his apostles:

But you shall receive power when the Holy Spirit has come upon you; and you shall be my witnesses in Jerusalem and in all Judea and Samaria and to the end of the earth.[2]

---

[1]Matthew 28:18.

[2]Acts of the Apostles 1:8.

After that he was lifted up in a cloud from a mountain near Jerusalem. While the apostles were gazing up into heaven, two men in white robes appeared and said to them:

> Men of Galilee, why do you stand looking into heaven? This Jesus, who was taken up from you into heaven, will come in the same way as you saw him go into heaven.[3]

The apostles were not very effective in getting started, but they did elect another man to take the place of Judas, a man called Matthias, so their intentions were to continue the work of Jesus. It was the day of Pentecost which marked the turning point in their relationship to Jesus, from being students to becoming successors, those leading a movement in his name. They were together in a room and there appeared tongues of fire resting on each one of them. They were filled with the Holy Spirit and began to speak in tongues.

They went out into the open and began preaching. The odd thing about it was that Jews from the dispersion, used to other languages, understood the men from Galilee, each hearing in his own language. The essential Kerygma, or preaching of the church, is reported in the Acts as a speech of Peter:

> Jesus of Nazareth, a man attested to you by God with mighty works and wonders and signs which God did through him in your midst, as you yourselves know—this Jesus delivered up according to the definite plan and foreknowledge of God, you crucified and killed by the hands of lawless men. But God raised him up, having loosed the pangs of death, because it was not possible for him to be held by it. . . . Let all the house of Israel therefore know assuredly that God has made him both Lord and Christ, this Jesus whom you crucified.[4]

The hearers asked what they could do. Peter responded:

> Repent, and be baptized every one of you in the name of Jesus Christ for the forgiveness of your sins; and you shall receive the gift of the Holy Spirit.[5]

About three thousand people were reported to have believed, been

---

[3]Acts 1:11.

[4]Summary from Acts 2:22-36.

[5]Acts 2:38.

baptized, and added to the faithful on that day. For many Christians Pentecost is the birthday of the church of Jesus Christ.

The apostles seem to have expected Jesus to return and establish the Kingdom of God at any time, so the faithful of Jerusalem thought it important to spend their time together learning about the Kingdom, fasting and praying. Many sold their goods and donated the proceeds to the group; it was reported that they had all things in common. Besides teaching the faithful and administering provisions for members of the assembly, the apostles seem to have carried on a ministry of teaching and healing in public, seeking to expand membership of the followers of the Way. Peter healed a lame man begging in the temple and used the occasion to teach about Jesus as the Christ. He said that the stone rejected by the builders had become the head of the corner.

The trigger for the explosion of persecution, when it came, was not an apostle but a deacon. When the Hellenists in the church complained about how their widows were being neglected in the daily distribution, the apostles decided that they should not themselves stop teaching to serve tables, so they established an order of worthy men called deacons, whose job it was to tend to the table. Seven were chosen, among whom was a man named Stephen. Stephen, regarded as being full of grace and power, did more than tend tables; he got into a dispute with a group of Jews from the synagogue of the Freedmen. Unable to best him in a straightforward argument, they went behind his back and accused him of blasphemy, a charge which landed him in front of the high priest.

When the high priest asked Stephen whether the charge was true, Stephen did not deny it outright but used the occasion to deliver a sermon which included the words, "You stiff-necked people, uncircumcised in heart and ears, you always resist the Holy Spirit. As your fathers did, so do you."[6] They were enraged against him. He continued, in a vision, "Behold I see the heavens opened, and the Son of man standing at the right hand of God."[7] That was enough for them to find him guilty of blasphemy, and not waiting for any permission from Rome, they took Stephen into their own hand, dragged him out of the city, and stoned him to death. One young man held the coats of the people who did the stoning. He was Saul of Tarsus.

The violent death of Stephen was a signal to crowds of Jews and the priests to go after the followers of Jesus in a serious way. Many followers

---

[6] Acts 7:51.

[7] Acts 7:56.

of "the Way" fled for their lives, going as far as Judea and even Samaria. Wherever they went they preached salvation through Jesus as the Christ. In persecution the message which had been largely confined to Jerusalem was widely scattered among the Jews. For those who did not escape soon enough, life was grim. Saul of Tarsus went into house after house where there were people believing in Jesus as the Christ and dragged them off to prison. Nor was he satisfied with imprisoning those in Jerusalem; he sought writs so that he could journey even to Damascus and arrest anyone he found belonging to "the Way."

Saul reached Damascus, but not as a persecutor of members of "the Way." Before he came to the city, a light flashed around him and he fell to the ground blinded. He then heard a voice saying to him, "Saul, Saul, why do you persecute me?" To which Saul responded, "Who are you, Lord?" The response was, "I am Jesus, whom you are persecuting; but rise and enter the city, and you will be told what you are to do."[8] So it was in that stunned and blinded condition that a helpless Saul was led to Damascus. A follower of "the Way," Ananias, found him and healed his blindness. Saul spent several days with the disciples in Damascus and learned the message about Jesus as the Christ. Then he went into the synagogues and preached Jesus as the Son of God. There was clearly a change in his appearance from a persecutor of the followers of "the Way" to a champion preacher for the cause of the Christ. Although some members of "the Way" were still uncomfortable around a man who had been so dangerous to them, the Jews who had rejected Jesus were convinced that he had joined their enemies. These Jews sought to kill Saul. It was only through the Christians secretly helping him over the city wall at night that he was able to escape Damascus with his life and return to Jerusalem. He did not fare much better there, and it was necessary for him to be evacuated through the port at Caesarea in order to escape to Tarsus.

Thus far the followers of "the Way" had been limited to Jews, either the Hebrews or the Hellenists. It was Simon Peter who had to make the tough choice of whether to admit Gentiles to "the Way." He was approached by messengers from a man named Cornelius, a centurion of the Italian Cohort. He was a worshipper of God and gave liberally of alms to the people. The point of his request, when Peter arrived at Caesarea, was that he wanted to hear the preaching of Peter about Jesus. And as Peter was preaching the standard message about Jesus as the Christ, the Holy Spirit fell upon Cornelius and his household, all who heard the

---

[8] Acts 9:1-6.

words of Peter. The Jews were amazed, for this was the first time in their experience that the Holy Spirit had been given to Gentiles. But that was enough for Peter. He baptized those Gentiles who had received the Holy Spirit into the name of Jesus Christ. Philip had baptized an Ethiopian eunuch who was traveling through the country, but here was a household of Gentiles who would be accepted into congregations of "the Way" along with the Jews of that persuasion. When Peter returned to Jerusalem he did not escape the criticism of the circumcision party, those who argued that one must be a Jew before one could become a member of "the Way."

Barnabas and Paul, the Christian name taken by Saul, used Antioch, in Syria, the third largest city of the Roman empire, as their home base for missionary activities. In spite of either praise or persecution of the missionaries, churches were established, for part of the scriptures of the New Testament preserve Paul's letters to people all over the empire indicating that they had accepted the Christ.

Whatever his failures, Paul was an extremely effective founder of Christian churches. He was well equipped by birth, by education, and by experience. He was a Roman citizen, a fact which saved his life on a number of occasions when he ran into hostile officials. He was a Pharisee Jew, trained by the rabbi Gamaliel. He knew Jews from his own family, but he also knew gentiles from his life in Tarsus, a center of commerce and intellectual ferment. Upon him fell the awesome task, if Christianity was ever to be anything more than a special sect among Jews, of translating the essential ideas about Jesus the Christ from a Jewish intellectual and cultus setting into the thought forms and practices of Greeks and Romans. What he produced in doctrine and in practice was a hybrid of two cultures, a life that was neither Jewish nor Greek nor Roman but distinctively Christian, bearing the stamp of the greatest founder of churches, Paul.

If Paul, the former Saul, was so good at his job, why was he always embroiled in controversy? Why was he an object of persistent pursuit and persecution? It was in part because his teachings of Christian morality and religion went against the grain of Greek or Roman practices of worship. But most of his opposition came from Jews and from Jewish Christians. The Jews had never forgiven Paul for turning from a persecutor of Christians to a founder of Christian churches. There were also Christians, such as most of those in the Jerusalem church, who fervently believed that one had to be a sound and solid Jew before one could become a Christian. Christianity for them was a special emphasis within Judaism by those who had accepted Jesus as the Christ. Paul had worked out an arrangement with the leaders of the Jerusalem church, such as James, which permitted him to accept converts without having them undergo the Jewish rite of circumcision. To many other Jews and Christians this was a polluting of their faith; they were not going to permit such corruption if they could help it.

Since it was the custom of Paul to begin his teaching about the Christ in a synagogue if there were Jews in the community he was visiting, the Jews and Judaizing Christians had a reason for concern. They therefore made it their business to keep track of Paul and to follow him to each new place and try to turn against him as many Jews as possible in the city where he was working or where he had just been. If they could stir up such a disturbance of the peace that local pagan officials had to step in to remove the catalyst, so much the better. Although the enemies of Paul were very effective in moving him out of cities, unwittingly they were effective in helping him found churches in new places.

His enemies were also helping Paul establish doctrines of Christianity which separated it from Judaism. For Paul, the only thing necessary for one to be saved was to believe in Jesus as the Christ, the Son of God. Those who were elected by God and predestined to salvation would respond in faith and be saved. All humans had sinned and fallen short of God's requirements since the sin of Adam, their father. They had been required to keep the Torah, but due to their sin they could not. God had to make it possible for them to fulfill His requirements. The life, death, and resurrection of Jesus Christ, through his blood shed on the cross, washed away human sins and prepared the elect, who believed in faith, for a new life in Christ on earth and for resurrection into a life everlasting after death of the earthly body. The law which was impossible to keep before Christ was now unnecessary, for it was fulfilled through the law of love when one was in Christ Jesus. Morality was still strict, however, for one's body is the temple of the Holy Spirit. If one did marry, the vows were sacred and to be kept. Outside the marriage, celibacy was the ideal life: fornication, adultery, homosexuality, and bestiality were definitely outlawed. All life was to be lived in the full spirit of love, in the spirit of freedom in Christ, rather than according to a slavish following after the letter of the law, for one could never earn salvation through the impossible task of fulfilling every letter of the law. Salvation was a gift of God to be received by faith; that is how one is justified, made right, with God. These were the doctrines Paul made clear in his letters to the congregations he had founded, and especially in the letter to the church in Rome, which he had not visited when he wrote it.

Once in Jerusalem, even with the large gift from Gentile Christians for the Jerusalem church, Paul was not warmly welcomed, for his very presence threatened the precarious relationships between the Christians and the non-Christian Jews. His enemies found their opportunity while

Paul was in the temple. Although Gentiles were permitted in the outside courts, they were subject to immediate execution if they were found in the courts limited to the circumcised Jews. The enemies of Paul circulated the rumor that he had brought a Gentile, Trophimus, into the court reserved for the Jews alone. The charge was entirely believable to the people who hated Paul for his work with the Gentiles. The crowd mobilized immediately in order to put Paul to death. Only the fast action from a tribune named Claudius Lysias, who rushed to intervene in the riot, saved Paul from immediate death. With some order restored, Paul requested, and received, permission from the tribune to address the crowd. However, it was of no use to him. He had to be kept in protective custody until some fair trial could be arranged. When it was learned from reliable sources that forty men had vowed not to eat or drink until they had murdered Paul, he was removed under heavy Roman guard to Caesarea.

Over a period of time his case was heard by Felix and then Festus, both Romans, and by Agrippa, of Jewish heritage. Unable to resolve the matter within the region, Paul appealed to Caesar. He was then guaranteed an opportunity to plead his case before the emperor. He was taken under guard to Rome, suffering along the way extreme hardship from storms and a shipwreck, not to mention also being snakebitten on Malta. Eventually he did arrive in Rome, being met by Christians when he landed in the port some miles from the city. There he lived in a house under guard, providing for his own upkeep. Meanwhile he continued to teach and bear witness to Christ. The Acts of the Apostles and the letters of Paul are silent about his trial. Whether the case was dismissed after a time or whether it went contrary to the wishes of the Christian writers is not known. Tradition says that Paul died in Rome during a period of persecution.

When a fire broke out in Rome in July of 64 A.D., destroying much of the city, Nero turned the wrath of the population against the Christians, who made excellent scapegoats since the population already despised their holier-than-thou attitudes. Tacitus writes in his *Annales* that when crowds of Christians were placed on trial, they were convicted not so much for arson as because of their "hatred of the human race." Their punishments set precedents in the persecutions which were to ensue under other emperors:

> Besides being put to death they were made to serve as objects of amusement; they were clad in the hides of beasts and torn to death by dogs; others were crucified, others set on fire to serve to illuminate the night when daylight failed. Nero had thrown open his grounds for the display, and was putting on a show in

the circus, where he mingled with the people in the dress of charioteer or drove about in his chariot. All this gave rise to a feeling of pity, even toward men whose guilt merited the most exemplary punishment; for it was felt that they were being destroyed not for the public good but to gratify the cruelty of an individual.[9]

According to tradition, Peter and Paul were imprisoned in the Mamertine Prison in Rome. Both are believed to have died in the persecution under Nero. Peter is believed to have been crucified upside down, and Paul is thought to have been beheaded.

The persecution of Christians at that time was limited to Rome. It was not spread throughout the empire nor was the religion persecuted for being illegal. However, worse things were in store, not only for the Christians of the empire but for the Jews themselves, especially those of Jerusalem. Tension between Romans and Jews was strong in Judea, and the quality of the procurators sent by Rome was only making matters more desperate each year. The revolt that simmered as a rumor in the days of Jesus was ready to boil over and consume all in Judea.

---

[9]Tacitus, *Annales*, xv. 44, in Henry Bettenson, ed., *Documents of the Christian Church* (New York: Oxford University Press, 1943), p. 2.

SUGGESTIONS FOR ADDITIONAL READING

Barclay, William. *The Mind of St. Paul*. New York: Harper and Row, Publishers, 1975.

Bouttier, Michael. *Christianity According to Paul*. Naperville, Illinois: Alec R. Allenson, Inc., 1966.

Brown, Raymond E., Donfried, K. P. and Reumann, John eds. *Peter in the New Testament*. Minneapolis, Minnesota: Augsburg Publishing House, 1973.

Cullmann, Oscar. *Peter*. Translated by Floyd Filson. Philadelphia: The Westminster Press, 1953.

Dibelius, Martin. *Studies in the Acts of the Apostles*. Edited by H. Greeven. London: S. C. M. Press, 1956.

Dodd, C. H. *The Meaning of Paul for Today*. Cleveland, Ohio: William Collins and World Publishing Co., Inc., 1974.

Gasque, W. W. *A History of the Criticism of the Acts of the Apostles*. Grand Rapids: William B. Eerdmans Publishing Co., 1975.

Hunter, Archibald M. *Paul and His Predecessors*. Philadelphia: The Westminster Press, 1961.

Jackson, F. J. Foakes and Lake, Kirsopp. *The Beginnings of Christianity*. 2 volumes. London: Macmillan, 1922.

Schmithals, Walter. *Paul and James*. Translated by Dorothea Barton. London: S. C. M. Press, Ltd., 1965.

Schoyes, H. J. *Paul*. Translated by Harold Knight. Philadelphia: The Westminster Press, 1961.

Shepard, J. W. *The Life and Letters of St. Paul*. Grand Rapids, Michigan: Wm. B. Eerdmans Publishing Company, 1970.

Williams, C. S. C. *A Commentary of the Acts of the Apostles*. New York: Harper and Brothers, 1957.

CHAPTER 13

INSTITUTIONS SUCCEED PERSONS

By the time Muhammad appeared in history, in the seventh century A.D., the Christian Church was firmly established in the Mediterranean world. Persecutions by various emperors had not destroyed it. Its weaknesses were due primarily to divisions within it which had developed over the years, beginning in the first century. Its institutions remained although its leaders had come and gone.

The passing of Jesus, of Peter, Paul, and the other apostles did not mean the end of "the Way," as it might have, for the leaders had done their work very well. During their lifetimes they had established forms of activities which were to be maintained even after their deaths. The structure of the church, while always influenced by human leaders, was not totally at their mercy. The basic form of that structure was Jewish although it was modified according to local situations, depending upon whether the church, the assembly, the ecclesia, was limited entirely to Jews, as it sometimes appeared to be in Jerusalem, or whether it embraced a majority of either Greeks or Romans.

The order of public worship was based upon that of the synagogue. Prayers, hymns, reading of scriptures, preaching and teaching, and a call to service were likely to be found in any church service which was open to the public. Some sort of leadership was exercised, perhaps by a layman, as in Judaism, or gradually by persons with more qualities of leadership, set aside for the purpose, such as a bishop who served as an overseer or superintendent, or as a presbyter or president. The meeting places of the synagogue did not long serve those who became followers of the Christ, and they had to find their own places of meeting, whether in homes, in public rooms, out of doors, or even in caves or underground tombs, such as the catacombs of Rome. Separate buildings for worship, constructed by Christians for their own use, came in time, but they were not a primary concern in the first century.

One of the rites of the early church that was not a part of the synagogue service was the agape or love feast. Although the Jerusalem church at the time of Stephen had appointed deacons to serve tables, because Christians had all things in common, even daily meals, there was also a meal reserved to those who had been baptized as followers of Christ. It was based upon the Last Supper of Jesus with his disciples where he broke bread as a symbol of his broken body and drank wine as a symbol of his blood to be poured out in a sacrifice for mankind. It was referred to as the eucharist, based upon a prayer of thanksgiving observed during the ritual. This rite seems to have been the most sacred observance in the estimation of those who were already baptized Christians.

The rite of baptism which Jesus and his apostles had adopted from John the Baptist was continued after the days of the apostles. It was still the act that marked one's acceptance of Jesus as the Christ, the forgiveness of one's former sins, and the entrance into a new life in Christ. In the days of Peter and of Paul it seems to have been administered at the time of decision by the convert. As time proceeded, however, the time between decision to become a Christian and the time of baptism seems to have been lengthened and increasing care was taken to see that the convert had some developed knowledge of the teaching of the Christian church. The gift of the Holy Spirit that was so much a part of the early ministry of Peter which preceded or succeeded the rite of baptism seems to have received less attention as the churches became more established institutions.

The writings based upon the teachings of the apostles became, however, one of the most important factors in the formation of Christian churches. As long as the apostles who knew Jesus were alive their words of recollection had primary importance; however, as they died of old age or by violence, it became of utmost importance to preserve their knowledge. The teachings of Paul, also, were recalled and renewed as he revisited the churches which he had established. In his absence the letters of instruction and exhortation which he had written to congregations in various cities and regions became valuable literature to the church, gradually gaining a status among Christians almost as important as the Jewish scriptures.

In some ways the simplest surviving gospel, which may be the earliest, is the gospel of Mark. It is in many ways quite concise, omitting the stories of the birth of Jesus and any mention of a childhood, beginning rather with the account of Jesus going to John the Baptist for the rite of baptism.[1] It has a vivid account of the events in a day of the life of Jesus, but it avoids any long account of discourses or sermons of Jesus, concentrating on events and summary sayings. As in all the gospels, a lot of attention is devoted to the final days of Jesus in Jerusalem, his arrest, trial, and crucifixion. It has been a no-nonsense gospel which understandably had a favored place in the church in Rome.

Matthew, on the other hand, has a particular interest in showing that Jesus lived in a way which fulfilled the prophecies of the Jewish prophets. The genealogy of Jesus is of great importance, showing that he was born of the lineage of King David in the city of Bethlehem.[2] The story of his birth from a virgin is important, and so are the accounts of how he was recognized by Magi as a great person and by King Herod of the Jews as a king who would be a rival for the throne. Thus Matthew has a lot of material not to be found in Mark. Moreover it is in Matthew that one finds the lengthy collection of teachings of Jesus known as the Sermon on the Mount.[3] On the other hand, nearly all of the material of Mark appears somewhere in the gospel of Matthew.

Luke has a concern for the relationship between Jesus and John the Baptist and takes considerable space to show the relationship of the mother of John and the mother of Jesus and the experiences of John's father who was a priest.[4] Instead of emphasis upon kings and Jewish scriptures, Luke concentrates upon the shepherds of the field to whom angels of heaven announced the birth of Jesus. Luke also used a considerable amount of the material which is found in Mark. As did Matthew, he included long passages of teachings of Jesus, such as the sermon on the plain. There are also places where Matthew and Luke agree word for word on material which is not found in Mark, which led

---

[1] Mark 1.

[2] Matthew 1.

[3] Matthew 5, 6, 7.

[4] Luke 1.

some scholars in the nineteenth century to hold that they used a common source (in German, *Quelle*) which has not been found, however, as a separate document. Scholars refer to this hypothetical document as the "Q" document.

The gospel of John stands alone as a separate approach entirely. Scholars of the gospels can place the first three gospels, Matthew, Mark, and Luke into parallel columns and show remarkable similarities among the three. The fourth gospel, John, is strikingly different. Its prologue has the ring of Platonist philosophy until it reaches the point where the Logos took flesh and dwelt among men.[5] Jesus is painted in a portrait of the eternal reason principle clothed in the fleshly tent of a human being. He openly pronounces from the beginning who he is, namely, the Son of the Father who is in heaven. His discourses are loftly and enigmatic, more a dialogue for the powerful and the educated rather than the humble student of Jewish Torah or the shepherds of the field. Yet, some of the most striking figures of Jesus in the minds of his followers come from the Gospel of John: "I am the good shepherd." "I am the way, the truth, and the life." "I am the vine." "I am the door." The beautiful summary of Christianity in the words of Jesus are in this gospel: "God so loved the world that he gave his only begotten son that whosoever believeth in him should not perish but have everlasting life."[6] Other words read:

> Let not your hearts be troubled, you believe in God, believe also in me. In my father's house are many mansions, if it were not so I would have told you. I go to prepare a place for you. And if I go and prepare a place for you I will come again and receive you unto myself that where I am there ye may be also.[7]

The gospels are, then, each different in the sense that each presents Jesus from a different point of view. Yet all of them agree that he is the Christ and that through believing in him one is freed from sin and prepared for life in the presence of the reign of God. All agree that the life, death, and resurrection of Jesus as the Christ was an episode essential for the salvation of mankind. The earliest date usually assigned for the earliest gospel is around 40 A.D., some ten or more years after the death

---

[5]John 1.

[6]John 3:16.

[7]John 14:1-3.

of Jesus. This theory makes the assumption that the earliest gospel may have been written first in Aramaic, the language spoken by Jesus and his people, rather than in the *koine*, or marketplace, Greek. The latest date usually assigned is to the gospel of John, placing it around 120 A.D. Most liberal Christian scholars of the twentieth century have placed the synoptic, or first three gospels, after 70 A.D. It is in favor of the reliability of the gospels on the biography of Jesus that they were composed of material that was probably written during the lifetime of people who were his contemporaries.

The gospels show just how much Christian ideas were distinctive from mainstream ideas of Judaism, for they show how he criticized the rabbis, especially the Pharisees of his day. It was a theme which was preserved and even developed by Paul of Tarsus as he adapted the Christian message to non-Jews, or Gentiles. To a great extent it was Paul who laid a foundation for Christianity to stand alone, apart from Judaism.

One of the great monuments to the genius of Paul is the letter he wrote to the church in Rome before he ever visited the city. The book of Romans has captured the imagination and inspired the zeal of many of the greatest thinkers in Christianity for centuries.[8] In it Paul makes the point that salvation under God is not dependent upon being either Jew or Greek, but upon being in the right relationship to God. The Jews have a right to have pride in the law and to respect it as a guide to salvation. The truth is, in fact, that one cannot keep all of the law in practice, for sinful human beings, no matter how hard they try, violate the law at some points. Under those circumstances, instead of becoming an instrument of salvation the law becomes an instrument of condemnation. The law has the effect of making one guilty. The law should be fulfilled, yet one finds it impossible, and then the law which was given to bring about one's salvation actually confirms one's condemnation.

Salvation must, then, be sought in some other way. Ritual, such as circumcision, is an outward sign of an inward change in one's relationship to God. Unless the inward relationship has changed, the external sign alone does not effect the salvation one seeks. The key to salvation is elsewhere. In the study of Jewish scriptures Paul thought he had found the key element. In the father of the Jews, Abraham, one had an example of one who had the right relationship with God even before the law was given to Moses. How was Abraham justified before God? The answer, Paul concluded, was that Abraham was justified by his faith

---

[8]Romans.

in God. He needed nothing else in the beginning, for the ritual of circumcision and other covenants grew out of the relationship of faith which preceded any law.

On the other hand, faith is not something one can turn on at will. Faith itself is a gift of God, bestowed through his grace on people who had not earned it. The means of extending this grace was in Jesus as the Christ, who died, shedding his blood, for human beings while they were still sinners. For Paul, all human beings are descendants from Adam who sinned against God. From the sin of that parent of the human race, every human being carries the mark of sin, which explains why even when one wants to do so, it is impossible to fulfill the letter of the law. God, through Christ, had to do for human beings what they could not ever do for themselves. In his grace, he sent the Christ, an innocent being, God who had become man, to shed his blood and die for them. Through their faith in him the sinner could be saved. Therefore, human beings lost in sin through Adam are saved by the grace of God through their faith in the Lord Jesus Christ.

Since salvation is through faith and the spirit of God in Christ rather than through the law, one should live in the spirit, in freedom in Christ, rather than bound by the letter of the law. "All who are led by the spirit of God are sons of God."[9] One should enjoy freedom in the spirit of God rather than slavery to the conventions and rituals and bondage of the law. This new kind of life is open to all mankind, regardless of nation or race or human circumstance in social station or economic level. Even Jews could be saved; it was just more difficult for them because they had such pride in the law that they could find it difficult to lower its priority below that of faith.

While the letter to the Romans was an assertive position of freedom welcomed by some Jews and by many Gentiles, it is easy to see how it was a challenge to severe condemnation by the members of the Jewish establishment. For, generally speaking, they did not look upon the story of Adam as implying that his sin has extended to all other human beings. They believed that it was possible to have salvation by keeping the law; indeed that was the only way of salvation for a Jew. They also believed that if anyone wanted salvation one should receive circumcision and become a Jew.

If Paul freed Christians from bondage to the Jewish law he did not free them for immorality. In his letter to the Corinthians, Paul had to

---

[9]Romans 8:14.

remind Christians that although they were not saved by the law, there were moral requirements to be kept by people who were saved through Christ.[10] Living in freedom of the spirit means that a Christian is a temple and that God's spirit dwells in that person. Since one is the dwelling place of the spirit of God, one should keep one's body in the kind of purity appropriate to such an edifice. One's body is a member of the body of Christ, for the church is the body of Christ, and Christians are members of that body. So one should not corrupt one's body with a prostitute or other forms of intemperance or immorality. While marriage should be faithful, it is preferable not to marry so that one can give all of one's life in Christian service, as did Paul.

Freedom means that many things are all right for the believer which might have been frowned upon by Jews. On the other hand, one has to consider Christians who are still immature in the faith and non-Christians who might misconstrue one's actions. One should, for example, avoid eating meat which has been offered first to an idol, not because there is anything wrong with the meat or with eating it, but one's eating that kind of meat might mislead other people about one's beliefs. Though one has freedom in Christ, one also has responsibilities to other members in the body of Christ. One's goal is to do all things so as to bring praise to the glory of God.

The guide to every action of the Christian should be love. It is superior to any other act or relationship in the world. Without love, all other acts are empty of value in the sight of God. With love, all things can be understood. It is the only enduring thing in the world, for whereas many valuable things will pass away, love will never end. As Paul concludes his great hymn in I Corinthians 13, "So faith, hope, love abide, these three; but the greatest of these is love."

Other literature in the New Testament reflects a belief that the time of the return of Jesus the Christ to help carry out the last judgment of the world is about to occur at any moment. Paul believed that those who are dead will be raised again at the last day to meet Christ as he descends from heaven on a cloud, as he ascended on a cloud when he left the earth and his disciples. Paul also told the Christians of Thessalonica that the day of the Lord would come as a thief in the night, a time of wrath and destruction when one is complacent and peaceful. However, the time of wrath and judgment for most people will be a time of reward for Christians who have been faithful to Christ in their lives. For that reason,

---

[10]I and II Corinthians.

the most important thing one could do in life is always to live ready for the Christ to return at any moment.

The book of the Revelation of St. John is an apocalypse, sharing several of the characteristics of the book of Daniel. It is also a message of encouragement to Christians who are undergoing persecution, perhaps from the Roman government. The symbolism is difficult to interpret for the reader of later centuries, but it must have been rather clear to the Christians of the first century who understood the symbols of nations and their leaders, as an informed citizen of today might grasp the meaning of cartoons as political satire. Nevertheless, some of the vision of the last judgment is clear even to people of other centuries:

> Then I saw a new heaven and a new earth; for the first heaven and the first earth had passed away, and the sea was no more. And I saw the holy city, new Jerusalem, coming down out of heaven from God, prepared as a bride adorned for her husband; and I heard a great voice from the throne saying, "Behold, the dwelling of God is with men. He will dwell with them and they shall be his people, and God himself will be with them; he will wipe every tear from their eyes, and death shall be no more, neither shall there be mourning nor crying nor pain any more, for the former things have passed away." (Rev. 21:1-4)

The vision of Heaven remained with Christians through the centuries, but it was not exclusive with them. Some Jews shared the vision with them. Muslims, when they arrived, also held a dream of a better life after death in Paradise.

SUGGESTIONS FOR ADDITIONAL READING

Baird, William. *The Corinthian Church - A Biblical Approach to Urban Culture.* New York: Abingdon Press, 1964.

Barrett, C. K. *A Commentary on the Epistle to the Romans.* New York: Harper and Row, 1957.

Barth, Karl. *The Epistle to the Romans.* Translated by E. C. Hoskyns. London: Oxford University Press, 1965.

Conybeare, W. J. and Howson, J. S. *The Life and Epistles of St. Paul.* 2 volumes. London: Longmans, Green, and Co., 1877.

McGiffert, Arthur Cushman. *A History of Christianity in the Apostolic Age.* New York: Charles Scribner's Sons, 1916.

McGiffert, Arthur Cushman. *A History of Christian Thought.* Volume I. New York: Charles Scribner's Sons, 1932.

Munck, Johannes, *Paul.* Richmond, Virginia: John Knox Press, 1959.

O'Neill, J. C. *Paul's Letter to the Romans.* Harmondsworth, Middlesex: Penguin Books, Ltd., 1975.

Weiss, Johannes, *Earliest Christianity.* Translated by T. C. Grant. Gloucester, Massachusetts: Peter Smith, 1970.

CHAPTER 14

THE DAYS OF THE ZEALOTS

The faith that Jesus of Nazareth was the Christ and was in control of history satisfied some Jews who became members of "the Way." But Jesus was not accepted as the Christ by anything like a majority of Jews. Once the High Priest succeeded in having Jesus put to death, the masses of people in Galilee and Judea seem to have accepted the decision and to have looked further for means of deliverance from Rome. They concluded that Jesus and his followers had no program of improving the physical and political welfare of the Jews. Indeed, it was demonstrated on several occasions that they were more likely to be victims of Rome rather than victors. The hopes of most Jews in Jerusalem, and certainly the political leaders, had to find fulfillment elsewhere because for them Jesus plainly was not the Messiah but a false prophet. And the organization of his followers was a kind of subversive effort, weakening the Jewish faith and increasing tensions with Rome without any possibility of gains.

For a while, during the reign of Herod Agrippa I who was well-liked by the Jews, the Procurators were not sent to govern Judea and the tensions of the past eased somewhat. Upon the death of Herod, however, the stream of Procurators was resumed and tensions resumed. There were severe rifts among the people of the area, not only between Jews and Romans but also between Jews and Gentiles and between Judeans and Samaritans. A high priest, considered too lax by some Jews, was assassinated. Quarrels were rampant among the inhabitants of the land and Rome was determined to keep the whole boiling pot under their control. It was a situation made to order for the Zealots, for open war was ready to break out at any time.

Not all Jews were consumed by politics, however. One of them, a pacifist and a teacher, was concerned to continue studies of the law and preserve the religion of the fathers in some place more stable than Jerusalem. Johanan ben Zakkai persuaded the Romans of the innocence of his request to leave Jerusalem and to establish a school in the little town of Jamnia, which had not been involved in the battles which had broken out by that time. To the Romans it was innocuous, but as it turned out in history, when this request was granted, it made possible the survival of Judaism despite the defeat of its political and military force.[1]

Defeat may have been inevitable for those forces, but it was neither swift nor painless. The first leader of the Roman forces was Vespasian who returned to Rome upon the death of Nero in order to become emperor. The task of defeating the Jews was completed by his son Titus who, not without mercy, was completely devoted to crushing the rebellion and preventing a recurrence. The Zealots were within the walls of Jerusalem fighting for their lives. The Romans broke down one wall to find that there was yet another defended to the death by Zealots. Titus called upon the defenders time and again to surrender, but they would not. One estimate is that a million Jews died in the fighting. Nevertheless, the frenzy of the Zealots was no match for the calculating military executions of the Roman army and finally the temple was won by the Romans. The fighting had broken out in 66 A.D. and the temple was destroyed by fire on the ninth of Ab in the year 70. The western wall was the only thing left of the sacred temple constructed under Solomon and restored over the centuries.[2]

Titus executed by crucifixion many of the survivors. Some of the more handsome he took to Rome with him to march in his victory parade. He also took gold furnishings from the temple, pictured on the arch of Titus in Rome which marks his victory over Jerusalem.

---

[1]James Parker, *The Foundations of Judaism and Christianity* (Chicago: Quadrangle Books, 1960), book 3, *The Emergence of Rabbinic Judaism.* Herbert Danby, *The Mishnah* (London: Oxford University Press, 1933).

[2]John B. Noss, *Man's Religions* (New York: Macmillan Publishing Co., Inc., 1974).

Some Zealots either escaped from Jerusalem or gathered from other centers and installed themselves in a rock fortress at Masada. They endured for three more years but in the end they committed suicide rather than surrender to the Roman troops. The final remnant of the Jewish army that revolted against Rome was eliminated. In many ways it may have seemed that the nation had come to an end. There was no longer any place for a priesthood to function, for there was no temple and none would be permitted by the Romans. The political power of the Sanhedrin was also gone. The flame of Judaism which had burned since the days of Moses had never been lower.[3]

But just as the study of literature had flourished during the Babylonian exile and the synagogue had developed in the absence of a temple, so these activities resumed a major role in the survival of the essential faith of the Jews. The men who retained a growing power were not the priests or Sadducees but Pharisees, or more particularly, rabbis. Johannan ben Zakkai was looked upon as a disciple of the Hillel school. In spite of his personal leanings to Hillel, Johanan be Zakkai tried to reconcile the teachings of that school with those of Shammai. The teachings of the masters were collected to guide a defeated and perplexed nation.

The second step taken by Johanan ben Zakkai was just as important as the first. He reestablished the Sanhedrin as the High Court binding on all Jews and exercising as much power as Rome would allow. No longer controlled by priests and Sadducees, it was an instrument of the Pharisees speaking to the religious areas of a Jew's life but without power to give a death sentence. What the Bet Din could do was fix a Jewish calendar with exact dates for fasts and festivals so that all Jews could observe those days which gave their existence meaning.

The successors of Johanan ben Zakkai assumed responsibility for taking other steps to preserve Judaism. They decided what books of Scripture would be regarded as sacred and which ones were merely of some literary interest. In short, they established the Jewish Bible. The standard form of worship was also developed under Rabbi Gamaliel. Although it was adapted to the fact of life that the temple was destroyed, it included a prayer for the restoration of the temple and the worship which belonged in it. Any layman could lead prayers in the synagogue services. The Pentateuch was, of course, the primary scripture in use but

---

[3]Leo Trepp. *A History of Jewish Experience* (New York: Behrman House, 1962).

the prophetic books also had their place. These were studied along with the Writings and an unwritten law, or Halakah, developed under the leadership of the rabbis. Judaism took a form which would allow it to endure in spite of the severe blow it had suffered in the burning of the temple.

It was well that so much progress was made at Jamnia for the tragedies for Jerusalem were not yet ended. Unfortunately, some part of the next tragedy had to be shared with a rabbi who was for the most part a good and creative man. Rabbi Akiba ben Joseph did not have the rank of a scholar when he married his employer's daughter, but with her support he devoted himself to becoming a great scholar. Although he believed the scriptures to be divine revelation with nothing in them without special meaning, his method of interpretation allowed him to find in the ancient writings grounds for the customs of the Jews which had, until his time, not been tied to the written law. He also codified the Oral Law, arranging it into six major headings with appropriate subheadings. But for all his interest as a scholar, he became entangled in politics and thought that he had found the Messiah. It was that belief that led to another tragedy for the Jews.

Rabbi Akiba loved his people and had reason to hope that deliverance could be found. Bad matters were, in his view, about to become worse. It was bad enough that after the destruction of the temple Jews still had to pay a half shekel tax to support it. The tax, moreover, was being used to support a temple to Jupiter. The emperor Hadrian ordered that a temple for Jupiter Capitolinus be erected over the site of the old Jewish temple. That was more than the Jews could stand. Rabbi Akiba took a leading role in the revolt that broke out in 132 A.D. and lasted for three-and-a-half-years.

When the Jews were finally defeated Hadrian resumed the building of Jerusalem as he had planned. Since the Jews did not approve, he ordered that they were not to enter the city which was now a Roman colony. The only time a Jew could return to Jerusalem was during the month of Ab, the anniversary of the destruction of the temple. By bribing a guard a Jew could go to the remaining wall of the temple of his fathers and mourn his losses. The place became known as the Wailing Wall. Not until 1967 did Jews regain political control of the Wall. Muslims and Christians know well the reluctance of Jews to weaken their control over it.

Jamnia had become involved in the revolt, so the scholars moved to a town in Galilee called Usha, and there they continued their work. Two scholars of note developed there, Rabbi Meir and Rabbi Judah. Judah was a Patriarch and thus head of the High Court. He was a man of great learning and also wealth, two things which together with his political position made him a man of uncommon authority. His great work was the Mishnah, a collection of rabbinic teachings.[4] In it he relied on Rabbi Akiba's six headings or Orders: Seeds, or agriculture; Seasons, or festivals and fasts; Women, with laws of marriage; Damages, on civil and criminal law; Fathers, ethical teachings of the fathers of Israel; Holy Things, dealing with ritual and worship; and a sixth Order, Purities, relating to ceremonial purity and impurity. Under each order was a tractate, chapters, and paragraphs. While some minor changes may have been made to the Mishnah after the death of Rabbi Judah, it is recognized as his great work and it carries very weighty authority. At his insistence it was issued in the Hebrew language rather than Aramaic.

As the schools of Palestine lost their prestige in scholarship, leadership passed to the established Jewish community in Babylon. Under men such as Abba, better known simply as Rab, or Master, and Rab Samuel rabbinic discussions flourished. Under Rab Ashi the combining of the Mishnah and the Gemara, of the Haggadah and Halakah, bagan and was almost completed at his death in 427 A.D. By 485 A.D. the completed work was known as the famous Babylonian Talmud.[5] It was the foundation for Jewish life and practice for all Jews from that time forward through the middle ages. Regardless of the hostile environment in which Jews might find themselves, as long as they had the Talmud they had a guide and a means of preserving their faith and their culture.

While pursuing the mainstream development of Judaism through Palestine and Babylon, one should not forget that a vital Judaism flourished in another country which had a long history of providing a home for a great many Jews. Egypt had a large colony of Jews, particularly in Alexandria. And although they also followed the mainstream of Jews after the destruction of the temple of Jerusalem, they also had the problem of living in a culture which was strongly influenced by Hellenism. In the first century of the Common Era, they had to see how their ancient Jewish faith compared to the teachings of the Greek philosophers such as the Platonists and the Stoics. In Alexandria, Philo, known also as Judaeus (20 B.C. to 40 A.D.), faced the problem as he tried to integrate Greek and Jewish thought systems.

---

[4]Herbert Danby, *The Mishnah.*

[5]Jacob Neusner, *Invitation to the Talmud* (New York: Harper and Row, 1973).

If the Greek philosophers are taken seriously and the Jewish Scriptures are taken literally, then there seems little way that the two can be related in a common thought system. They belong to two different worlds. However, Philo thought that he had found a way of relating them while remaining true to both. The key to his work was the use of the allegorical method of interpreting the Jewish Scriptures. While there was a literal meaning of the Scriptures, he said, there was also a spiritual meaning. When one reads with understanding the spiritual meaning, one sees that there is no conflict between the philosophy of Plato and his followers and the law and the prophets of Judaism. The essential truth is that while man is a physical being, he is also a spiritual being. The soul should seek to rise from the realm of the physical world, from imprisonment in the lusts and passions of the body, to the realm of the mind and the spirit. The Jewish Law is a means of accomplishing this act. Philo differed from Paul in that he thought that the law was essential and helpful in making progress in the life of the mind and of the spirit.

Philo speaks of a Logos, or Word of God, which comes from God and gives all things in creation order and intelligibility. The Logos is the reason principle running through all things. It is in knowing it and following it that one is led through higher being to God.

Philo's attempt to accommodate Judaism to Hellenism had a place, and it may have set some sort of example for those Jews who became Christians and tried to form a faith that was acceptable not only to them but also to Gentiles of the Greek and the Roman worlds. But it was not acceptable to the tradition of the rabbis, who emphasized the unique faith of the Jews as the chosen people of God rather than their kinship with other thought systems. The Jews wanted their own country with their own laws and customs without having to accommodate themselves to other peoples. They usually sought no converts, although they would accept some people who came to them wanting to become Jews. They were interested in themselves as the chosen people of God and in receiving in full the promises that went with that calling. The attitude of the rabbis prevailed in Judaism.

Jews had experienced anti-Semitism throughout their history. The Egyptians practiced it against them and so did the Syrians, Babylonians, and, at times, the Persians. The Romans could not understand their Sabbath observance, their lack of three dimensional art, their absence from the games of the arenas, their observances, such as the Passover, celebrated in privacy, the act of circumcision, and their concern with the family and with sexual morality. The Talmud, which preserved their peculiar identity, set them apart from their neighbors. Their concern for

Jerusalem and the sending of money out of the countries of the diaspora to support either the old temple, or later, the Patriarch, was not understood or appreciated. To attack them and humble them, proving to them and to oneself that they were not so special or superior after all seemed much more rewarding than trying to understand them.

The Christians did not forget that Jesus had been condemned by the High Priest and that scribes and Pharisees had been his enemies. The persecution of the Jerusalem church which stoned Stephen and sent followers of "the Way" throughout Palestine and to other countries to escape the deputies sent to arrest them was there in the Christian Scriptures for each new generation to study and digest. It seems to have been easy for peoples throughout history to prove their loyalty to their cause by taking out their personal prejudices on some perceived enemy. The Jews were ready victims for the purpose. For brief periods they were tolerated in peace, in one country or another. But quite often they were suddenly the victims of an outpouring of resentment and bitter hatred.

The Jews believed that Jesus was not the Messiah which they had longed to receive. But it was also apparent that neither were the Zealots nor Bar Kochba.

SUGGESTIONS FOR ADDITIONAL READING

Baron, Salo and Blau, Joseph L., editors. *Judaism*. Indianapolis: Bobbs-Merrill Company, Inc., 1954.

Blau, Saul. *The Story of Jewish Philosophy*. New York: Random House, 1962.

Bonsirven, Joseph. *Palestinian Judaism in the Time of Jesus Christ*. Translated by William Wolf. New York: Holt, Rinehart and Winston, 1964.

Guinebert, Charles. *The Jewish World in the Time of Jesus*. New Hyde Park, New York: University Books, 1959.

Hereford, R. T. *Christianity in Talmud and Midrash*. Clifton, New Jersey: Reference Book Publishers, Inc., 1966.

Neusner, Jacob, ed. *Understanding Rabbinic Judaism*. New York: K. T. A. V. Publishing House, Inc. 1974.

Sandmel, Samuel. *The First Christian Century in Judaism and Christianity*. New York: Oxford University Press, 1969.

Strack, Hermann L. *Introduction to the Talmud and Midrash*. Philadelphia: Jewish Publication Society of America, 1931.

Unterman, Isaac. *The Talmud*. New York: Block Publishing Company, 1952.

CHAPTER 15

THE CHRIST OF THE CREEDS

The Jews who were widely scattered found it necessary to establish unity through a common set of beliefs and practices. The same kind of problem confronted the Christians. In their beginning stages diversity helped their growth. But eventually there were beliefs and practices creeping into some groups which could threaten the strength of the Christian movement. The churches had to reach some agreement on the essential points of faith and practice.

The canon of the New Testament separated the acceptable material to the Church from that which was only of local interest or which was unacceptable to all persons who understood the main thrust of the teachings of the apostles. Yet, the material of that canon did not mean that intellectual activity in the churches had ceased. The New Testament was full of intriguing ideas which invited vigorous minds to continue analyzing and developing them. Each student and each teacher was, for the most part, free to pursue an idea and even to teach the results of his speculation.

Early Christians, in spite of their sporadic problems with Roman requirements which would compromise their faith, took full advantage of a variety of ideas. The details of their further doctrinal development can be maddening to any serious scholar trying to digest every step that occurred in the first five centuries. Nevertheless, even though the picture may have to be distorted somewhat by brevity, some notion of the doctrinal struggles of those centuries is essential for anyone who would understand the various positions within modern Christianity.[1]

One of the most attractive ideas to the non-Jews who were drawn to Christianity was that of Docetism. Named for the Greek word "to seem" or "to appear," *dokesis*, Docetists believed that the divine Logos did not ever really become flesh but only appeared to do so. In much of Greek thought, even in that of Plato, the mind is superior to the body. Salvation comes in freeing the mind from the body, which is ensnared in passions and corruption. The mind is more of the nature of the divine. The Pythagoreans spent much effort in strengthening the mind so that it could be free from the body and thus eternal. To philosophers of this order and for adherents of the mystery religions which popularly shared this view of flesh and the world, it was almost impossible to think that a divine principle could stoop or sink to the low point of assuming a physical nature. Such an occurrence would jeopardize the divinity of a being. Jesus only appeared to become a man.

Docetism fit in rather nicely with a larger thought system which is hard to define in terms of locality or period of history since in various forms it covered several centuries and several regions. Essentially gnosticism emphasized a special, secret knowledge or, in Greek, *gnosis*. This secret knowledge which led to salvation was only made available to the initiated. Again, the emphasis was on the mind and knowledge with a disparagement of the world of nature and of history. Also disparaged was the simple faith of simple people, for Gnosticism appealed to the intellectuals. It syncretized the insights of many religions, including astral beings from Babylonia and Egypt. There was usually a hierarchy of divine beings, the highest of which would never have soiled his hands by stooping to create a physical world. Like one of their representatives, Marcion, they could never accept the crude god portrayed in the Jewish Bible as the same God revealed in the New Testament. The Jewish god was obviously a lower being and not a god worthy of worship. Terms such as "truth," "wisdom," and "word" were more akin to the thinking of the Gnostics.

The people who had composed the Christian Bible could never tolerate Gnosticism without undermining the essential position of their understanding of the work of Christ. The salvation of man, for them,

---

[1]Williston Walker, *A History of the Christian Church* (New York: Charles Scribner's Sons, 1959). Also, Kenneth Scott Latourette, *A History of Christianity* (New York: Harper and Brothers, 1953).

depended upon God becoming a real man and suffering death as a real man. Without those historical facts there could be no salvation of mankind bound in sin since the sin of Adam. The Christ could not save were he not God. But he could not save human beings unless he had become a human being and died for their sins. There was also no Christian hope that believers would be raised from the dead if Christ had not been raised as a human being by God, the first fruit of many to follow him in victory over death.

The response of those who claimed to follow the teachings of the authors of the New Testament devised a statement of their beliefs. Such a statement in the Christian Church is referred to as a creed, based on the Latin word for "I believe," or *credo*. The creed which was advanced by Christians to deal with Gnosticism is known as "The Apostles' Creed," although the present version may not have existed until the sixth century, A.D. It purports to set forth a minimum of faith established by the Apostles themselves. Many of the ideas in it can indeed be found expressed from the earliest years of the churches. But it has an emphasis upon facts in history, in spite of the preferences of the Docetists and other Gnostics. One form found in Epiphanius purports to have been left with Julius, Bishop of Rome in 340 A.D.[2]

1. I believe in God almighty
2. And in Christ Jesus, his only son, our Lord
3. Who was born of the Holy Spirit and the Virgin Mary
4. Who was crucified under Pontius Pilate and was buried
5. And the third day rose from the dead
6. Who ascended into heaven
7. And sitteth on the right hand of the Father
8. Whence he cometh to judge the living and the dead
9. And in the Holy Ghost
10. The holy church
11. The remission of sins
12. The resurrection of the flesh
13. The life everlasting

Current usage of the Apostles Creed can be found in most recent hymnals and prayerbooks of Christian orders or denominations.

Another problem that was made perennial through the Christian

---

[2]Henry Bettenson, ed. *Documents of the Christian Church* (New York: Oxford University Press, 1943), p. 33.

canon of scriptures, was that of the relationship of the Holy Spirit to the Son and to the Father. The gospels state that Jesus as the Christ was the Son of God. Jesus speaks clearly about our Father in heaven, to whom he prayed. Jesus also promised the gift of a Holy Spirit which would give comfort and power. The book of Acts of the Apostles makes the Holy Spirit a main character, along with Peter and Paul. If the Christ comes from God and the Spirit comes from God, what is the relationship of the Spirit and the Christ? Is the Spirit a replacement for Christ? Are all three of these really God? If so, how can God still be one, as Jews and Christians and later, Muslims, have all agreed? The problems can be formulated in many different ways and answered in even more different ways. Two well-known choices were presented at the beginning of the third Christian century, one from Rome and the other from the rival city of Carthage.

Sabellius was teaching in Rome around 215 A.D. the truth that God is one. The Father, Son, and Holy Spirit are really one and the same, each appearing under its own *Prosopon*, a term used in theater for the masks worn by an actor portraying more than one character in a drama. For Sabellius there is no doubt that God is one and only one, although he may appear in different forms on different occasions. Even as the sun can be hot, bright, and round, so God can be Father, Son, and Holy Spirit. The problem the Christians found with Sabellius, which led them to reject his explanation, was that Father, Son, and Holy Spirit are mere appearances and not real entities at all. One is faced with the unpleasant scene of God talking to himself when Jesus prays to his Father in heaven. Most Christians thought that each entity was a separate personality and that some way had to be found to preserve that threeness without winding up with three separate gods.

Tertullian of Carthage, who lived about the same time as Sabellius, is known to have come from training in Stoicism and legal expression. He combined legal concepts and philosophical concepts to give a clear expression to how the Father, Son, and Holy Spirit fit together in one Trinity which preserves at the same time the oneness of God and the triune experiences of the Christian Community. God is *una substantia*, one substance, in three person, or *personae*. The personae were parties in legal cases in Roman courts. They have their *oikonomia* (Greek), economy, that is, administrative activity, in God. There were problems with Tertullian's views, such as that of the Son being subordinate to the Father and the Holy Spirit proceeding only through the Son, which had to be worked out later by other fathers of the church. But Tertullian had sketched the parameters of orthodoxy; there had to be three separate beings or persons and there could only be one entity, or God. The mainstream of the Catholic, or universal, church always came back to those two points so clearly set forth by Tertullian. It has remained an intellectual problem for millions of Christians who have nevertheless accepted it on faith. It is unthinkable to Jews and Muslims.

At the beginning of the fourth century there broke out in Alexandria, Egypt, a dispute between the bishop, Alexander, and a presbyter, Arius. Whereas Alexander taught that both God and the Son always were, the Son being equal with the Father, Arius maintained that although God always was, the Son was not, but was the most important of all things created by God. Jesus was not God. The Son is clearly subordinate to the Father, in the view of Arius. The dispute between presbyter and bishop grew, and each party attracted followers. The bishop wrote his fellow bishops and explained the importance of maintaining his position on the doctrine. The eastern part of the Roman empire was being caught up in the controversy.

Then a shocking development took place. The emperor, Constantine, stepped in to help settle the quarrel. The persecutions of Christians by various emperors from the time of Nero on had continued to the days of Diocletian, whose edict of 303 A.D. ordered destruction of church buildings and the burning of Christian books throughout the empire. Had the persecution been continuous, uniform, and equally severe at all times during that period it is likely that the church could have been destroyed. Only ten years after Diocletian's edict Constantine established a policy of toleration for Christianity in the empire. The previous year he had been engaged in a battle with Maxentius when through a vision and a dream he was shown the symbol of a cross and the words, "Conquer by this." The emperor made such a standard and proceeded to the battle at Milvian bridge near Rome where he was victorious. The power of the Christian symbol was firmly fixed in his mind from that day onward. Essentially, the Christians were free to practice their faith, even their proselytizing, and Jews were forbidden to stone their members who decided to leave them to join Christianity. Although Constantine did not make Christianity the official state religion of the Roman empire, he gave it the status it needed to grow without interference from the state.

Christianity had contributed to his own strength in battle, Constantine may have reasoned, and it could contribute to the strength of the empire. Nevertheless, there was enough of the Roman administrator in him to know that a powerful force divided and at war with itself could be a divisive element in his empire. So Constantine took the initiative and called a council of Christian bishops, paying their traveling expenses from state funds, to meet at Nicea, in Asia Minor, in 325 A.D. Everybody who was anybody in the church was there, three hundred bishops, the eastern part of the empire being well represented, except that the absent bishop of Rome was represented by two presbyters. The whole thing was presided over by a person who was only a catechumen, yet unbaptised but under instruction in the Christian faith, but who was welcomed to the office since he was the emperor.

The result of the council was that Arius not only lost the fight but was anathematized (condemned) along with anyone else who contended that there ever was a time when the Son was not, or that he did not exist before he was begotten, or that he was made out of nothing, or was of any other substance than of the Father. Moreover, the Son was not subject to change. The Nicean Creed clarified the issues for all times, showing what the majority of bishops attending Nicea in 325 A.D. concluded about the nature of the Son in relationship to the Father.

> We believe in one God, the Father Almighty, maker of all things visible and invisible, and in one Lord, Jesus Christ, the Son of God, the only begotten of the Father, that is, of the substance (*ousias*) of the Father, God from God, light from light, true God from true God, begotten, not made, of one substance(*homoousion*) with the Father, through whom all things came to be, those things that are in heaven and those things that are on earth, who for us men and for our salvation came down and was made flesh, and was made man, suffered, rose the third day, ascended into the heavens, and will come to judge the living and the dead.[3]

The creed, together with its denunciation of these who held a contrary position, was believed to settle the matter. It was a war to end all wars. However, as was the case with most ecumenical councils, it became but a stage in the development of a controversy. The Arians kept on contending for their position and when Constantius, a son of Constantine, became sole ruler of the empire in 353 they had his support against the Nicean party. Numerous councils were called and another issue was joined with the theological one, that is, whether the church should submit to the opinion of the ruler, as the Arians contended, or whether it should be independent from the emperor, as the Nicean party

---

[3]Latourette, *A History of Christianity,* p. 155; cf. Bettenson, *Documents,* pp. 34-37.

maintained. With subsequent emperors the Arian party lost ground and new personalities entered the discussion to add strength to the Nicean point of view.

In 381 a second ecumenical council was held at Constantinople. One conclusion was that Father, Son, and Holy Spirit were not created and are to be worshipped together as one God. The majority of Romans held to the Nicene position, and Arianism was eclipsed. If the Son was really God and really man, how were the two natures related in him? Each bishop had an opinion, and all did not teach the same thing. Apollinaris believed that in the human Jesus the mind of the human had been replaced with the Logos, or divine reason. While the divine nature was complete in this view of Apollinaris, his fellow bishops thought his solution left the human nature of Jesus incomplete. Cyril of Alexandria held to the presence of the Logos in Jesus, but found the humanity not that of an individual man but of humanity in general. Thus Jesus was not a man. Maintaining emphasis on the divine element, he referred to the Virgin Mary as Theotokos, God-bearing, rather than as Christotokos, "Christ-bearing," as preferred by Nestorius of Constantinople. Nestorius emphasized the human nature of the Christ more than did Cyril.

A third ecumenical council was assembled in Ephesus in 432 A.D. to settle the controversy between Nestorius and Cyril, but political manipulation exceeded sound theological discussion and there was no agreement. The controversy continued, with each side asking the emperor to assist in its cause. Nestorius was eventually exiled, and his party found a home for their position, considered heretical by the Catholic church, in the Persian empire. Seemingly outside the controversy, the regions of Egypt, Ethiopia and parts of Syria were given to a position known as Monophysitism. There was only one nature in Christ,the Divine, which wholly subsumed the human, leaving only a few human characteristics to be seen. They emphasized the divine at the expense of the human. The main body of the church could not accept that position.

The question of the two natures of the Christ and their relationship was stated in a fourth ecumenical council held in Chalcedon, near Constantinople, in 451 A.D. The bishop of Rome at that time was Leo I, a man of outstanding ability. He wrote a letter to Flavian, which came to be known as the "Tome of Leo." In it he reaffirmed the position taken earlier by Tertullian on the two natures of Christ, that is, that there are two complete and independent natures together in one person in the Christ. Leo's tome was presented to the council of six hundred bishops in Chalcedon by legates representing him, for he could not be present himself. The tome of Leo was approved, and a creed was prepared to set forth the views he had espoused. The resulting definition was considerably more brief than the tome which Leo had written:

> Therefore, following the holy fathers, we all with one accord teach men to acknowledge one and the same Son, our Lord Jesus Christ, at once complete in Godhead and complete in manhood, truly God and truly man, consisting also of a reasonable soul and body; of one substance (homoousios) with the Father as regards his Godhead, and at the same time of one substance with us as regards his manhood; like us in all respects, apart from sin; as regards his Godhead, begotten of the Father before the ages, but yet as regards his manhood begotten, for us men and for our salvation, of Mary the Virgin, the God-bearer (Theotokos); one and the same Christ, Son, Lord, Only-begotten, recognized in two natures, without confusion, without change, without division, without separation; the distinction of natures being in no way annulled by the union, but rather the characteristics of each nature being preserved and coming together to form one person and subsistence (hypostasis), not as parted or separated into two persons, but one and the same Son and Only-begotten God the Word, Lord Jesus Christ; even as the prophets from earliest times spoke of him, and our Lord Jesus Christ himself taught us, and the creed of the Fathers has handed down to us.[4]

Once again the statement became a milestone in further controversy as sides continued to discuss how the two natures in the Christ are really related. But as time went on it became clear that the position of the fourth ecumenical council was definitive for the great body of churches which centered their leadership around the powerful bishop of Rome, the church which was known as Catholic, or worldwide. Jews and Muslims would reject it all, believing Jesus to be only a man.

In order to understand the development of Christianity for the next thousand years, it is necessary to go back in history for a century to discuss the life of a man who has been regarded by many as the most powerful force in the development of Christianity since St. Paul. He was Aurelius Augustinus, who became known as St. Augustine, Bishop of Hippo.

---

[4]Bettenson, *Documents,* p. 73.

SUGGESTIONS FOR ADDITIONAL READING

Ayer, J. C. *A Sourcebook for Ancient Church History.* New York: Charles Scribner's Sons, 1913.

Cross, F. L. *The Early Christian Fathers.* London: Gerald Duckworth and Co., Ltd., 1960.

Danielou, Jean. Translated by Smith and Baker. *The Origins of Latin Christianity.* Philadelphia: The Westminster Press, 1977.

Pelikan, Jaroslav. *The Christian Tradition.* Chicago: The University of Chicago Press, 1972.

Eusebius, *The History of the Church from Christ to Constantine.* Translated by G. A. Williamson. New York: University Press, 1966.

Grant, Robert M. *After the New Testament.* Philadelphia: Fortress Press, 1967.

Gwatkin, H. M. *Early Christian History to A.D. 313.* 2 volumes. London: MacMillan and Co. Ltd., 1909.

Harnack, Adolf. *The Expansion of Christianity in the First Three Centuries.* Translated by James Moffatt. 2 volumes. New York: G. P. Putnam's Sons, 1904.

Johnson, Paul. *A History of Christianity.* New York: Atheneum, 1976.

Nichols, Robert H. *The Growth of the Christian Church.* Philadelphia: The Westminster Press, 1941.

Richardson, C. C. *The Church Through the Centuries.* London: The Religious Book Club, 1938.

Stauffer, Ethelbert. *Christ and the Caesars.* Translated by K. and R. Gregor Smith. Philadelphia: The Westminster Press, 1955.

CHAPTER 16

AURELIUS AUGUSTINE

By the time Jovian succeeded Julian the Apostate as emperor in 363 A.D. Christianity was the established religion of the Roman empire. This official recognition was just in time to give the Christian Church a firm foundation that could withstand a decay that would crumble the foundations of the political government of Rome. Economic, moral, social, political, and military weaknesses were raising a specter of collapse upon the greatest city of the world. Constantinople was already an alternative capital of the once superb empire. Only a few more years remained before Rome would have to endure the humiliation of being invaded and sacked by Aleric the Goth in 410 A.D. At that time it would be the bishop of Rome to whom those who remained would look for strength and assistance. It would be the beginning of the "Dark Ages" of the Western world.

Shortly after the death of Constantine and half a century before the arrival of Aleric in Rome, a development was taking place in another part of the empire which would help Christian and Roman culture endure after the collapse of the Roman empire and the fragmenting incursion of the force from northern Europe. More than any other one man, it was Aurelius Augustine who packaged Christianity so that it would endure the challenges of the barbarian hordes.

Born the son of a somewhat insignificant Roman official in the North African town of Tagaste, west of Carthage and fifty miles south of the Mediterranean Sea, in 354 A.D., Aurelius Augustine was also the product of a Christian mother.[1] From his parents he received, revised, and recommended a whole new way of regarding the sacred world and the secular world. His vision was to be shared by bishops and emperors alike for many centuries.

With the help of a fellow citizen of Tagaste, Augustine's ability as a scholar was developed at home, then in Madaura, and then in Carthage. He was almost baptized a Christian at the insistence of his mother, Monnica, but escaped when he recovered from illness. He was a pagan, as was his father, Patricius, at the time, and besides the good life of teaching and writing, which he began in his nineteenth year, he also began the convenient life he enjoyed for many years with a mistress. From that union with a beloved woman he never named—even in his most public disclosure of his lifelong private thoughts, *The Confessions*—was born a son Adeodatus. Monnica thought primarily of his conversion to Christianity; he thought primarily about the glory of being a great author and a teacher of rhetoric, a worthy follower of the mighty Cicero. There was only one major concern which diverted his attention. He thought lusts of the flesh were entirely contrary to the life of philosophy he had willed for himself. Yet, his will was not strong enough to overcome his lusts. How could he explain and deal with what he believed to be the force of evil in his own life?

For many years in North Africa the answer he found was in terms of the religious philosophy of Manicheanism. It had such a hold upon him that for several years after he left the sect he still wrote against them until he had expunged them from him system. Developed by disciples of one Mani, Manicheanism explained evil in terms of a dualistic war between forces of light and forces of darkness. Manicheans stressed that one should refrain from fleshly desires, especially sex, which might imprison more soul in flesh. Augustine gradually lost faith in their explanations, and when their greatest teacher, Faustus, whom Augustine finally met, seemed to him to be a fraud, he began looking for another philosophy.

He left North Africa and his mother, Monnica, to begin a new life at the hub of the world, Rome. He was not destined to escape his mother's influence, however, for he fell seriously ill, and in time she arrived to nurse him back to health. When he recovered he was involved in a new philosophy, that of some successors of the Academy of Plato known as the Academics. They held that nothing can be known—a serious

---

[1] Whitney J. Oates, ed., *Basic Writings of Saint Augustine,* 2 volumes (New York: Random House, 1948): *Confessions.*

skepticism about the capabilities of the human mind. With only that to profess, Augustine was not prepared to make much progress in his philosophical or in his personal problems. He was also unprepared for the students of Rome, who, though more settled than those of North Africa, often left their professor without paying their tuition. When a job was offered him in Milan he took it.

Augustine was moving toward a serious breakdown in his life. He was filled with doubts about everything. At his mother's insistence he sent his mistress back to Africa and prepared to marry a rich young woman two years later when she would become of age. Disgusting himself, he took another mistress in the meantime. He was unhappy in his work and developed a chest problem that made it difficult for him to speak. But something else was happening to prepare him for a break with all of his former loves for glory in his profession.

He had gone to hear Ambrose, bishop of Milan, famed for his oratory, out of a professional interest in his style. Then, as he studied the style, he became aware of the great truths that the bishop spoke. He tried to visit with Ambrose, but he found that the bishop was too busy. Instead Augustine visited with Simplician, who gave him some Platonist books to study. Thus in one source, the Church, he found Chrisitianity and a new philosophy presented together. Moreover, he learned of monasticism and began to see that in such a lifestyle he might find the life of philosophy and abstinence he had sought since he was nineteen years old.

In a very dramatic scene he reached a climax in his life as he was in the garden of his home in Milan. Guided by a voice saying, "Take up, take up," he picked up a copy of the Bible and read the words of Paul which seemed addressed from God directly to his situation:

> Not in rioting and drunkenness, not in chambering and wantonness, not in strife and envying, but put ye on the Lord Jesus Christ, and make not provision for the flesh, to fulfill the lusts thereof. (Romans 13:13)

He decided then to become a baptized Christian. Monnica was overjoyed, for her lifetime of prayer had been rewarded. Augustine, Monnica, his friend Alypius, and Adeodatus all moved to a farm outside of Milan in order for the males to prepare themselves through a study of philosophy and Christian doctrine for baptism the next Easter. Augustine resigned his teaching position for reason of health; however, he continued to teach a few pupils on the farm. The dialogues produced between the fall of 386 A.D. and Easter of 387 A.D. show how Augustine's new philosophy and theology were shaping his life. He saw his new life of Christian Platonism as a fulfillment of the life Plato had envisioned for mankind but had never attained.

Augustine remained in Ostia, the port he planned to leave to return to Africa, longer than he intended. His mother had died there a few days after she and he together had a lofty mystical experience. These two events remained firm in his memory. In Ostia he continued to write against the Manicheans and to explore the scriptures which he had once despised as inferior to the writings of the Latin classics. In time he did return to Africa and continue his monastic life of philosophy with a few friends and students. After the loss of Monnica no female was present in their community. Adeodatus did not long survive her death.

In 391 A.D., when he was visiting the town of Hippo Regius, he was seized by the Christians of the city and impressed into service as a presbyter, a clergyman training to succeed their aging bishop, Valerius. While he had resisted any such move that would take him from his contemplative life for one of involvement in the daily cares of the world, once he was in the office he threw himself into his task with vigor. While the teachings of the church had guided him since his conversion experience, much of his emphasis had been upon philosophy, for he found no essential conflict between philosophy and the teachings of the church. Nevertheless, one of his letters to his bishop just after his ordination expresses a need for time to study the Scriptures in preparation for his more arduous duties as a parish priest.[2]

Augustine was a good teacher, preacher, counselor and administrator. The Church, he thought, was a replacement for Plato's Academy, much more suited to the needs of all mankind and much more efficient in helping them attain the life of which Plato only dreamed. When he became a bishop of Hippo Regius in 396 A.D., he turned all of his talents to the expounding of the Catholic Christian faith. Almost immediately there was a conflict between the Catholic teachings and a position that was based largely on grounds of human reason alone.

The Donatists took a position that on the surface seemed reasonable enough. They said that the priest in any sacrament is an important factor in its effectiveness. If the priest is immoral and not right with God, then the sacrament is affected adversely. The sacrament might be without efficacy if the priest was not morally acceptable to God. Augustine saw a problem. How could a worshiper ever know whether any sacrament had

---

[2]J. H. Baxter, ed., *St. Augustine: Select Letters* (Cambridge: Harvard University press, 1930), letter xxi.

saving power? How could he judge the morals of his celebrant from the standpoint of God? Augustine concluded that it is the priest's ordination into an office and the conduct of the established institution of the sacrament that makes the sacrament effective, not the personal moral purity of the officiating priest. A properly ordained priest administering the established sacrament of the Catholic Church was all a worshiper had to know, concluded Bishop Augustine.[3]

An even sharper conflict arose in a dispute with the monk Pelagius. Pelagius argued that anyone could take steps to obtain salvation in the church. By effort and striving, man could achieve a life of such merit that God would give grace and save. The invitation to salvation might have read, "Whosoever will, let him come." With proper human merit, one could be sure God would recognize and save.

That position also had a certain attractiveness to Augustine, for he had started early after his conversion writing a dialogue on the free will in which he argued for human freedom and responsibility in conduct. Often Augustine had spoken of an ascent to God through various stages, as the soul freed itself from the lower natures of the body. With the Neoplatonists he believed in human responsibility based on a free choice. On the other hand, he had become acquainted with the Scriptures of St. Paul and he agreed that salvation from God is not based upon the merit of a human being in keeping the law of God. He followed Paul's doctrine that in Adam all men die and in Christ they are all made alive. We are saved by faith, yes, but God must give that faith. It is a gift of God. We are then saved in spite of ourselves rather than because of ourselves. So strongly did he state the position that Augustine is often referred to as the "doctor of grace."[4]

Augustine retained his concept of human freedom as given to man by God at creation. He maintained that God's foreknowledge that man would sin does not make God responsible for that sin which has afflicted all human beings since Adam. But once that sin and its penalty had become a fact human beings no longer had freedom of will to return to their former state, that is, before the fall of Adam. Now only God could create the conditions whereby man could be reinstated. Man could not

---

[3]G. G. Willis, St. *Augustine and the Donatist Controversy* (London: S. P. C. K., 1950).

[4]Gerald Bonner, St. *Augustine of Hippo* (Philadelphia: The Westminster Press, 1963).

arrange it or even earn it; he was totally dependent upon God. Augustine was as insistent as Paul or even more so as he tried to meet what he considered to be the very serious threat of Pelagius. The Catholic Church gradually modified that view and in the days of Luther, came to a doctrine of grace based to some extent upon merits of the believer.

The best known book of Augustine to modern readers is his *Confessions.* Published around 401 A.D. as an autobiography addressed to God the work is a classic in world literature, not only for its style but also for its psychological insight into the development of a human personality. Covering the period from his birth to his return to Africa as a Christian, it is at once the most personal of accounts and the most universal. In some sense it is an account of every person's struggle with the problem of evil—the desire to do good and be the best but lacking the will to accomplish it; the hope for a saving change sometime before it is too late, but not just at the moment. As Augustine put it, "O Lord, save me, but not just now!" Augustine's conviction that he had finally made it led him to write the book for others. His belief that only God could have brought about his new life was the rationale for his addressing the whole story to God.

The truly crowning work of philosophy and theology in Augustine, the fine example of faith and reason combined into a philosophy of history that had profound influence on bishops and emperors alike in the middle ages, is *The City of God.*[5] Charlemagne is reported to have had great respect for the work. This classic was written in response to the catastrophic fall of Rome before Aleric and the Goths in 410 A.D. There were those who claimed that the fall came because the Romans had forgotten the honor of ancient Roman gods who had built the city. These former gods were angry at being deserted in favor of the Christian religion. Augustine's first task, then, as a churchman, was to deal with that vicious opinion which could, if left unanswered, have had disastrous effects for Christians in the Catholic Church as the barbarians continued to make inroads into the territory of the Romans.

Augustine also was impressed with the achievements of the earlier Romans. Their system of justice was world renowned. Their administration of government was superior in the ancient world. In human achievements they were the best. They had splendid vices. But such a kingdom cannot endure forever in the scheme of God, he wrote. It

---

[5]St. Augustine, *The City of God,* in Whitney J. Oates, *Basic Writings.*

can endure for a time and then it will fall into decay, for its flourishing carries seeds of its own destruction.

Within that same city, a city of Man, existing for glory of self rather than the glory of God, there was another city growing. It was the city of God, composed of those persons who lived for the glory of God rather than for the glory of self. While many of these persons were in the Catholic Church, not all the members of the Catholic Church were citizens of the city of God, for some of them were self-serving rather than God-serving persons. What a person loves, or whom a person loves, determines the city to which one belongs. It must be either the city of Man or the city of God.

Augustine came to this interpretation of history from a study of the Scriptures, similar to the extensive one he had made in the *Trinity*. Throughout the Scriptures he found evidence of the two cities existing side-by-side and yet always distinct. The city of Man must be subject to change and decay. Only the city of God can grow and endure from age to age, for only it participates fully in the eternal nature of God. It will come in its fullness in God's own fullness of time and endure from age to age. Until then, human beings are confronted with a choice of how they want to live. By the grace of God they may be called into the city of God or they may cling to their human nature and remain members of the city of Man. The relationship of the earthly church and the earthly state could not completely escape the influence of Augustine's *City of God* for the next thousand years in Europe.

Even in his great work as a theologian Augustine gave evidence that he had continued to read and to practice philosophy of reason through the years. He had also grown in his depth of study of Scriptures, his skills as an administrator, and his influence as a church politician. In it all his professional training as a writer and a speaker remained apparent. And for all of his involvement in the practical world, he always maintained after his conversion a simple, monastic life for himself and for his students.

Augustine was an appropriate symbol for the close of one age and the beginning of another. He packaged the best of Christian and Roman culture in a combination that could endure and influence the Western World through those centuries known as the Dark Ages. As Augustine lay dying in his beloved city in North Africa in 430 A.D. the barbarians were literally at the gates of the city, ready to crush the last remnants of that splendid empire which had so dazzled the old saint as a young man. The city of Man was no longer his concern; for more than forty years he had lived in the city of God. The best known sinner in the world is also the best known saint in the world.

SUGGESTIONS FOR ADDITIONAL READING

Barrow, R. H. *Introduction to St. Augustine the City of God.* London: Taber and Taber Limited, 1950.

Bourke, Vernon J. *The Essential Augustine.* Indianapolis, Indiana: Hackett Publishing Company, 1974.

Deane, Herbert A. *The Political and Social Ideas of St. Augustine.* New York: Columbia University Press, 1963.

Markus, R. A. *Saeculum: History and Society in the Theology of St. Augustine.* Cambridge: Cambridge University Press, 1970.

Portalie, Eugene. *A Guide to the Thought of Saint Augustine.* Translated by R. J. Bastian. Chicago: Henry Regnery Company, 1960.

CHAPTER 17

MUHAMMAD

It was well for the Jews and for the Christians that they had settled the major issues of their faith by the sixth century A.D. The Babylonian Talmud was an effective guide for the Jews under the most trying conditions, and with the Council of Chalcedon the Christians had a settlement that could serve them well for posterity. What neither could have foreseen was that their greatest challenge was not to be either from Rome or from the plundering hordes of Europe. Their greatest challenge in history would come from another people who also claimed Abraham as their father, and who admired and embodied many of the values which both Jews and Christians traced back to their common patriarch.

The Arabs, of the Arabian peninsula, inhabited an area no more promising in natural endowments than had been the regions of Palestine inhabited by the early Jews or the early Christians. In spite of the fact that trade routes crossed Arabia, it was essentially an island surrounded by sand on the north, the Syrian Desert, and water on the other three sides, the Persian Gulf, the Arabian Sea, the Indian Ocean, and the Red Sea. With the exception of a small area of fertile land in the southwest, the country is extremely arid. Seldom did it ever produce enough food to support all of the population, which was predominantly Caucasian.[1]

---

[1]Caesar E. Farah, *Islam* (Woodbury, New York: Barron's Educational Series, Inc., 1970).

The Arabs considered themselves descendants of Abraham through his son Ishmael, the son of Abraham and Hagar. In fact they regarded a well in Mecca, Zam Zam, as the water source the infant had kicked up in the desert which saved his life and that of his mother when she appealed to God for his life. While they had no part of the inheritance claimed by the descendants of Abraham's son Isaac, they did share a reverence for the same patriarch, and recognized a certain kinship with Jews and with Christians. Both of these groups were present in Arabia. Small groups of Jews could be found in some towns, and the ones in Yathrib became particularly important in the future developments of the Arabs.

On the other hand the Arabs had their own religion, bearing traces of Persian types of divine beings and perhaps influences of the teachings of Zoroaster. Angels which were good, ghouls which were bad, and jinn who could work either way seem to have been a part of their thought world. One religious center was in the city of Mecca, located in a mountain pass and very much dependent upon pilgrim visits for its economy, since it was so barren that even the hardy date palm would not grow there. It contained the famous Kabah, a cube housing paintings and stautes of various deities inside the giant room and embodying the sacred black stone, thought to be a meteorite, in its southeast corner at a height convenient for a pilgrim to kiss on his circumambulation of the building. The area for one mile around the Kabah was sacred and no warfare was to take place there nor was any blood to be spilled.

It was really only in Mecca that warring or feuding tribes of Arabs could meet for worship and trade with any assurance that there would not be fighting and bloodshed. Thus the tribe responsible for administering that sacred city played an important role in the life of the Arabs. They were the Quraysh, who highly prized their political powers and the economic advantages which came to them as keepers of the sacred city. The very multiplicity of deities and religious duties and customs were highly valued by them, for they offered something for every tribe and every worshiper, no matter what his personal preferences. They jealously guarded anything which might threaten their privileged position within the Arab hierarchy.

It was into that city that the future leader of all Arabs was born. Muhammad (or Mohammed), the son of Abdullah and Aminah, was born about 571 A.D. The fact that his father died before Muhammad was born and that Aminah died when he was around six years old probably had a profound influence upon the later moral teachings of Muhammad. The duty of raising him, a poor orphan of the impoverished Hashemite clan, fell to his powerful grandfather, Abd-al-Muttalib, as long as he lived, and then to his uncle, Abu Talib. As was the case in the life of Jesus, very little is known about the prophet's childhood and adolescence. Nevertheless, that has not prevented speculation. There is considerable speculation about travels for purposes of trade Muhammad may have made with his grandfather or with his uncle and what philosophies and theologies he may have encountered while traveling. Aside from the fact that he seems to have been familiar with some of the teachings of the Jews and some of the teachings of the Christians, there is not much more than conjecture about his life until Muhammad was twenty-five years old. At that time he married a prosperous widow, Khadijah, who was forty years old.[2]

He had served Khadijah as an overseer of her camel caravans and so brought some necessary skill to her enterprise. He seems to have found all in her that he wanted in a wife, for it is said that contrary to Arab custom, he did not take another wife as long as she lived. They had an ideal relationship, except that the two sons born to them died in infancy, which had a deep influence on what developed in Arabia after the death of Muhammad. They did have four daughters, however, and at least one of them, Fatima, is extremely well known to all Arabs.

Along with an able character as a practical man of the world, effective in economic competition, Muhammad also developed a meditative side of his character as he grew older. He made a habit of going to Mount Hira, near Mecca, to spend time in meditation. It was on such an occasion, "the night of power and excellence," thought to have been in the month of Ramadan, that the angel Gabriel appeared to him and brought him a message from God, Allah:

> Read: In the name of thy Lord who createth,
> Createth man from a clot.

> Read: And thy Lord is the Most Bounteous,
> Who teacheth by the pen,
> Teacheth man that which he knew not.[3]

Needless to say that a man of the practical nature of Muhammad was deeply shaken by his experience. He talked it over at length with Khadijah, who seems to have supported him in accepting it as a valid religious experience. Waraqa ibn-Nawfal, a blind man acquainted with

---

[2]H. A. R. Gibb, *Mohammedanism* (New York: The New American Library of World Literature-Mentor Books, 1955).

[3]Quran 96:1-5. Farah, *Islam*, p. 40.

scriptures of the Jews and of the Christians, could see that Muhammad was being called by God in the tradition of the early prophets of the Jews, and he warned him that there would be much opposition and suffering in his future. The next appearances of the angel to Muhammad made the same point and forced him to a crisis; he had to decide whether he would champion the cause of Allah or not. He could hide as a coward or stand up and be a man.

Muhammad accepted the challenge to preach the word of the one true God. He made some converts among his family and friends. Khadijah, of course, was loyal. Abu Bakr, a merchant of Mecca who was well respected, was persuaded by his words. His cousin Ali, the son of Abu Talib, joined him and his adopted son Zayd, a former slave and Christian, completed his ranks. Outside of that circle his converts were slow. At most he probably reached a hundred and twenty-five families. However, that was enough to cause deep concern among the Quraysh. Muhammad was an object of their wrath and, when he would not stop his insistence that there was only one true god and that all the idols in the Kabah should be destroyed, he was the object of their torments which included throwing filth upon him and his followers. Had Muhammad not had powerful protectors in his family he probably would have been killed when he refused to cease and desist in a teaching which could have threatened to destroy the economic and political base of Mecca and the Quraysh. Still they continued to harass him at every turn. Muhammad sought relief for his followers if not for himself.

The first group to seek refuge consisted of a dozen or more families and later some eighty individuals who went to Abyssinia. The Negus received them and refused to hand them over to their enemies. Muhammad and a few staunch followers stayed behind in Mecca to continue their witness. The flight to Abyssinia did not seem to promise any real advance in his cause. What he needed was an environment more friendly to his teachings so that he could establish a community of faithful without daily fear for their lives. The opening came when two warring tribes of Yathrib, the Khazraj and the Aws, sent representatives, ten of the twelve being Jewish and the other two pagan, to invite Muhammad to come to their city and be their leader. The Jews thought that he might possibly be the promised messiah. Shortly thereafter about a hundred followers of Muhammad's religion left Mecca and traveled to Yathrib where they were well received.

The Quraysh, who had wanted to silence Muhammad or to get rid of him, were now frightened that the Meccan families and the Yathrib tribes might join forces under Muhammad's leadership and cause problems for Mecca. Their strategy was to prevent Muhammad from leaving Mecca. Aware of their fears and their plans, Muhammad and two companions, Ali and Abu Bakr, slipped out of Mecca and made their way to Yathrib in the year 622 A.D. The eleven day journey, which was made this time in eight days, concluded on September 24. To Muslims today it is known as the Hijrah.

The fears of the Quraysh proved well founded. Muhammad established a political cause in a new commonwealth in Yathrib, whose name was changed to Medina, the city of the prophet. There was, however, some factionalism in the new community. The Ansar, or helpers, were those who had invited Muhammad to the city and the Muhajirun or emigrants were those who came from Mecca to be with him. A third group, mostly Jews, later came to be referred to as the Munafiqun or Hypocrites, for their expectations of finding the messiah in Muhammad turned to disappointment. In the beginning, nevertheless, Muhammad was successful in uniting all of the groups behind him so that they had a stronger government and more unity than they had previously known. Proving to be an able administrator, he introduced laws and customs which were binding on the community, giving it character distinct from other Arabs and pioneering the unique style of life that would come to characterize his followers when he later expanded his kingdom of converts.

Although his position was vastly superior to what it had been in Mecca, not everything was sweetness and light. In order to maintain unity, he had to denounce the recalcitrant Jews and subdue them, permitting them to leave with what they could carry but abandoning their lands to the community. Then he had to defend himself from the Quraysh. In response to their minor attempts to stifle his economic survival, Muhammad led a raid on one of their caravans to Mecca. In response to that the Quraysh led an attack on Medina. In January of 624 A.D., Abu Jahl of Mecca led an army against Muhammad, who met them at Badr, defeating the superior force of the Meccans. The victory was sufficient to establish Muhammad as an able warrior in the eyes of the bedouins and they rallied to his leadership. In a second battle the following year the Muslims were not so fortunate, for in addition to being defeated in battle they almost lost their leader. The Meccans missed an opportunity for total destruction of the movement when they failed to press their attack and destroy Medina.

In 627 A.D. a new attempt was made against Medina by Abu Sufyan of Mecca who had succeeded in attracting as allies the disenchanted Jews who had left the commonwealth of Medina. Their force could have been overwhelming except that a Persian convert to Islam had persuaded Muhammad to take the precaution of strengthening the defenses of Medina by digging a trench around it. The battle which finally came is known as "the battle of the ditch," for it was that element of defense which gave the Muslims the necessary edge to survive the combined forces of their enemies. After a month of siege the attackers withdrew.

Muhammad now felt strong enough to make his move toward a return to the holy city of Mecca. His first step was to win over the tribes around Mecca who had traditionally joined with the Quraysh against their enemies. Having succeeded there, Muhammad negotiated with the Quraysh in Mecca a ten year truce which would allow him to make an annual pilgrimage to Mecca and also to proselytize people whom he met. Thus he gained recognition as a major leader and also opened a gateway for new converts so that his movement would continue to gain strength. One more factor leading to Muhammad's rejection of the Jews occurred when a female member of the Jewish tribe at Khaybar attempted to poison him and his companions. Retaliating, Muhammad subdued them and made them yield all of their lands to the Muslims.

His only able enemy now was the Quraysh of Mecca, except the Ghassanid Arabs who had violated a truce by killing a Muslim envoy sent to convert them. Muhammad sent an army under Zayd to extract retribution, but the expedition ended in the death of Zayd. Chosroes of Persia made an enemy of the Muslims when he tore up their invitation to become members of Islam. The Muslims thought that the Quraysh had violated their truce by attacking a tribe in alliance with the Muslims, so Muhammad amassed an army and marched on Mecca, determined to resolve the Quraysh problem for all times. It turned out not to be necessary to defeat the city of Mecca with actual use of his army, for a delegation headed by Abu Sufyan came from Mecca and offered to submit to Muhammad's faith. An agreement was reached and Muhammad entered Mecca as victorious ruler in the eighth year of the Hijrah, the point from which the Muslim calendar reckons time. Thus, in the year of the Christians 630, ten years after the conversion of Khadijah, Muhammad won the support of his fellow inhabitants of Mecca.

Muhammad dealt compassionately with Mecca. The one place where he was deliberate in destruction was in the Kabah itself, where he is reported to have destroyed 360 idols, nearly one for each day of the year. Henceforth, the only inhabitant of the Kabah would be Allah. Muhammad's teachings and laws and customs were accepted by the inhabitants of the city.

Next he moved to consolidate all of Arabia under his faith. Besides the Quraysh, who had finally given in, there remained two tribes who had to be subdued with the sword. They were the Thaqif and the Hawazin, and in the ninth year of the Hijrah they submitted to him. Christians and Jews were also to be subdued, for although Muhammad dealt differently with persons who had a scripture, that is, who were not pagan, the word of Allah was that he exact tribute from them if he could not convert them, for both the Jews and Christians had let the worship of other deities than God enter their practices.

> Fight against such of those who have been given the Scripture as believe not in Allah nor the Last Day, and forbid not that which Allah hath forbidden by His messenger, and follow not the religion of truth, until they pay the tribute readily, being brought low.[4]

For Muhammad thought the Jews regarded Elijah as the Son of God and the Christians regarded Christ as the Son of God, both then worshipping some deity other than only the one true God.

Medina was still the locus of Muhammad's life, even after he had subdued and cleansed Mecca. He made his final pilgrimage to the city of the Kabah in February of 632. Before leaving, realizing that it might be his last time, he assembled his followers on Mount Arafat and gave them his final words from Allah. Among those statements prized by Muslims are these:

> Know ye that all Muslims are brothers. Ye are all one brotherhood; and no man shall take ought from his brother unless it is freely given to him. Shun unjustice. And let those here assembled inform those who are not of the same who when told afterwards may remember better than those who now hear it.[5]

His task of speaking for Allah accomplished, Muhammad returned to Medina to live out the final year of his life. Sensing that his death was not far in the future, Muhammad tried to bring together the loose ends of his work. There was the Byzantine ruler who had taken the life of Zayd who had to be subdued. The tribes who had submitted to his new religion still had to be taught how to live according to it. A system had to be established to unify the country under law and to collect the tithes which

---

[4]Quran 9:29. Farah, *Islam*, p. 56.

[5]Farah, *Islam*, p. 59, from Ibn-Hisham, p. 651.

were essential for the brotherhood. It was fortunate that he could have that year to consolidate, for no successor had been decided upon either by him or by the community.

His favorite wife after Khadijah was a younger woman, Aishah, the youngest daughter of his early convert, Abu Bakr. He spent most of his time in his final illness with her, leaving as necessary to lead the community prayer. About three days before his death he made his settlement with the community of prayer and early on the day he died he spoke his farewell words to his daughter Fatima. He died at home with Aishah on June 8, 632 A.D., the eleventh year of the Hijrah.

The man who was eventually chosen as his successor, Abu Bakr, is reported to have announced to the community:

> "O Muslims! If any of you have been worshipping Muhammad, then let me tell you that Muhammad is dead. "But if you really do worship God, then know ye that God is living and will never die!"[6]

---

[6]*Ibid.*, p. 60.

SUGGESTIONS FOR ADDITIONAL READING

Cragg, Kenneth. *The House of Islam.* Belmont, California: Dickenson Publishing Company, Inc., 1969.

Rodinson, Maxine. *Mohammed.* Translated by Anne Carter. New York: Pantheon Books, 1971.

Watt, W. Montgomery. *Muhammad at Mecca.* Oxford: Clarendon Press, 1953.

_____ *Muhammad at Medina.* Oxford: Clarendon Press, 1956.

_____ *Muhammad: Prophet and Statesman.* Oxford: Oxford University Press, 1961.

CHAPTER 18

ISLAM

Muhammad was a person of extraordinary ability and achievement. But what were the contents of the remarkable faith that he struggled so hard to have his fellow Arabs accept? In many ways it is simple, sharp, and clear. In others, to an outsider, its presentation in the Quran (Koran) is somewhat frustrating. Nevertheless Muhammad was not so different from an Isaiah or a Jeremiah or a Jesus, leaders he regarded as prophets before him. That is, his thoughts came piecemeal as they were revealed to him for a specific occasion. His teachings were applied to real-life situations rather than systematically ordered by some logical plan as he labored away as a scholar in some library or monastery. It is for his followers and those who would study him to try to bring order to what he had made known.

Perhaps the most important teaching of all was the absolute singleness of God. Al-ilah is, in a shortened form "Allah," the word for "The God." Muhammad took the old Arabic concept and purified it of any polytheism so that God was absolutely single.[1] It is not necessary to list the ninety-nine most beautiful names of God that Muslims have compiled; it is sufficient to say that he is transcendent creator and sustainer of the universe. He is judge of good and evil and judge of all mankind. God is everywhere and never sleeps. There is no other Being

---

[1]Caesar E. Farah. *Islam* (Woodbury, New York: Barron's Educational Series, Inc., 1970).

alongside of him. The worst affront one can make upon God is to attribute being to anything else that would share his rule with him. Muhammad utterly rejected the Christian notion that the Christ or the Holy Spirit could also be God or equal to God. He also assumed that Jews shared a similar concept in thinking of Elijah as the son of God. Both religions were, in his eyes, dishonoring Allah with their beliefs that his power was shared with other beings of divine nature. Such a mistake is *shirk*, the opposite of *ikhlas*, the giving of one's entire devotion to God without any mixture of allegiance to others.

It would have been difficult for Muhammad not to include angels in his scheme of higher beings since it was the angel Gabriel who communicated the contents of the Quran to him over the period of a decade. He also included in the hierarchy an Angel of Death and the Holy Spirit, who announced the birth of Jesus to Mary. Opposite to the angels are devils who are fallen *jinn* rather than fallen angels. *Jinn* are created beings as humans are, but they are made of fire rather than earth. The leader of the evil spirits is *Shaitan* or *Iblis*.[2]

A second central doctrine of Muhammad was that of the prophets. God had sent his spokesmen at various times and places to make known his unity and purpose. All of these prophets were, according to Muhammad, to be honored by the people of Islam, those who submit to the will of Allah. Twenty eight prophets are mentioned in the Quran, only four of whom are Arabian. Three are Christian and eighteen are from the Jewish Bible. Muhammad considered himself the last of the prophets and the bearer of God's most complete revelation to mankind. No other revelation was necessary for salvation. Very emphatically Muhammad held, and so did his followers for all times, that he was a human being and not a divine person. He did not share the nature of God any more than did any other human being. His special place came because he was the one chosen by God to receive from Gabriel the most complete revelation for mankind and because he faithfully carried out his commission to make known that message and lead mankind to submit to the will of Allah. Even to call a Muslim a "Muhammadan" is out of order, for Muhammad did not seek followers for himself but people to submit their lives to Allah. One who does submit his life to Allah is a Muslim.

There was no doubt in the experience of Muhammad that there would be a last judgment, a Last Day. While the time of its arrival was

---

[2]H. A. R. Gibb, *Mohammedanism* (New York: New American Library, 1953).

known only to God, the events that would take place had been made known to Muhammad. The trumpet would sound, the ground would open and both men and *jinn* would be called upon to give an accounting of their lives. Each would have his guardian angel to bear witness to his life and each would be weighed in the balance. The blessed would be separated to the right hand and be invited to the Garden of Paradise, a mansion having all the joys of a palace, including the company of dark maidens and pure wives. No more pleasant place could be imagined than was the reality of that paradise. On the left hand would be the believers and worshipers of other gods than the true God, Allah. The essential ingredients of the Muslim Hell are fire and heat. Presenting unbelievers with a clear choice was a duty accepted by Muslims and carried out with vigor; it was an act of mercy to save those otherwise condemned to Hell for the joys of Paradise.

Another major doctrine of Muhammad was that every Muslim should fulfill the daily duty of prayer. Prayer was to be said while bowing in a prescribed way, probably well established by the time of Muhammad's death. Each *rak'ah* or bowing is composed of seven separate movements and recitations: (1) The hands are placed open on each side of one's face as one recites, "Allahu akbar," (God is Great). (2) One stands upright while reciting the opening sura of the Quran and other passages. (3) One bows from the hips. (4) One straightens from bowing from the hips. (5) In one movement one smoothly goes to one's knees and prostrates oneself with face to ground. (6) One rises to the position of sitting on one's haunches. (7) A second prostration is made. Starting with the second bowing, one begins with the second movement and ends each pair of bowings with the *shahada* or profession of faith, "la ilaha illa-llah muhammadun rasulu'llah," in English "There is no God but Allah and Muhammad is his prophet."

Prayers are, of course, a duty five times every day. Muhammad picked the noon prayer on Friday as the primary prayer time for congregational participation. The Christians had a preference for Sunday morning and the Jews for Saturday. By choosing Friday at noon he gave Muslims a distinctive time of their own. Of course, the ritual washing of head, forearms, hands and feet was enjoined prior to engaging in prayer. While water was preferred for the purpose, due to the nature of their habitation Muslims were permitted to use clean sand where water was not available. Muhammad's preference for a human voice to call the faithful to prayer seems to have stemmed from his dislike of bells being struck or wooden clappers being hit together.

Another absolute duty of every Muslim is the giving of alms, *zakah*.

Remembering his own days as an orphan and the poverty of so many of his people, Muhammad required an offering, not a tax, of every Muslim. It is used to meet the needs of the poor, needy, wayfarers, debtors and prisoners. By some Muslims it is seen as a loan to God.

Also established at Medina was the practice of fasting. It is obligatory that every Muslim fast during the ninth lunar month, Ramadan. Fasting is to be observed from first light of morning to last night of evening (light being as long as a black thread can be distinguished from a white thread held side-by-side). Those who are ill or on a journey are permitted to postpone the fast until later, when they are required to fast an equal number of days.

During his days at Medina Muhammad also set the example of a religious duty for every Muslim to make a pilgrimage, or *hajj*, to Mecca. The tradition favored the twelfth month and the circumambulation of the Ka'bah. Runnng back and forth between the small hills of Safa and Marwa imitating Hagar searching for water for Ishmael, visiting the well Zam Zam, and assembling on the ninth day at the hill of Arafat, twelve miles east of Mecca, and offering sacrifices at Mina on the way back to Mecca were traditions which go back to the days of Muhammad. Such a sacred obligation is carried out with great care that the worshiper is in a state of purity or ritual consecration, *ihram*. The head is shaved and ordinary clothes are replaced by two unsewn sheets which leave the head and face uncovered. No adornment or primping is permitted, only women may cover their heads, and no sexual relations are permitted until after one leaves Mina to return to regular life.

Taken together, there are five obligatory acts of devotion of every Muslim: (1) Repetition of the Shahada, (2) Prayer, (3) Almsgiving, (4) Fasting, and (5) The Hajj.

Although the ceremonial obligations may be the most visible to the outside observers of Islam, the Prophet also taught by word and example many moral obligations for those who submit to the will of Allah. One is taught to care for others for the sake of Allah without thought of reward for oneself. The needy, the orphan, and the prisoner were singled out as examples of persons for whom one should have mercy and generosity. One who devours the wealth of orphans is devouring the very punishments of hell in oneself. Kindness towards one's parents is expected.

Muhammad is said to have had eleven wives, but apparently he was a firm believer in restraint in sexual relations. He had only Khadijah as long as she lived and Aishah was the only virgin bride he ever took. The others seem to have been widows of comrades or, in the case of the wife of

Zayd, unable to live peaceably with a husband. The view of some Muslims is that the prophet simply had compassion for them and gave them a home and security when they had none. They also point out that while Muhammad had more wives than did Jesus, he had many less than did King Solomon. A husband is not to devour the wealth of his wife or to be unfaithful in his relationships with women. Wives, on the other hand, are taught to be modest, displaying their charms only for their husbands or to their own very near relatives.

The Muslim was taught to do his duty. There was a great leveling process of social distinctions which cast itself upon all who entered the faith. The prophet envisioned one vast fraternity of believers, all equal before God. Where there was want or need it was the duty, not an optional privilege, for Muslims to contribute until it was overcome. In all things one was taught to deal justly with other people.

The accumulation of wealth while a fellow Muslim was in need was contrary to the teachings of the prophet. In the day of judgment such gathering of wealth on earth while others starved will be used against a person, and the mass of his wealth will be turned into the mass of his suffering. Usury is similarly condemned.

Individual characteristics of truthfulness, courage, humility, and mercy are strongly enjoined by Muhammad, but he also emphasized that individual pride and boastfulness over one's fellows, even those doing wrong, were to be avoided. Individualism had to take its place within the solidarity of the whole Muslim community. The divisiveness of early Arab pride in self and tribe had made the nation weak. Pride in the community of the faithful had to replace it if the new religion was to grow and prosper.   The faithful were expected to avoid certain other vices that did not contribute to the strength of the community. As were the Jews, the Muslims were prohibited from eating the flesh of swine. Unlike the Jews, they were also forbidden to drink wine. Gambling was strictly forbidden. Old ways of worship of Arab deities were also cast aside.

Of course there has long been some question within Islam about exactly what the prophet did say and do as he set the pattern of life for the believers in the religion he taught. The primary source book is the Quran. It is the bible of the Muslims, giving them a special status along with Jews and with Christians, possessors of sacred books. Like so many of the prophets before him, Muhammad did not write anything down, so he had to trust what others memorized or wrote to preserve his teachings for posterity.

The Quran was regarded by Muhammad as the only miracle necessary in Islam. He challenged his critics to try to compose ten verses of poetry as beautiful as the recitations he had made to them. There was no doubt in his mind that what he recited was not composed by him but that it had revealed to him by the angel Gabriel. What Gabriel had revealed to him was the exact message written on a prototype book with Allah in heaven. Thus, what Muhammad received and recited to the Arabs was the very word of God. To try to trace Jewish and Christian influences upon the prophet and thus upon his message would be to ascribe a human origin to the Quran or at least a human influence upon what God had revealed. Both ideas are unacceptable to orthodox Muslims. They would explain the similarities of their teachings to Judaism and Christianity to the belief that, after all, the message given was from the same God and the same line of prophets. The Quran simply sets straight the errors that had crept into the messages of earlier prophets of Jews and Christians.

The most obvious order in the Quran is that the chapters, or surahs, are arranged according to length with the longest coming first and the very shortest ones last in the book. To the faithful each surah is known by a name rather than a mere number. For example, the first surah is entitled "al-Baqarah," the cow, and has 287 verses. Two surahs have only three verses, "al Nasr" and "al-Kawthar." While some scholars argue that there is another logic of order which runs through the surahs as one reads them continuously, the casual reader is not often fortunate enough to find it. There is usually a note at the end of each surah, however, which indicates the place where the revelation was received.

Among the first surahs in the Quran are ones revealed at Medina, which means that they were from the middle period of revelation experiences which spanned two decades. They reflect the need Muhammad faced for very practical instruction to a community of converts in matters of faith and morals. Tensions were present in the community and they are reflected. They do not, moreover, have the same quality of those surahs revealed in Mecca when the prophet was almost alone against the hostile Quraysh. In them all the logic and reason he could muster are used to persuade the Quraysh to worship the great and merciful Allah alone.

> Say: He is Allah, the One! Allah, the eternally Besought of all! He begetteth not nor was begotten. And there is none comparable unto Him. They surely disbelieve who say: Lo! Allah is the third of three; when there is no God save the One God. If they desist not from so saying a painful doom will fall on those of them who disbelieve.[3]

---

[3]Caesar E. Farah, *Islam,* p. 88. Quran 112:1-4 and Quran 5:74.

The very first surah of the Quran belongs to the Meccan period, and is regarded by some Muslims as equivalent to the Lord's Prayer for the Christians:

> Praise be to Allah, Lord of the Worlds, the Beneficent, the Merciful. Owner of the Day of Judgment, Thee (alone) we worship; Thee (alone) we ask for help. Show us the straight path, The path of those whom Thou hast favoured; Not (the path) of those who earn Thine anger nor of those who go astray.[4]

It is this prayer that is repeated twenty times a day by every Muslim who carries out his daily ritual of prayers.

When Muhammad died many of the surahs had been written down as well as memorized. However, when more than one person memorized, a problem arose if some memorized differently from others. What had the original of the prophet been? One could then turn to written notes or copies of the message. But suppose more than one copy in writing existed, each differing in some way? Who was right? As did the Jews and the Christians, the Muslims stressed the great importance of coming as close as possible to the word of the prophet, who was believed to have delivered faithfully the very word of God.

Unlike the Jews and the Christians with their scriptures, the Muslims saw the absolute necessity of acting at once to compile an authoritative version of the Quran. Muhammad had not appointed a successor who was clearly recognized by all Muslims, and the previously warring Arab tribes might revert to their former ways when the strong leader was not on the scene. As a matter of fact Muhammad's successor, Abu Bakr, had to fight to reconquer Arabia and in that bloody conflict many of the companions of the prophet, the huffaz or memorizers, were killed. The man who would be the next successor, Umar, is said to have persuaded Abu Bakr to complete the Quran as soon as possible.

The person given this task was a young man named Zayd, twenty two years old, who had been an aide of the Prophet. He pulled together the best sources he could find and relied heavily on the companions of the Prophet. Before Abu Bakr died in 634 A.D., only two years after the death of Muhammad, he had in his hand a completed copy of the Quran. This copy is reported to have been turned over to Umar, the successor of Abu Bakr in 634 A.D. and then given by him to his daughter Hafsa, a widow of Muhammad.

---

[4]*Ibid.*, p. 90.

The assembled copy was not official and not widely known. It failed to provide the cohesion needed for spiritual unity of the Arabs and warfare among them and Muslims of other countries continued. Future military campaigns could be seriously undermined by disputes over the proper text to follow. For that reason the caliph Uthman (644-656) attempted to have assembled one universal and official version of the Quran.

The man to do the job was again Zayd, the assistant to Muhammad. He assembled all of the available material that he could and did his best to make a copy as true to Muhammad's revelations. Four copies were made, and the work was completed in 657. One copy was kept in Medina and others were sent to Muslim centers in Basra and Kufa in Iraq and to Damascus in Syria. In order to prevent further disputes all other copies were destroyed. Thus there is no longer any evidence with which to compare the work of Zayd in an attempt to evaluate the quality of his scholarship.

The Quran is a very important source of understanding Islam but it is not the only one. What the Prophet said and what he did became increasingly important to the community in later years and an additional body of information about civil and religious teachings was developed from that information. But that was a separate and longer development, one which can better be described after some sketch has been made of the expansion of Islam shortly after the death of Muhammad.

SUGGESTIONS FOR ADDITIONAL READING

Bell, Richard. *Introduction to the Quran*. Edinburgh: At the University Press, 1958.

Gatje, Helmut. *The Qur'an and its Exegesis*. Translated by Alford T. Welch. Berkeley, California: University of California Press, 1976.

Parrinder, Geoffrey. *Jesus in the Qur'an*. London: Taber and Taber, 1965.

Smith, James T. *An Historical and Semantic Study of the 'Islam' as Seen in a Sequence of Qur'an Commentaries*. Missoula, Montana: Scholars Press, 1975.

Wansbrough, John. *Quranic Studies*. Oxford: Oxford University Press, 1977.

CHAPTER 19

JIHAD (HOLY WAR)[1]

Muslims are taught by the Prophet to strive in the Way of God. In Sura 2:186ff., they are told:

> Fight in the way of Allah against those who fight against you, but begin not hostilities. Lo! Allah loveth not aggressors. . . And slay them wherever ye find them, and drive them out of the places whence they drove you out, for persecution is worse than slaughter. And fight not with them at the Inviolable Place of Worship until they first attack you there, but if they attack you (there) then slay them. Such is the reward of disbelievers. . . But if they desist, then lo! Allah is Forgiving, Merciful. . . And fight them until persecution is no more, and religion is for Allah. But if they desist, then let there be no hostility except against wrongdoers.

Again, in Sura 9:5 they are commanded:

> Then, when the sacred months have passed, slay the idolators wherever ye find them, and take them (captive), and besiege them, and prepare for them each ambush. But if they repent and establish worship and pay the poor-due, then leave their way free. Lo! Allah is Forgiving, Merciful.

---

[1]H. A. R. Gibb, *Mohammedanism* (New York: The New American Library, 1953), pp. 57-58. On the term "Jihad," see Majid Khadduri, *War and Peace in the Law of Islam*, p. 55.

In Sura 9:29, Muslims are told:

> Fight against those who believe not in God nor in the Last
> Day, who prohibit not what God and His Apostle have
> prohibited and who refuse allegiance to the True Faith from
> among those who have received the Book, until they humbly
> pay tribute out of hand.

In his lifetime, Muhammad set the example for the faithful to follow.
The true faith was to be brought with all its power to persons who
divided loyalty to God by worshipping other deities. If they resisted, they
were to be fought with military power until they agreed to listen without
bearing arms. If they were then Jews or Christians, they could pay a
tribute to the Muslims without abandoning their own faith. If they were
pagans, peoples without a book, they were to submit to Islam. The
tradition of expansion was ingrained in the followers of Muhammad and
as soon as they were able to do so they continued the momentum which
he began.

The death of Muhammad was the occasion for a revolt of the Arab
tribes in order to regain their former independence. It was the task of the
first caliph, or successor, Abu Bakr, to fight against Arab tribes until he
could reunite the force of Arabia behind the true faith. He amassed a force
of between ten and twenty thousand troops to launch against the world
outside of Arabia. Abu Bakr's one year reign was followed by a ten year
rule of Umar, again one of the Companions of the Prophet, who saw
some of the most successful military expeditions of medieval times.
General Khalid ibn al-Walid marched on the city of Damascus in Syria
and after six months of siege took the city in the year 635. The Byzantines
who were to remain bitter enemies of the Muslims for centuries
responded with their emperor, Heraclius, sending fifty thousand
Christian troops to repel the aggressors. They met defeat in battle
conditions of heat and dust which gave the experienced warriors of the
Arabs the advantage. All of Syria fell to Islam.

The response of the Jews and the Christians living in Syria may have
at first appeared surprising to the Arabs and the Byzantines alike. They
actually welcomed the Muslim occupation of the land. As they had been
enjoined by the Prophet, the conquerors treated fairly the Jews and
Christians once the fighting had ceased. Of course, the conquered people
had to pay the poll tax required of non-Muslims in their conquered lands,
but they found that to be a lighter burden than they had borne under the
Byzantines. The Arabs were not too demanding, for to their tastes,
impoverished by desert life, the life in Syria and Damascus was very rich
indeed.

The defenders lacked the fervor of the attackers who fought the holy war in the belief that if they fell in battle they would go directly to Paradise. The Muslim forces were successful against Jerusalem in 638 and against Caesarea in 640. With those cities all Palestine became theirs. During the same period Muslim forces marched on Iraq, which fell in 637, and into Persia, beginning in 640. The conquest of the Persians took longer because their resistance was more fierce. Egypt fell in 640. A campaign was also launched into Asia Minor which lasted for a dozen years.

Umar was succeeded in 644 by Uthman, a son-in-law of Muhammad, who reigned until 656 when he was assassinated because he had allowed corruption to enter the office through so many appointments from his family, the suspected Ummayads. He was succeeded by Ali, the husband of Fatima, a daughter of Muhammad, who had two sons who were the only male descendants of the Prophet. Ali lasted until his assassination in 661 A.D.

Feelings ran high over the wealth and power of the caliphate. While the caliph was not the spiritual leader of the faith, he was definitely the administrative head. The wealth pouring in from tribute in occupied lands seemed stupendous to Umar, though it could be shared with the family of the Prophet and with other Arabs. Now as new territory was added year after year the tribute grew until it was not only difficult to manage but also a strong magnet to covetousness and corruption. Gaining the caliphate and controlling all of that military power and all of that inpouring wealth became a goal of powerful groups whose strength was greater than that carried by the tradition of being a companion of the Prophet.

One such contender was Mu'awiya who raised an objection to Ali and set out to replace him as caliph. Ali was strongly supported in the struggle and moved his camp from Medina to Kufa in Iraq. With a strong army he began his march to destroy Mu'awiya. Then for some reason not at all understood by his partisans Ali agreed to let the dispute of leadership go to arbitration. Absolutely disgusted with him, Ali's followers concluded that he was, after all, an usurper not chosen by God or he never would have submitted such an important matter to the arbitration of human beings. While the matter was under consideration Mu'awiya worked very hard to make himself the chosen one while Ali, on the other hand, sat back to let fate take its course. And take its course it did, in a way that has caused a permanent split in the Muslim community, for the disgusted followers of Ali took it upon themselves to assassinate him. Mu'awiya, an Ummayad, came to power in 661. That family controlled the caliphate until 750 when they were overthrown by the Abbassids.

During the time that the Ummayads were in control, the Muslim empire expanded into Spain, Turkestan, Mongolia, and India. Only the fierce resistance of Charles Martel, who defeated Muslim armies at Tours in 732 A.D., prevented their takeover of France. How much more territory they might have gained in Europe can only be conjectured. The high water mark of the growing strength of Islam was reached by the year 750. After that time, under the Abbassids, the capital was moved to Baghdad where oriental splendor was fabled throughout the world, both East and West. Nevertheless the strong power of Jihad had diminished, for the Muslim armies contained thousands of persons who were not Arabs, and the holders of power were perhaps more intrigued with the wealth they possessed already than they were with the religious commandments of the Prophet who called upon his followers to witness to the world as to the revelation he had received from God. Indeed, there was a split in the Muslim empire, with rival caliphs ruling for a time in Spain and in Egypt.

The Quran had settled many disputes among the expanding numbers of Muslims. But there were so many situations which arose that the Quran did not speak to directly. Yet in his lifetime the Prophet had said and done things apart from the sacred revelation that indicated how he thought the will of God should go in similar matters. The companions of Muhammad, as long as they lived, were fond of relating such sayings and incidents that they believed set a precedent for the Muslim community to follow. Their stories became part of the oral tradition that helped guide Islam.

Different traditions arose from the stories that happened to be remembered by particular people. In time one story might have several versions in circulation. Again it was necessary to make an attempt to arrive at a single, official collection of *Hadith* (or tradition account) canons. So two centuries after the death of the Prophet projects were begun to arrive at the authentic tradition. All *hadiths* in circulation were examined and their *isnad*, or chain of attestors, traced as well as possible. From this process the strength of the *hadith* was classified as strong or fair or weak. Of course, who did the collecting and evaluating made a difference, and a half dozen or more projects were under way about the same time in the eighth century. The one that emerged most highly regarded was that of al-Bukhari, followed closely in regard by a version prepared by Muslim. Al-Bukhari's collection is regarded as second only to the Quran itself.[2]

---

[2]*Ibid.*, p. 65.

As in Judaism the concern in Islam was with the development of a community of the faithful, based upon the will of God rather than upon intellectual or theological speculation. Life had its ritual side and its legal side, but both sides were part of one Law. In Judaism there is Torah. In Islam there is the Sharia. Whereas in Judaism the whole application of Torah to daily life reached a formidable compilation in the Babylonian Talmud, in Islam there has been resistance to such an official compilation, perhaps because Islam is a much younger religion.

Quran and Hadith, or Tradition, form the sources of Muslim law. The Quran sets the standard of absolute Good or Evil, since it comes directly from God. On the other hand, there are many situations in life which are not clearly and definitively spoken to by the Quran. The method used then is that of the *qiyas* or analogy, to apply the principles of the Quran to a situation not explicitly spoken to in the Quran. Upon this basis the law, or Sharia, of Islam was developed. One more principle was involved, however.

The principle of consensus is called *Ijma*. It refers to the consensus of the Muslim community, traditions carried out by the community in its earliest days and believed to be in keeping with the Quran and Tradition or Hadiths. In practice, the spokesmen for the community were the scholars who were for Islam comparable to the scribes of Judaism. While Islam has no well-established priesthood to correspond to the Levites in Judaism, the *Ulama* or learned doctors of Islam do compare in some ways with the scribes or in very limited ways with some functions of rabbis. The rule of the community, or Ijma, in reality being the opinions of the Ulama, early became one foundation upon which the Sharia was based.

Ijma, as does the Church for Roman Catholics, gurantees the very survival of the sacred writings and the sacred traditions. It has been the collector, the judge, and the preserver of those things believed to be holy, sacred, desirable, true and required. Ijma carries weight as a third force of infallibility, as the Church does for Roman Catholic Christians. Again the doctrine of consensus in Islam may be compared to the place of the Councils of the Christian Church, setting the limits of divergence of opinion and practice within the community. The caliphate of Islam rests upon Ijma, even as the papacy of the Christians rests to a great extent upon tradition in the Christian community.

The Sharia, based upon the revelation of God, the Quran, and upon the words and examples of the Prophet, the Hadiths, and upon the inspired consensus of the community, Ijma, is understandably in the highest sense completely authoritarian. God is the sole legislator; to violate the law is to sin against God. Not all human actions are covered in the Sharia. There is some room for individual liberty on matters where the Sharia is indifferent. It recognizes five grades of action. The first is composed of actions which are absolutely obligatory for all Believers. The second comprises those actions which are highly desirable for Believers but not required. The third grade is in the middle of the scale, comprising actions which are neither good nor bad, being indifferent. The fourth moves toward the negative end of the scale, comprised of those actions which are undesirable but not forbidden. The fifth grade consists of those actions which are prohibited.

Considering the role of the community and the fact that many of the traditions and opinions were not written down in early decades, it is easy to understand why separate traditions of Sharia should have occurred even in Sunni, or traditional Islam. The Sharia developed apart from the everyday enforcement of law under the Ummayads, where the civil and military officers took care of most enforcement. Sharia development was in the hand of theologians and lawyers who had little contact with laws and customs outside of Arabia. The Sharia was not largely enforced as a full system of law until the ascent to power of the Abbassids. Four schools soon became apparent in the interpretation of the Sharia.

One can easily see that the Hanifi school would be the favorite of the Abbassids since their capital was in Iraq and the school arose there under one Abu Hanifa, who died in 767 A.D. Although the founder himself refused office, two of his pupils who held high judicial offices took it upon themselves to collect and publish his teachings on the law. Based upon the old Iraqi sunna, the school had a strong reliance on personal reasoning to adapt it to the changing traditions of the Prophet.

The Maliki school was named for Malik ibn Anas, who died in 795 A.D. Essentially it was the school of law of Medina. Growing out of the established practices of the city of the Prophet, it was collected and practiced by the practicing judge of Medina, Malik ibn Anas. He called his corpus al Muwatta, the Levelled Path.

The Shafite school was developed a generation later by a pupil of Malik, as Shafii, who died in Egypt in 820 A.D. He attempted to separate the later tradition of Medina, which had crept into the Medinan or Malikite school, from the tradition of the Prophet himself. He relied upon the method of analogical deduction, or qiyas.

These three schools of the Sunni or traditional Muslims recognize a fourth school which is much more conservative than themselves and which does not as readily recognize their legitimacy. The Hanbalites tried to do away with so much analogy and reasoning and to get back to more basic traditions. It was largely the product of the efforts of Ahmad ibn Hanbal of Baghdad who died in 855 A.D. The school gained some following in Iraq and Syria down until the Ottoman conquest. It was revived in the eighteenth century in central Arabia under the name of Wahhabi.[3]

The Sharia was laid upon foundations completely separate from the secular authorities, and since it was divine, it had to be left inviolate and applied by the proper appointment of *qadis*, or judges, wherever Islam was in control. In a limited way there existed beside it the application of laws of secular authorities in courts known as *mazalim*. The religious laws formed a basis for these settlements of wrongs by the secular leaders. In both the religious courts and in the secular courts the custom arose of submitting the findings to a consultant for review. The Consultant was a *mufti* whose reply comprised a *fatwa*, and a collection of the fatwas became very important for helping shape the future application of the Sharia. But in spite of the various interpretations and applications practiced with it, the Sharia formed the basis for the common culture of Islam through many countries and over many centuries. It is the ideal, resisting changes, yet changing enough to keep it relevant to the changing conditions of a dynamic religion.

Almost no religion ever escapes strong division of opinion about who is truly faithful to the essentials of their religious faith, and Islam is no exception. Muhammad had to take charge of the situation in Medina and eliminate those who could not be brought into line with his teachings. As the movement gained power, however, somewhat more tolerance was allowed for theological positions as long as persons outwardly gave allegiance to the persons in power. The early supporters of Muhammad always felt that they were the truly faithful, and they resented the late comers, the Ummayads, who had come into Islam only after Muhammad had gained the power to defeat them militarily, having opposed him with the sword up until that time. When Ali showed signs of giving in to a compromise with Mu'awiya by submitting his case to arbitration, the anti-Ummayads, the Kharijites, separated or seceded. So angry were they that some of them later killed Ali. They were the puritans or separatists who wanted to keep the faith pure and essentially what it was under Muhammad at Medina.

Opposing their views was the more tolerant and permissive view of those who had swelled the ranks of Islam after Muhammad's conquest of the Arabians. Everyone who would give nominal allegiance to the basic tenets of Islam was welcome, regardless of their past performance. Purity of motive or action was not as important as following a few basic outward

---

[3]Caesar E. Farah, *Islam* (Woodbury, New York: Barron's Educational Series, Inc., 1970), p. 224.

works, which was all that was necessary to be an acceptable Muslim. It was this view that prevailed as Islam expanded into other countries, but the bitterness between Murjites, who wanted to keep everyone in the broad body of Islam, and the Kharijites who wanted only the most pure, continued for centuries.

Some middle ground in the controversy developed among a group known as the Mutazilites. They were outsiders too, familiar with Greek, Christian, Jewish, and Zoroastrian thought before they became converts to Islam. With their perspective on ideas other than Arabian they could arrive at a position which translated the essential teachings of Islam into terms understandable to other religions and cultures. While it would be going too far to call them rationalists or freethinkers, it would be fair to think of them as apologists explaining their faith in terms of thought that could be understood by rational philosophy and rational systems of other religions. They accepted the authority of the Quran, but they held the position that there could only be one Truth and that Truth is not contrary to reason. Allah desired the free ascent of the human will to his will, and he is a just God, bound by justice in his action. He would not predestine a person to sin and then hold him responsible for that sin too. The main body of Muslims, nevertheless, saw the concept that God was not completely powerful and able to do anything he desired at any time as divisive and limiting. They had to oppose the ideas of reason and of justice of the Mutazilites as too limiting of the power of Allah.

Another possibility for division within religions is upon the proper choice of leaders. Just as the Kharijites thought that the choice of Ali had been a terrible mistake, a group arose that believed even more fiercely through the centuries that the assassination of Ali and his two sons, the grandsons of Muhammad, Al-Hasan and Al-Husayn, had been the greatest tragedy of all history. The true and legitimate leaders of Islam were Ali and his descendants, so they did not accept Mu'awiya and the caliphs who succeeded him. But then, which of the descendants of Ali are the legitimate caliphs? The majority of the Shiites belong to the twelvers, who accept all descendants down to Muhammad al Muntazar (d. 878), the twelfth iman, who disappeared at the age of five, leaving no descendants. It is their theory that he will return as the Mahdi to judge the world and carry out the last judgment. Other sects break off on legitimate descendants before number twelve. The Zaidites look upon Zaid as the proper fifth imam rather than Muhammad Al-Baqir (d. 731), and the Ismailites regard Ismail as the seventh Imam rather than Musa Al-Kazim (d. 797).

The Ismailites have given rise themselves to a number of sects which have gained a certain notoriety both within and without Islam. One group, known as the Qarmatians, formed a secret communistic society in North Arabia and became so powerful that they could disrupt whole governments. Taking their name late in the ninth century from a man named Hamdan Qarmat, they occupied much of Arabia and withstood the forces of the caliphs of Baghdad. They were so bold as to raid Mecca during the pilgrim season, and they even stole the sacred Black Stone of the Kabah and retained it for twenty years.

SUGGESTIONS FOR ADDITIONAL READING

Cash, W. W. *The Expansion of Islam.* London: Church Missionary Society, 1928.

Khadduri, Majid. *War and Peace in the Law of Islam.* Baltimore: The John Hopkins Press, 1955.

Lammens, H. *Islam.* Translated by E. D. Ross. London: Frank Cass and Company Limited, 1969.

Lewis, Bernard. *Islam in History.* London: Alcove Press Limited, 1973.

Lewis, Bernard. *The Assassins, A Radical Sect in Islam.* London: Weidenfield and Nicholson, 1967.

CHAPTER 20

MUSLIMS, CHRISTIANS, AND JEWS

The children of Abraham acknowledged one father, but they had developed a fierce sibling rivalry. That rivalry was not, however, full-blown immediately. Just as the Jews had received infant Christianity as a newborn which needed to be trained in the way that it should go through mild chastisement of errors, so the Jews and the Christians regarded the infant faith of Islam. Those in Arabia, Syria and Palestine soon learned that Islam was something more than a collection of madmen led by a false prophet of Judaism or Christianity. At first the Jews had found Muhammad to be something of a heretic, as did the Christians later. Only those who had firsthand experience of the new religion came to a clear understanding that they were confronting a separate religion. That is understandable, for it took Muhammad himself a few years to realize that he had to establish a separate identity for his followers, with separate days for prayer and separate ways of worship. The Muslims might be a correcting continuation of the descendants of Abraham, but that correcting influence could only succeed, thought Muhammad, if his followers had the correct way and could somehow confront the other children of Abraham with it. The family tie was acknowledged by him and by the Jews and the Christians, but brotherhood had varying shades of meaning as the siblings grew in maturity alongside each other.

There have been two extreme views of how the Christians and Jews fared once the jihad had been launched from Arabia. In one view, the Christians of the areas of Syria and Palestine welcomed the change from the harsh rule of the Byzantines of Constantinople, the old Roman center which was under the influence of the Greek Christians. They preferred the tolerant and less demanding Muslims who seemed to be satisfied with a little tribute money as the price for their not converting to Islam. On the other hand, one can read stories of great hardship against Christians and Jews and that the newly converted Muslim hordes, bent on wealth gained through plunder, perpetrated all sorts of excesses against innocent populations in the name of their newly acquired faith. Which view is correct?

Perhaps both views are true at one time and place or another, and yet neither extreme may give a picture of what life was like through so many centuries of what is often referred to as the Middle Ages. One view is that there was not all that much interaction between Christians, Jews, and Muslims. That is, where Muslims clearly ruled, there was so much advantage to being a Muslim that conversions took place on mass scale. Where the Muslims did not rule, the Christians generally did in the areas around the Mediterranean.[1] These may have been Latin centered, looking at the Bishop of Rome if they were under the influence of the western capital of the Roman Empire, or Greek centered, looking to the Metropolitan of Constantinople if the territory were under the influence of the emperor of the eastern part of the Roman Empire.

From the Muslim point of view, Europe did not hold a great attraction. The center of the world seems to have been considered by them in early centuries to have been in Iraq. The only nations that counted as civilized as far as they were concerned were the Arabs, the Persians, the Indians, and the Byzantines. Even those nations were not equal. The Indians had only anonymous books, so they were deficient; the Greeks had logic and philosophy, but they were deficient in oratory; the Persians had oratory, but they could not improvise anything, relying on their ancestors for everything. Only the Arabs had the beauty of language and the ability to compose beautiful poetry on the spot. One only had to visit Arabia to see that the Arab was superior to all in that art and in the beauty of language.

Add to that view of the world the view that the Arab had been chosen by God for a final revelation that had been given imperfectly or received imperfectly by the Jews and the Christians and one can understand much of the foundation for interaction of the three major religions of the western world during the Medieval period. The Arab took pride above all

---

[1]Gustave E. von Grunebaum, *Medieval Islam* (Chicago: The University of Chicago Press, 1953).

in the beauty of his literature. His love for the sciences was secondary and developed considerably later in the history of Islam.

Early Christian understanding of Islam was just as biased in its own direction. The Christians did not doubt that they had succeeded the Jews as the chosen people of God, that they now and for all time possessed the final form of Truth. The first word about Muhammad, as seen by John of Damascus, was that Islam was a heresy within Christianity. During the days of the emperor Heraclius there was a false prophet by the name of Mamed. Familiar with the Old and New Testament and the teachings of an Arian monk, he feigned piety and led away his people to his own sect. He claimed that his teachings had been sent him directly from heaven.[2]

Another view of Muhammad was given by the Byzantine theologian or historian named Theophanes Confessor, who died in 817 A.D. He did not reveal the sources he used for his work, which also attracted later writers as a source.[3] He was aware that some misguided Hebrews at first thought that Muhammad was the Messiah. They forsook the religion of Moses and remained with him until the end, even though they had seen him eat camel flesh and knew then that he was not the one whom they expected. Khadijah discovered that her husband was an epileptic and covered his illness with a story of his encounter with an angel Gabriel. Khadijah sought the advice of a false abbot who was her lover and on having Muhammad's story confirmed spread the word that her husband was a prophet. He succeeded in winning others by describing Paradise as a place of carnal pleasures such as carousing, drinking, and making love to women. Two centuries later a story circulated that an excommunicated monk put together heretical doctrine after the nature of Arius and wrote it into a book he called the Koran. He taught that Christ was not God but just a great prophet. This monk handed the Koran to Muhammad and claimed that the book had come down to Muhammad from heaven through the angel Gabriel. Gullible people followed Muhammad as the final prophet. Other accounts had Muhammad failing to rise from the dead as he had predicted and his body being eaten by dogs or, in another account, by pigs while he was in an epileptic seizure. Other literature, such as the *Chanson de Roland*, speaks of the polytheism of the Muslims with Muhammad considered one of their gods, along with Apollon, Jupin, and Tervagant.

Although more factual information came to light when the Crusaders

---

[2]*Ibid.*, p. 43.

[3]*Ibid.*, pp. 43-44.

of the Christians engaged the Muslims in Palestine and when, under the influence of Peter of Cluny, the Quran was translated for the first time in 1141 A.D., inhabitants of the Western world had already formed their favorable impressions, as well as their unfavorable ones. There was far more attraction to Westerners in the mysterious East than there was in the West for the Easterners. Westerners were aware of a much higher standard of living in the East. They had been intrigued since the time of Herodotus with tales of the wonders of the East. Jerusalem was the center of things, the capital of the Holy Land. China and India were places of marvels and wisdom, as was the great land of the Persians. There was a certain amount of envy and admiration mixed with the deliberate distortions which played down the origins and beliefs of the Muslim religion. There was even a belief that civilization flowed from East to West.

By the late Middle Ages the admiration was reciprocal. If Westerners learned their Arabic and loved the poetry and wisdom of the Saracens, the Muslims had come to appreciate the sciences and the philosophy of the West. There was by that time a respect between the enemies of the Byzantines and the Persians. Worthy adversaries not only had great respect for each other but also inquired after each other's health. Mutual understanding had, over the centuries, come to replace the early attempts to belittle and smear each other.

People of the Book, Jews and Christians, enjoyed the status of *dimmis*, possessors of a protective treaty *dimma*, in which they renounced certain rights in order to gain certain privileges.[4] Non-Muslims were essentially isolated within their own religious groups. Permanent status as second-class citizens was the price they paid for their personal safety and property. Of course tribute always had to be paid, as Muhammad had established. Other requirements have often been forgotten by recent writers. Under a so-called "Covenant of Umar" Christians agreed, in return for the safety of themselves, their families and their properties to pay tribute and to let Muslims stop at their churches for three days and nights, also feeding them. They would beat the wooden board, naqus, that summoned worshippers, quietly and not be noisy in chanting. They were not to build any new structure for their religious observance, such as a church, hermitage, or convent nor even make repairs to existing structures. Assembly in a Muslim quarter was forbidden, as was assembly in the presence of Muslims. Any sort of

---

[4]*Ibid.*

display that would mark the place of worship of non-Muslims or invite others to it, such as a cross, was forbidden. On the other hand, they were not to try to learn the Quran or teach it to their children. However, should someone desire to become a Muslim, a *dimmi* was not to attempt to prevent it. Imitation of Muslims in dress or appearance was not tolerated. Houses of *dimmis* were to be no higher than Muslim houses. *Dimmis* were not to possess weapons or carry them within Muslim territory; violence against a Muslim, such as striking him, was forbidden. One was not to keep a slave that had once belonged to a Muslim. *Dimmis* who broke those rules were beyond the protection of the Muslim community.

In the early relationships of the three religions, the Muslims preferred the Christians to the Jews. As time went on however, they developed a much stronger hatred for the Christians, so that after the Crusades the Christians who had launched fierce battles against them were often despised. The effect gradually reached all Christians living in Muslim lands. In the West there was no considerable group of minorities in either Christian or Muslim territories, with the exception of Jews. In the East, Christians were largely forced to live to themselves and to rely on their own courts. Sometimes they were tolerated in public life. The caliph al-Mutawakkil (847-61) disliked Christians so much that he would not allow them outside of their houses without special clothing, such as a belt and girdle; even their slaves had to have special marks on their clothing. Their new churches were pulled down.

Muslim society enlarged itself to encompass the new converts of Persians, Copts, Greeks, Nabataeans, Negroes, and Turks. They obtained affiliation with an Arab tribe that would give protection to them. In turn, they were considered as the clients of the Arabs, *mawali*. Something of the meaning can be understood in that a former slave of a master, once freed, was a client or *maula* of his master. In the early years everyone tried to become Arabicized. Strangely enough, as time went on and city life replaced rural living, the Persians became the ideal to follow. While not the ideal, Negroes were accepted in the society. From 946 to 968 Kafur, a former slave and a Negro, governed Egypt.[5]

By the eleventh century of the Christian era, a number of factors were at work which led the Christians to attempt to regain the centers important in the beginnings of their religion, such as Jerusalem. The unified Muslim faith which had swept over Palestine shortly after the death of Muhammad was now divided into three major, conflicting

---

[5]*Ibid*, p. 210.

centers. There were caliphs at Baghdad, at Cairo, and at Cordova, dividing the political power of Islam. There were new political and religious powers at work in the area of Palestine; the somewhat tolerant Arabs had been replaced by Turks and Mongols and tribes from central Asia. They threatened the Greek emperor in 1071 and threatened the stream of pilgrims which tried to reach the holy places through a route in Hungary, which had become a Christian country with the conversion of King Stephen. These fierce warriors took Jerusalem in 1078. That gave them control of all the holy places, for which they did not have the kind of respect the Arabs had held. Pilgrims were not guaranteed safe conduct to venerate the shrines that they had once enjoyed. The Christians had already learned to hate the Muslims through the contact they had had in the Mediterranean and through their long struggle in Spain. There was also a new sense of devotion in Christendom through the reform movement from Cluny. All these reasons were crystalized by an outright appeal from the Greek emperors in face of the Muslim invasions.

The mood of the times favored going on holy crusades. Merchants in Venice and Genoa liked the idea because it provided them new business in transporting crusaders. Kings liked it because some of their restless and somewhat threatening young warriors could find a less threatening way to spend their time and energy. The crusaders could dream of the rich spoil they would plunder from their foes. Moreover, in preaching of the clergy, such as that of Urban II at the Council of Claremont in 1095, there was promise of a reward in heaven for those who might die in order to defend the honor of Christ against the false prophet Muhammad. So attractive was the project of crusades that several were launched without official sanction, and for their impatience they perished in Hungary or Asia Minor.

The first Crusade was in response to an appeal from Alexius I (1081-1118) in Constantinople, to Pope Urban II for assistance.[6] Urban proclaimed the Crusade at Claremont in 1095, not only to help Alexius and deliver the Holy Places from the "Infidel" but also to grant forgiveness of sins and eternal life to those who might fall in battle. Peter the Hermit, a popular preacher, took up the project and won much support for it. His own bands of crusaders fell upon hard luck in Hungary and in the Balkans. Their recruits were sometimes beyond control and not only massacred Jews in the cities of the Rhine but also pillaged the

---

[6]Williston Walker, *A History of the Christian Church* (New York: Charles Scribner's Sons, 1952); and Kenneth Scott Latourette, *A History of Christianity* (New York: Harper and Brothers, 1953).

countries they passed through to the point that reprisals were taken against them that ended their mission. Peter the Hermit escaped this fate to join the more organized force of the first Crusade.

The first Crusade was essentially composed of several separate armies of feudal nobles in Europe. The most famous noble was Godfrey of Bouillon who led an army from Lorraine and Belgium, along with his brothers Baldwin and Eustace. From northern France came an army led by Hugh of Vermandois and Robert of Normandy. From the south of France came a force commanded by Count Raimond of Toulouse, and from Italy there was an army led by Bohemund of Taranto and a nephew of his, Tancred. Working without an overall, single leader, each army in the Crusades was to make its way as best it could and the forces were to join in Constantinople. Gradually the Crusade assembled in Constantinople in the winter and spring of 1096 and 1097. Though Alexius had sent for them, they caused plenty of problems for him with their conduct and their demands.

Focusing upon the closest target, Nicea, the Crusaders forced its surrender after a siege of a month in the spring of 1097. Antioch was the next destination, and after a long siege the city fell in June of 1098. Jeursalem was next, and again after a siege, it fell in July of 1099. It was at that time that Godfrey of Bouillon was named the Protector of the Holy Sepulchre. Upon his death he was succeeded by his brother who took the title of King Baldwin I and ruled until 1118 A.D. Latin influence was everywhere in establishing the feudal organization of the country and in the formation of religious orders, such as the Templars and the Hospitalers.

The concept which began in such glory of purpose and achievement soon degenerated into some pathetic attempts and results. The second Crusade, launched by Bernard of Clairvaux and Emperor Conrad II left Germany in 1147. Most of its forces were lost in Asia Minor and those who did reach Palestine were defeated in Damascus in 1148. The third Crusade is well known from the participation of King Richard the Lion Hearted of England. He was joined by Emperor Frederick Barbarossa, a great soldier who drowned on the campaign, and King Philip Augustus of France. Their limited result was the recapture of Acre; Jerusalem remained Muslim. The fourth Crusade was most disastrous to Christendom in terms of lasting results, for the Crusaders, though not approved in plan by Pope Innocent III, joined the Venetians who transported them in conquering and plundering Constantinople, a Christian center, in 1204. Relics of the saints were removed and transported to the West. A Latin patriarch replaced the Greek head of the

Greek Church, and the Greek Church was brought under the control of the Pope. The Eastern empire was weaker than ever and more vulnerable to Muslims. The animosity between the Latin and the Greek forms of Christianity could hardly have been more intense after that unfortunate diversion of Crusaders from their original purpose.

A "Children's Crusade," composed of bands of children on pilgrimage to the Holy Land, resulted in most of the children being sold into slavery in Egypt. The fifth Crusade was against Egypt and ended in failure. The sixth Crusade in 1229, under Emperor Frederick II, did secure possession of Jerusalem and Nazareth and a corridor to reach them from the sea. The results were short-lived, however, for the Holy Land reverted to Muslims in 1244. The Crusades were over.

On the whole, the Crusades were failures. They did not regain the Holy Land for the Christians. They cost thousands of Christian lives and untold wealth that could have been spent for better purposes. They intensified the hatred between Christian and Muslims. They stimulated Christian persecution of the Jews, and they resulted in Christian turning against Christian, making even deeper the gulf that separated the Roman Catholic Church from the Greek Orthodox Church of the East.

SUGGESTIONS FOR ADDITIONAL READING

Barton, James L. *The Christian Approach to Islam*. Boston: The Pilgrim Press, 1918.

Bell, Richard. *The Origin of Islam in Its Christian Environment*. London: Frank Cass and Company Limited, 1968.

Cragg, Kenneth. *The Call of the Minaret*. New York: Oxford University Press, 1964.

Geiger, Abraham. *Judaism and Islam*. New York: K. A. T.V. Publishing House, Inc., 1970.

Khadduri, Majid. *War and Peace in the Law of Islam*. Baltimore: The John Hopkins Press, 1955.

Lewis, Bernard. *Islam in History*. London: Alcove Press Ltd., 1973.

Lewis, Bernard. *Race and Color in Islam*. New York: Harper and Row, Publishers, 1971.

CHAPTER 21

MEDIEVAL RELIGIONS

One fact of Medieval religions was the division of East and West. In a sense, the basis for the division may have been established even before Christianity began. The Jewish people had been scattered into other communities since the Babylonian exile, and synagogues had sprung up in almost every community where there were ten Jewish males. While those communities of the faithful clung to some knowledge of the old customs and the old language, they gradually took on something of the culture of the peoples where they were located, especially their language and philosophy of life. The missionary journeys of Paul of Tarsus, the founder of so many Christian churches, are informative as to the differences which existed in Judaism when Christianity started.

The churches of Antioch, Jerusalem, Asia Minor and cities to the east shared a common language which was marketplace Greek. They shared in a common heritage of Hellenism which had endured since the time of Alexander the Great. They were colored by philosophies of the Platonists and of the Stoics. They enjoyed views of the divine dimension of the human being. Freedom of the congregation and a general fellowship of congregations were part of the relaxed process followed in their worship, their teachings, and their lives within the household of faith. The Greek background of Alexandria in Egypt was not without its influence too, and the Septuagint, the Greek translation of the Jewish Bible, was helpful in the feeling of fellowship among Christians in cities where Greek thought and customs were prevalent.

When Paul had arrived in Rome as a prisoner, he had been met by

Christians from the church in Rome. While not without some influence from Greek thought, Rome had developed its own thought and its own way of doing things. Its greatness did not lie in philosophy; for that it was content to borrow from the Greeks as could be illustrated in the life of the Stoic emperor Marcus Aurelius. On the other hand, law and administration became two strong contributions of the Romans to the part of the world which they ruled. Jerusalem, of course, had known both cultures as well as the Jewish way of doing things. The Roman way dominated until the empire was divided in leadership, when the Greek way crept back again. The emperors of Rome were the most powerful men of influence during the formative years of the Christian church, and it is not surprising that the organization of the churches in lands under their control should have taken upon their governments something of the spirit of the Roman emperors. Roman language, too, was different. Latin was the language of the realm, so the Christians in that part of the empire thought and spoke in a language different from the Christians at the eastern end of the Mediterranean Sea.

The combination of having two capitals for the Roman Empire (Rome and Constantinople) and the threat to the emperor of Rome from barbarian invasions helped the division become even clearer. As the emperor's role in Rome declined, the role of the Bishop of Rome increased. He had already been acknowledged as primary among bishops of the Latin speaking churches around the Mediterranean, for he was located in the city of the emperor. In order to fill a vacuum left by the emperors who looked to the East instead of to the West the Pope assumed many temporal duties. And when some of the invading tribes from the North were already converted Christians, there was a certain acknowledgment of power which came to the Bishop of Rome, the Pope.

The Roman emperors of the East, with their capital in Constantinople, concentrated more of their power there as Rome had more problems within and more threats from the North. Constantinople grew in stature and the Patriarch of the church there assumed a greater importance. The eastern churches were more under his care and his influence while the western churches were free to look more to the growing power of the Pope rather than to the remote power of the emperor.

The two different orientations of Christianity gradually separated, each organizing around a separate pole of the formerly united Roman Empire. The centers vied with each other in feelings of importance, and so did the leaders of the centers.

The story of growth of papal power is a fascinating one which is too long to trace here; however, a feel for it can be gained from the story of two Gregories, Gregory I and Gregory VII.

Gregory the Great was Pope from 590 A.D. to 604 A.D.[1] Born into a family of senator rank he came to office from a background of training in Roman administration. On the other hand he had great piety: he sold his property in Sicily and used it to found six monasteries and feed the poor. He lived a monastic life himself. In 590 A.D. his ability was openly acknowledged when he was made Pope in Rome. He immediately began expanded service from the office. He sent missionaries to Britain, worked to remove corrupt tax collectors in Italy, and assumed responsibility for Roman secular government when the Lombard invasion interrupted services from Constantinople. He had power to go with his services and he claimed that he was the successor of St. Peter. As Peter was over all other apostles of Christ, so was the Pope over all other bishops. Nevertheless, he made no claims to be equal to the emperor. He is also known for establishing schools for singers, and credited with establishing the use of the Gregorian chant in worship.

Pope Gregory VII, Hildebrand, did not hesitate to challenge Henry IV of Germany when the layman appointed a bishop of Milan. In the synod of 1076 A.D. Gregory denied Henry's authority in Germany and Italy and released Henry's subjects from allegiance to him. Henry IV backed down, went to Canossa in the winter and stood in the snow outside the Pope's residence for three days until Gregory forgave him and restored his power. No pope had ever exercised greater power until that time.

One further act of power was exercised by Pope Innocent III (1198-1216 A.D.). He had Otto II of Germany replaced by Frederick II. He forced Philip II of Spain to take back a queen whom he had divorced. When King John of England disagreed with him over the appointment of an archbishop of Canterbury, Innocent III excommunicated King John. He was released when King John acknowledged his kingdom as a fief from the Pope and paid a feudal tax to the Pope for it! That perhaps was the strongest exercise of papal power over the secular power.

Meanwhile in Constantinople the Roman Emperor was strong and the leader of the churches, the metropolitan, while under him, gained

---

[1]Kenneth Scott Latourette, *A History of Christianity* (New York: Harper and Brothers Publishers, 1953); and Williston Walker, *A History of the Christian Church* (New York: Charles Scribner's Sons, 1952); M. Deanesly, *A History of the Medieval Church* (London: Methuen and Co., Ltd., 1951).

power through him. But the metropolitan was in tension with the Pope. One bone of contention was the West's adding *filioque* to the Nicene Creed, claiming that the Holy Spirit proceeds from the Father and *from the Son.* The East could not agree. Charges and countercharges were exchanged until in 1054 A.D. a papal legate exceeded his authority and excommunicated the Patriarch of Constaninople.

Constantinople was a center of wealth long after Rome decayed. The Muslims were fascinated with Byzantium, as the Eastern empire was known, for in architecture, tapestries, and paintings their riches were inescapable.

Worship in the East had a distinctive character.[2] The dedication of the Holy Cross inspired a rich poetry of devotion and the service of kissing the cross and genuflecting before it was supported by the emperor. Icons, or two-dimensional figures, were more prevalent in the East, whereas the West favored three-dimensional figures of holy persons. Muslims criticized both forms as idolatry, and those Christians who were sensitive to the criticism tried to curb the practices. These iconoclasts were severely resisted.

The Eastern church, no less than the Western, was dedicated to missionary activity. The Greek church moved into the Balkans, Hungary, and into Russia by 860 A.D.

But the medieval times were not purely of political and religious struggles. In Judaism, Christianity and Islam there could be found excellent examples of holy lives, devoted to God instead of to the powers of the world.

Judaism had its saints, and it certainly had individuals, families, and communities living in devotion to God. But one does not find the buildings and books among them corresponding to the productions among Christians and Muslims. For while Jews had freedom in some communities and were allowed to flourish in learning and public worship, in much of Europe they were kept in separated quarters of cities and forced into the privacy of their homes. Often they were excluded from the institutions of higher learning. So they spent their time with Torah and Talmud, within the walls of their family homes, studying and observing the calendar of observances of the Jewish year. Even in their privacy and devotion, however, they were not safe from periodic purges

---

[2]Timothy Ware, *The Orthodox Church* (Baltimore, Maryland: Penguin Books, 1964). Harry J. Magoulias, *Byzantine Christianity: Emperor, Church and the West* (Chicago: Rand McNally and Company, 1970).

carried out by either local or crusading Christians. They had their martys at the hands of Christians.

Medieval Christendom, on the other hand, was a different story. The worldiness of the church which ensued after it became the official religion of the Roman Empire inspired other souls to seek within the church purer forms of Christian life. Monastic life became an accepted norm for men and women who were truly dedicated in living their lives for God.

One of the most famous designs for monastic life was based upon that of Benedict of Nursia, born about 480 A.D.[3] Monte Cassino, located between Naples and Rome, was the site of his new monastery founded in 529 A.D. It combined the elements of the family with the discipline of a military group and the monastery was self-supporting. Prayer, the first duty of every monk, was combined with manual labor out-of-doors so that monks would produce their own food and clothing. Every hour of the day was ordered around the devotion of God. In time other houses wanted to live under the rule and it eventually became standard for all houses in Europe. Monastic life, it turned out, needed to be reformed from time to time as some monks became lax and others wanted to be more rigorous in piety. The most famous monk of the order became Bernard of Clairvaux who joined the order in 1113 A.D.[4]

In the thirteenth century two orders emerged which were widely represented. One, known as the Gray Friars, from their gray clothing, was founded by Francis of Assisi. The wealthy young playboy took a vow of poverty and spent his days working in the fields and in caring for the sick.[5] He took no more thought of the morrow than did his "brother" birds or animals. Francis was a layman who worked with the poor. The other order was established by the "Black Friars," so called because of their black clothing, whose founder was Dominic de Guzman, 1170-1221 A.D.[6] Although he imitated the Franciscans in matters of vowing

---

[3]Williston Walker, *A History of the Christian Church* (New York: Charles Scribner's Sons, 1952), p. 138.

[4]M. Deanesly, *A History of the Medieval Church, 590-1500* (London: Methuen and Co., Ltd., 1951), p. 120.

[5]Paul Sabatier, *Life of St. Francis of Assisi*, translated by Seymour Houghton. (New York: Charles Scribner's Sons, 1928).

[6]Rosilind B. Brooke, *The Coming of the Friars* (London: George Allen and Unwin, Ltd., 1975).

poverty, he differed in that his order emphasized study and scholarship. Both orders produced active missionaries.

In Islam visions and revelations had always been a part of religion. A group known as the Sufis, while not particularly a separate branch of Islam, was a recognizable body.[7] Sufis sought an experience of personal union with God through a life of devotion. For them, the mystical experience was more important than keeping the letter of the Sharia. They pointed to the experiences of Muhammad to support their claims; although they sometimes differed with him in that some Sufis thought that the mystical life should rule out cohabitation with persons of the opposite sex. Their way of life was a striking contrast to the life of many Muslims after the wealth of conquests was distributed to believers.

Tension developed between supporters of the Sharia and the Sufis. The language of the Sufis spoke of attaining light, knowledge, and love; they, as did many other mystics, used the language of human love-making to express their desires for union with God. This approach made many supporters of the Sharia skeptical and even led to the Sufis being regarded as heretics. Abu Said, who died in 1049 A.D., thought that the Sharia was no longer necessary once one had attained the true path. He went so far as to say that the mystical dance of the Sufis should not be interrupted merely to respond to a routine community call to prayer.

Partly under the influence of Ibn-al-Arabi the Sufi groups organized into about twelve major orders. He claimed that through a special mystical interpretation of Muslim doctrines he was the "Seal of the Saints." Those who believed in him joined the fraternities which were parts of brotherhoods. Through membership in an order one became a *faqir* and might also be known as a *darwish*.[8] Like his Christian counterparts he sought repentance, abstinence, renunciation, poverty, and trust in God.

Whether Jew, Christian, or Muslim the children of Abraham who sought to escape the struggles of the political world found that they could do so only part way. They still had to deal with powers and doctrines, and they had to use human reason to choose their paths and to defend them.

---

[7]Nasrollah S. Fatemi and others, *Sufism* (New York: A. S. Barnes and Co., 1976).

[8]Idries Shah, *The Sufis* (Garden City, N. Y.: Anchor Books, 1971).

SUGGESTIONS FOR ADDITIONAL READING

Attwater, Donald. *The Christian Churches of the East.* 2 volumes. Milwaukee, Wisconsin: The Bruce Publishing Company, 1961.

Ayer, J. C. *A Source Book for Ancient Church History.* New York: Charles Scribner's Sons, 1913.

Breyer, Anthony and Herrin, Judith, editors. *Iconoclasm.* Birmingham, England: University of Birmingham Center for Byzantine Studies, 1977.

Chapman, John. St. *Benedict and the Sixth Century.* Westport, Conn.: Gatewood Press, Publishers, 1971.

Daniel-Rops, Henri. *Bernard of Clairvaux.* Translated by Elisabeth Abbott. New York: Hawthorn Books, Inc., 1964.

Daniel-Rops, H. *The Church in the Dark Ages.* Translated by Audrey Butler. London: J. M. Dent and Sons, Ltd., 1959.

Dudden, F. Holmes, *Gregory the Great.* 2 volumes. New York: Russell and Russell, 1905.

Englebert, Omer. *St. Francis of Assisi.* Translated by E. M. Cooper. Chicago: Franciscan Herald Press, 1965.

Florovsky, Georges. *Bible Church Tradition: An Eastern Orthodox View.* Belmont, Massachusetts: Nordland Publishing Company, 1972.

Lekai, Louis J. *The Cistercians.* Kent State University Press, 1977.

Matt, Leonard von and Hilpisch, Stephen. *Saint Benedict.* Translated by Ernest Graf. Chicago: Henry Regnery Co., 1961.

Meyendorff, John. *The Orthodox Church. New York: Pantheon* Books, 1968.

Nicholson. R. A. *Studies in Islamic Mysticism.* Cambridge: The University Press, 1967.

Paredi, Angelo. *Saint Ambrose.* Translated by Joseph Costelloe. Notre Dame, Indiana: University of Notre Dame Press, 1964.

Schimmel, Annemarie. *Mystical Dimensions of Islam.* Chapel Hill, N.C.: The University of North Carolina Press, 1975.

Schmemann, Alexander. *The Historical Road of Eastern Orthodoxy.* Translated by L. W. Kesich. New York: Holt, Rinehart, and Winston, 1963.

Shotwell, , J. T. and Loomis, L. R., editors. *The See of Peter.* New York: Octagon Books, 1965.

Sitwell, Gerald. Editor and Translator. *St. Odo of Cluny.* London: Sheed and Ward, 1958.

Workman, Herbert B. *The Evolution of the Monastic Ideal.* Boston: Beacon Press, 1962.

CHAPTER 22

REASON IN DEVOTION:

AL-GHAZALI, MAIMONIDES, AND AQUINAS

The piety of the monastic lives of devotion was sometimes, though not always, accompanied with rewards of learning. The cathedrals of Christianity had long operated schools to train workers in the church. The new monastic orders counted scholarship as part of their duties, so a school system grew up in them. The Jews of Babylon and Spain, in their studies of the law, also became interested in other branches of learning. Cordoba became a center of learning, as reflected in the Jewish academy there. Islamic learning was present in Cordoba and was increasing in Baghdad. Not only in mathematics and astronomy did the Muslims excel and contribute to Western thought, but also in philosophy they made a discovery that gave new impetus to learning among themselves, the Jews, and the Christians. Their discovery was Aristotle.

The teachings of the former student of Plato (427-347 B.C.), who died in 322 B.C., had to a great extent fallen into neglect and his works were lost to readers of Latin. To the early Christian apologists, Plato, with his theory of Universals, was much more in keeping with Christian doctrine. Augustine found the Platonists, whether Plato, his followers, or the Neoplatonists of Porphyry and Plotinus, superior to Aristotle. Aristotle was neglected to the point that later generations of Christians and Jews did not know him. The Arabs are the ones who rediscovered his works and translated them from Greek into Arabic. Probably in Spain the Arabic works were translated into Latin so that they could be handled by the learned men of Europe. The use of reason, especially in the form of logic known as the syllogism, was a major contribution of Aristotle, as was his insistence that the form which shapes substance is in the object itself and not apart from it in some ideal world, as the followers of Plato supposed.

Chronologically, the earliest of the three great scholars was al-Ghazali.[1] He was born in the northern part of Persia about 1058 A.D. Scholars were popular in the district, and al-Ghazali, whose full name was Abu Hamid Muhammad al-Ghazali, was brought up under a Sufi teacher. The way of the scholar appealed to him, and his ability attracted the attention of Nizam al-Mulk who appointed him, at age thirty-four, in 1091, to the chair of philosophy and theology at the Nizamyeh University of Baghdad. This great center of learning is reputed to have contained at the time 36 libraries and a center for translating into Arabic books from both East and West.

Fame and fortune came easily to al-Ghazali in an environment that rewarded success very handsomely. The Sufi training, nevertheless, made him suspicious of all the trappings of worldly success that surrounded the practice of the Faith of the Prophet. He was appalled at oppression and injustice in the leaders of the faithful and sought to arouse in his students a sense that reform was needed in personal lives of the faithful. Teaching three hundred students and keeping his emphasis upon matters of the intellect alone kept al-Ghazali under stress. He knew that there was another side of life as well, a life of the Spirit, which was as important as the intellect.

Four years after his appointment he began an experience which paralleled that of Augustine centuries before him. He faced a crisis in his life which had strong physical symptoms, although the real struggle was spiritual. He was existentially concerned that his own life not be lost to Hell because he had become too attached to worldly goods to live in such a way as to enter Paradise. He finally gave up his teaching post, sold all of his goods except some needed for his family, and became an ascetic, wandering about until his death in 1111 A.D.

His autobiographical work is *al Munqidh min ad-Dalal* or *Deliverance from Error*. Like Augustine's *Confessions* it contains a record of his spiritual growth from a life devoted to worldly success to one

---

[1]Nasrollah S. Fatemi and others, *Sufism* (New York: A. S. Barnes and Company, 1976), pp. 75-95.

lived in contemplation of God. He found a weakness in depending upon authority alone, realizing that first one had to know something of the truth in order to know whether an authority spoke the truth. His experience was that some people accepted everything as truth that was spoken by someone they liked, even though some of the teaching might be false. If one knew the truth first, one would then know which authority to follow. Sense perception and reason are superior to authority alone, but there is a higher form of knowing than those two. Intuition, or direct apprehension, is superior in knowing God and salvation, matters which are the utmost importance in human life.

Al-Ghazali continued to be a theologian after he stopped formal teaching of students about religion, so it is understandable that although he was critical of that profession, he was rather mild in his evaluation of it. He simply found it inadequate for his particular needs. The theistic philosophers, al-Farabi and Ibn Sina (Avicenna) were of more interest to him. They had gone rather far in combining the faith of Islam with the philosophy of the Neoplatonists. Al-Ghazali had mastered the logic of Aristotle and was able to work out a synthesis of Neoplatonism with Islam, being more careful than his predecessors not to give away those practices which were distinctively Muslim. Where Neoplatonism was irreconcilable with Islam, he pointed out why it was and abandoned it. He was hard on the Ismailiyah and Batiniyah who denied the use of reason and insisted on accepting the word of the Imam as infallible. As to the Sufis, he found their way of knowledge, through direct experience of God, most attractive. He differed with them in that he believed that it was possible to combine mysticism with the keeping of common religious duties.

The summary of what al-Ghazali learned in his spiritual journey was written in his work *The Revival of the Religious Sciences*, or *Ihya 'Ulum as-Din*. Among other things he accomplished in the book was a description of the ideal life of asceticism that should govern one's life in the world, especially in social relationships.

Al-Ghazali was the man par excellence who helped Islam come to grips with Greek philosophy and emerge strengthened by it. He used the methods of Aristotle to evaluate Neoplatonism and various forms of Islam. He knew where he could borrow to explain and strengthen the faith of the prophet and where he had to reject Neoplatonism. He could combine the life of the intellect and the life of the ascetic mystic not only in theory, but also in practice. Each of the major religions in the West needed such a man, and al-Ghazali fulfilled that role in Islam.

Maimonides played the part for Judaism. He was born Mosheh ben Maimon, in 1135 A.D. in Cordova, the capital of Ummayad caliphs of

Spain.[2] While Jews had been second-class citizens there also they nevertheless had a life of learning and scholarship and were not without their participation in the offices of government. Maimon, the father of Moses, had a good library and was something of a scholar. Many of those advantages were lost to young Moses in the year he was bar mitzvah, for the Almohads took Cordova, destroying much of the city, including the synagogue. Jews, like Christians, were severely persecuted, and some of them fled the country.

During travels, Maimonides kept working on his education without his father's good library which had been left in Cordoba. He was aware of gaps in his learning, but he devoted himself to the study of the Jewish writings and to as much of the secular learning of the world as he could read. By 1168 A.D. he published the *Commentary on The Mishnah*. He was immediately caught in the struggle between the traditional rabbinate and its interpretation of the law and the more radical Karaite movement which contended that every man could make his own authoritative interpretation of the law. Maimonides refused to make a living from his books, his teachings, or his study of the law. As did other Jews, he developed a trade by which he could earn the money necessary to support himself and his family. He became a physician, serving Muslims in the Fatimid court. Maimonides was the physician to Saladin's son during the last two years of the twelfth century. He was more than a tradesman of medicine, for he was a scholar of medical texts from the West and became something of an authority in that field.

Nevertheless, his love was the law, and his work with it was of primary importance to him. In 1178 A.D. he brought out his great *Mishneh Torah*. It contained his responses to knotty legal problems which had been addressed to him from all over the world. With it came fame as a scholar and interpreter of the law.

His major work, however, became that which he wrote to reconcile the problems of theology with the problems of science and reason. He needed to bring the faith of the Scriptures into relationship with all of the learning of his day. His means of bringing about this explanation was the one that he used with a Rabbi Joseph, who had grown up on the Scriptures of the faith and now had difficulty in relating that knowledge with what he had acquired in logic, cosmology, theology, and philosophy of the Greek and Arabic tradition. In a dialogue method as old as the time

---

[2]Jacob S. Minkin, *The World of Moses Maimonides* (New York: Thomas Yoseloff, 1957).

of Plato, Maimonides led the student from perplexity to an understanding of the relationship of all learning.

The *Moreh Nevukhim*, better known as the *Guide to the Perplexed*, was no mere polemic or apology for the faith. Maimonides used a doubting inquirer to lead him into an explanation of the Scriptures and of the faith of his people. He laid a foundation for an intellectual system which embraced all of the major learning of his day. Faith and reason were brought together for the inquiring believer rather than for the outsider who knew nothing of the faith. To the casual reader or the uniformed, there is still much to perplex in the order and the conclusions of the guide.

After an epistle dedicating the book to Rabbi Joseph, Maimonides moved into an explanation of how the treatise would proceed. It was not designed for an ignorant person but for one who had known reason and the law and was perplexed whether one should follow his own reason or renounce the foundations of the law. It was a matter, thought Maimonides, of analyzing terms and defining their meanings. The second purpose was to explain some passages of the prophets which are in parables having two meanings, an inner meaning as well as an external meaning. When one of knowledge interprets the parables according to the external meaning only, he is terribly perplexed, whereas when they are explained and interpreted by the inner meaning, the inquirer is delivered from being perplexed. Thus, in the title for the treatise, *The Guide to the Perplexed*, Maimonides did not promise to solve all problems for everyone but to remove most of the difficulties of great importance.

It was in the thirteenth century that a Christian scholar tried to bring together the faith and reason of Aristotle for the Christian intellectuals. The son of the Count of Aquino, Thomas, was born near Naples in 1225 A.D.[3] For nine years he studied at the abbey of Monte Cassino and then attended the University of Naples, where the Aristotelian texts were studied with Arabic commentaries. Peter, the Irishman who taught Aquinas, was so avid for Aristotle that he almost forgot his faith. Thomas was also enthusiastic for Aristotle but he held on to his faith and made the philosophy support it.

At the age of nineteen, Thomas decided to become a Dominican. His family violently protested and held him prisoner for a year while they tried all sorts of temptations to make him change his mind. At the end of

---

[3]Jacques Maritain, *St. Thomas Aquinas* (New York: Meridian Books, 1958).

that period, they recognized that he was beyond persuasion and let him continue to the University of Paris where he studied with Albrecht Gross, translated as Peter the Great, a German. Since Thomas listened carefully without speaking much, brooding within his corpulent body, his classmates referred to him as the "dumb ox." He was appraised otherwise by his teacher, who is reported to have said, "The bellows of this dumb ox will awaken all Christendom."[4]

Thomas was appointed professor of theology in Paris in 1259 A.D. Almost at once he was brought to the court of the Pope where he taught until 1268 A.D. He was back in Paris from 1268 to 1272 A.D. He died at the age of forty-nine, in 1274 A.D., while on the way to attend the Church Council of Lyons. He left behind numerous writings, sometimes dictated so prodigiously that he had kept four secretaries busy. His two greatest works are the *Summa Contra Gentiles* or *Summary of Arguments Against the Pagans,* and the *Summa Theologiae.*

Thomas believed that reason could tell one about the natural world and a certain amount about the world of faith. Reason could demonstrate *that* God is, but only Christian revelation can show fully *what* God is. Faith and reason are, however, complementary rather than two mutually exclusive disciplines.

The form of presentation of the *Summa Theologiae,* Part I, Question 2, Third Article, "Whether God Exists," has a form typical of how Aquinas dealt with problems. "I answer that the existence of God can be proved in five ways," said Aquinas. He then proceeded to describe five ways to prove from reason that God does exist. The first was from motion. Whatever is moved must be moved by another. However, that process cannot continue back infinitely, so there must have been a first mover, which everyone understands to be God. In a similar way he continued with the arguments from efficient cause, from possibility and necessity, from the graduation found in things, and from the governance of the world.

Having established *that* God is, Aquinas discussed *what* He is. While humans are limited in their knowledge of God, they are not prevented entirely from understanding his nature. As did Erigena, he acknowledged that one can proceed by the *via negativa,* saying that God is not identical with this or that, for He exceeds what any term can convey. Words that are superlatives in human language can be applied to God, as long as it is

---

[4]Wallace I. Matson, *A History of Philosophy* (New York: American Book Company, 1968), p. 237.

understood that they do not mean the same thing as when they are applied to human beings; they apply only by analogy. God's wisdom, power, glory, etc., can be spoken of as long as it is realized that they exceed anything we would mean were we speaking of human beings.

The world exists because God wishes it to exist. One can reason from the world to God, but one cannot reason from God to the world. God's creation of the world was a completely free act. He would have had all of His omnipotence had He not created it at all. Man is made of a substance of nature. The soul, however, Aquinas saw only somewhat in Aristotelian terms, for Aristotle did not recognize an immortal soul as Plato had done. Nor did he see the soul as substance. Aquinas made the soul a substantial form, capable of existing apart from matter. Thus, it could continue to exist after the dissolution of the body.

The goal of man is to spend eternity in heaven; happiness can only be obtained in its perfection in the next life. In this life, happiness is gained in the way described by Aristotle, that is, through the moral virtues and reason. Somehow, he was able to reconcile the doctrine of the "Mean" in Aristotle, that is, the mean between two extremes, as the guide for conduct, with the virtues of celibacy and the asceticism of the Dominicans. He was more in keeping with the Stoics, however, in his interpretation of morality as keeping the natural law, that is, life according to reason. In all things, human beings have free choice and are responsible for their actions. However, as did Augustine, he held that only by the grace of God can man freely choose to turn to God and be saved.

Thomas Aquinas followed Aristotle in looking at the state not as punishment for the fall of Adam and Eve, but as an expression of man as a political animal. While the state defends against criminals and enemies, it is also to labor to promote the general welfare of its people. That is God's intention, and for that purpose he established princes of the world. Church and state are two different powers, neither gaining its power from the other, but from God. The church is, according to Aquinas, the higher power.

The influence of Thomas Aquinas among Catholics was very great indeed. Less than a hundred years after his birth, in 1323 A.D., he was declared to be a saint. In 1567 A.D. he was declared a "Doctor of the Church," ranking equally with Augustine, Ambrose, Jerome, and Gregory. In 1879 A.D. Pope Leo XIII declared Thomas preeminent among philosophers. And in 1918 A.D. the Vatican directed that all theological education of priests be along the lines of Thomism. While Thomism is not required of all priests and not all other views are heretical, Thomas Aquinas does occupy a place among the Roman Catholic clergy that is without rival from any other thinker.

The attempts to reconcile faith and reason in the three great religions of the West both preceded the men sketched in this chapter and continued after them. But all three of the religions of the children of Abraham acknowledge Al-Ghazali, Maimonides, and Thomas Aquinas as the giants of the late medieval period in reconciling faith, knowledge, and practice.

SUGGESTIONS FOR ADDITIONAL READING

Field, Claud. *Mystics and Saints of Islam*. London: Francis Griffiths, 1910.

Maimonides, Moses. *The Guide of the Perplexed*. Translation and Notes by Shlomo Pines. Chicago: The University of Chicago Press, 1963.

Pegis, Anton C., editor. *Basic Writings of Saint Thomas Aquinas*. 2 volumes. New York: Random House, 1945.

Pieper, Josef. *Guide to Thomas Aquinas*. Translated by R. and C., Winston. New York: The New American Library of World Literature, 1962.

Yellin, David and Abrahams, Israel. *Maimonides*. Philadelphia: The Jewish Publication Society of America, 1903.

CHAPTER 23

LUTHER, CALVIN, AND HENRY VIII

Around the beginning of the sixteenth century A.D., Christianity experienced a bloody period of suffering. Jews and Muslims did not cause it; instead, they were sometimes victims of the warfare in Christianity. This time Christians were at war with Christians. In the name of the Christian faith, acts were committed which would strike terror in any civilized person of the twentieth century. It was the period of the Reformation and Counter Reformation.

The sympathies of the times were conducive to gestate an embryo which was conceived as a crisis in the life of one individual. Martin Luther did not start out as a revolutionary, and a more unlikely beginning would be hard to find. He was the son of a peasant miner. Born in 1483 A.D. in Eisleben, Germany, he was given every educational opportunity by his father in hopes that young Martin would make his fortune in the legal profession. The plan went well through his taking of the Master of Arts degree in 1505. Then something went wrong. Two incidents had a profound influence on Luther at that time. One was the death of a close friend. The other was his own narrow escape from death when he was nearly hit directly by a stroke of lightning. A religious crisis was reached in his life in which he found the salvation of his soul more important than any success the world had to offer.

Luther entered the German congregation of Augustinian hermits which had recently been established .in a reformed mode and was then under the guidance of Johann von Staupitz. The order represented the best of medieval monasticism, and Luther accepted Staupitz as a competent spiritual guide.Luther's ability was quickly recognized and he was ordained to the priesthood in 1507. He was to be more than an ordinary priest, however, for in 1508 his superiors sent him to the new University of Wittenberg, established by the Saxon Elector Frederick III, "The Wise." Luther made rapid progress: Bachelor of Theology in 1509, a representative to Rome on business for his order in 1510, and a Doctor of Theology in 1512.

He began his public career lecturing on the Bible, first on Psalms and then on Paul's letter to the Romans. He was also a preacher and a supervisor of eleven monasteries. In every way he was recognized as an able scholar, an able preacher, an able administrator, and a holy man of devotions. But he was deeply dissatisfied with himself. He worked as hard as possible to be acceptable to God, yet he felt completely unacceptable.

The answer to his problem came through his acquaintance with St. Augustine whom he had been studying since 1509. One thing he shared with the saint was a dislike for Aristotle. Gradually he discovered in his own lectures on the Scriptures the truths St. Augustine had found in the writings of Paul. Salvation, he realized, is a new relationship to God not based upon any human work but upon the grace of God. The believer accepts that grace of God in faith, and from that life lived in response to the grace of God produces a life of love and devotion. Salvation is a gift of God, not a work of any human being.

It was while Luther labored on his lectures on *Romans* in 1516 that he received the assurance within himself that God had granted him salvation. The sinner had been saved. That salvation was not through anything that he himself had done or anything that the church had done. It was solely through the grace of God, and Luther received it on faith, by which he was sure that he was justified before God. This was a deep, personal, transforming experience for the young seeker. He had discovered the deep meaning in the lives of St. Paul and St. Augustine. He did not then know it, but he had recovered a cornerstone that he would incorporate into a new structure, a new household of faith within Christianity.

The arrival of Johann Tetzel, seller of indulgences for the church, was the occasion for Luther to apply his new doctrine to practices of the larger church. Tetzel painted in glowing terms the value of indulgences which had been sold by the church in Rome since 1506. The proceeds were used for good works; namely, the building of St. Peter's basilica in Rome. Through buying an indulgence, a sinner could escape the penalties for his sin, for the church would grant that forgiveness from its treasury of merits deposited by the saints who had more merits than they needed to enter eternal life. Luther's scholarship led him to believe that indulgences were unscriptural and contrary to the way salvation actually comes, which is through the grace of God, rather than through good works such as building St. Peter's. In order to give the problem the attention it deserved, Luther wrote out 95 points or theses on which he wanted to hold a debate among scholars. In the customary manner, he announced his desire by posting the list in the place where such announcements were usually posted—on the door of the castle church. It was an act which grew out of feeling as well as out of intellect, but it was in no way conceived of as an act of revolution.

Luther was shocked at the result. Johann Maier of Eck, Professor of Theology at the University of Ingolstadt, charged him with heresy. The attacks and defenses grew. Luther wanted no fight with the pope, but in June 1518, Pope Leo X cited Luther to appear in Rome and asked Silvestro Mazzolini of Prierio to draw an opinion on Luther's position. Prierio asserted that Luther was a heretic. It was through the Elector Frederick, who was to save Luther more than once from the powers of the pope, that the hearing was transferred from Rome to the jurisdiction of papal legate at the Reichstag in Augsburg. At the hearing, Luther was ordered to retract his teachings on indulgences. He refused to retract, and he entered into a series of appeals. In the course of these appeals, Luther admitted that his position had some similarities with that of Huss and that the Council of Constance had erred in condemning Jan Huss. Luther allowed final appeal only to Scriptures interpreted by individuals rather than by the church. Eck was ready to finish him.

In 1520 Luther published *To the Christian Nobility of the German Nation* in which he asserted that the church is not superior to the state since all believers are priests. Therefore the church does not have exclusive right to interpret the Scriptures for this right belongs to every believer. He also asserted that persons other than the pope can call a council; indeed church reform councils ought to be called by the temporal authorities. It is easy to see, from this distance in time, why it was imperative that Rome silence a man who challenged the very foundations of its authority. It is also easy to see how princes and common people who were angry with the ways of the pope would find in Luther an outstanding champion of their causes.

In his *Babylonish Captivity of the Church* Luther attacked the doctrine of transubstantiation, in which the Catholic Church held that the bread and wine during the Holy Communion was transformed into the actual body and blood of Christ by action of the priest. For Luther the presence of Christ was real, but the substance underneath the appearance of bread and the appearance of wine did not *become* the flesh and blood of Christ. He believed that believers should be able to eat the bread and to drink the wine, and not be limited to taking only the bread. He said that the Lord's Supper is not a sacrifice to God, as it had been conceived in the Catholic Church. He even went so far as to say that the sacraments of Rome, such as confirmation, matrimony, orders, and extreme unction, have no basis as sacraments in the Scriptures.

When the Diet met at Worms in 1521, Luther attended, under safe conduct, to make his case before the Emperor and the Reichstag. He admitted that he had stated his cases against persons too strongly, but he would not retract the substance of his teachings until someone convinced him of the error of his knowledge, by use of Scriptures or some other adequate argument. Citing some other authority, even that of the pope, would not convince him. In conclusion he said, in effect, "Here I stand. God help me." He was placed under ban of the empire; he was to be seized and his books were to be burned. It was a sentence which was never lifted in his lifetime. Neither was it ever executed.

Luther had left the meeting before the sentence was passed, and friends seized him on his way home and placed him in protective custody in the Wartburg Castle. He was safe there under the protection of Prince Frederick, "The Wise." Luther used the time to translate the New Testament from Greek, other translation having been from the Vulgate, into beautiful German. His translation was to form the basis of a common German language and literature. This development, coupled with the use of the printing press, was soon to have Scriptures in the hands of lay people throughout Germany, making of every believer a priest who could read and interpret his own Scriptures.

Luther set the stage for a married clergy by taking as his wife a former nun, Katherine von Bora, in June of 1525. They had five children, and as the Lutheran cause moved back and forth between victory and tragedy in Germany, Luther was to find a solace in his life with his family. He was a robust extrovert and his happy family was an accompaniment to his own exuberant personality.

The emperor Charles favored Catholics in Germany and probably would have been tougher on Lutherans had he not been fighting away from Germany and had not the pope succeeded in angering him. Charles did not get his way, but neither did the Lutherans. The resulting compromise of the Reichstag meeting in Augsburg was worked out in 1555 and was known as the Peace of Augsburg. The principle of division was based on the Latin formula, *cujus regio, ejus religio.* That is, the religion of the prince of a territory would be the religion of all the people of that territory: the people themselves had no choice in the matter. Germany was finally divided, and Lutheranism was finally legally established.

In Switzerland John Calvin became the outstanding leader of the reformed movement in the church. Born in Noyon, France, in 1509, he grew up receiving income from ecclesiastical posts but he was never ordained a priest. His undergraduate training was in the University of Paris where he was prepared for theology. At the last moment, however, his father had him switch to law at the University of Orleans. He completed his course in law and went on with humanistic studies.

In 1533 Calvin underwent a conversion experience in which he concluded that he must follow the Word of God as it is given in the Scriptures. From that basis, he moved ahead with reform of the positions of the Catholic Church. In 1534 he resigned his benefices. After being imprisoned a brief time in Noyon, he knew that he had to escape from France to a safer country. He found refuge in Basel.

In 1536 the first edition of his most famous work appeared, *The Institutes of the Christian Religion.* Its preface was a letter to the king of France. The foundation for the doctrine he espoused was the teaching of Luther that man is justified by faith in God rather than through his own works in the law. But whereas Luther punched out his positions in a series of battles, discovering his doctrines as he took one step at a time, Calvin calmly and cooly set forth, in a way befitting one with legal training, a whole system of reformed theology.

Along with Paul, Augustine, and Luther, Calvin held that a man cannot initiate his own salvation. The initiation must begin with God. It is through God's grace that a man is saved through faith in Christ. Those who are to be saved have been elected from the beginning of the world and are predestined to turn to God. In gratitude to God for their salvation, they respond with lives of good works. The rigorous good works do not earn the salvation; they are the fruits of one whose sould is saved.

Along with the Scriptures Calvin stressed the importance of the church, the sacraments, and the civil government. The church on earth is not identical with the true church, which contains only the elect. The sacraments are two only, baptism and the Lord's Supper. The civil government has a duty to foster the welfare of the church and to discipline those persons whose punishment must exceed that of excommunication, which he believed to be within the power of the church to perform.

After Calvin joined Farel in Geneva in 1536 he soon decided that Geneva should be turned into the kind of model community he had pictured in the *Institutes*. In 1537 he proposed, and had adopted, a new ecclesiastical constitution, the *Ordonnances*. The four offices instituted were those of pastor, teacher, elder, and deacon. The key office in the church was that of the elder, a layman. Elders were representatives of the laymen. They joined with the ministers to compose the Consistoire which met weekly to administer church discipline. Calvin gave the teacher charge of the Geneva school system. Eventually he developed a teaching tool known as the catechism, a standard set of questions and answers designed to teach the essentials that every Christian believer should hold.

Calvin's fame became international not only for his practical administration but also for his scholarship in the *Institutes* and other writings. He strengthened his reputation further in 1559 by founding the Genevan Academy, which later became the University of Geneva. Outside of Germany, where Luther was supreme, Calvin was the inspiration for reform. In France, the Netherlands, England, and particularly Scotland, his influence on changing the church was very great. He died in Geneva in May of 1564. He too had married, and he was more of a humanist than some people like to grant. He was, however, more reserved, more systematic, and more thoughtful in many ways than Luther, the great giant of Germany. Considered together, they set in motion doctrines which not only changed the face of Europe but also of the new world in the next century.

Reform in England had its spiritual leaders and translators too. But the most influential man in the reform there was not a scholar or a monk, but a lusty king. Henry VIII made the most of the feeling of his subjects that England was for Englishmen. His break with Rome came not through a conversion experience or through study of Scriptures, but through disagreement with the pope on who could legally be the wife of Henry VIII. Henry VIII had started his reign opposed to Luther, defending the seven sacraments against Luther's two. A grateful Pope Leo X gave him the title of "Defender of the Faith." But titles were not as important to Henry VIII as having a male heir for his throne.

Henry had married the widowed wife of his brother Arthur, Catherine of Aragon, the daughter of Ferdinand and Isabella of Spain. Mary was the only one of their six children who survived. Henry wanted a son, which Catherine could not give him. So he tried to have the marriage declared illegal so that he could marry his new love, Anne Boleyn. The annulment was not secured from the pope. Henry planned to have Cardinal Wolsey tried for treason, but he was cheated of it by the death of Wolsey on his way to trial in 1530. In 1531 Henry accused the clergy of breach of the old statute of *Praemunire* in their recognizing Wolsey as a papal legate. His fine upon the clergy was heavy. And he declared that he was "single and supreme head in earth of the Church of England." Monks and bishops alike who opposed the Act were executed. Parliament gave Henry about 376 monasteries to do with as he pleased. Death claimed Catherine of Aragon, and Anne Boleyn was beheaded for adultery. A new bride, Jane Seymour, gave him a son Edward, in 1537, but she died eleven days later. Henry had his way with the church, brides, and heir.

Before Henry VIII died in 1547, the doctrines of the church of England had taken something of a protestant form. He made his concession to the movement in his Ten Articles which he drafted in 1536. The Bible, the Apostles' Creed, the Nicene Creed, and the Athanasian creeds, together with the first four councils, were the foundations of teaching. He mentioned only three sacraments—baptism, penance, and the Lord's Supper. One is justified by faith in Christ, but confession and absolution are also required. In the Supper Christ is physically present. One could honor saints and images but not to excess. He denied that the bishop of Rome can deliver the soul of a departed one from purgatory.

An English translation of the Bible was made based on Tyndale and Coverdale versions, and it was for sale in 1537, largely through the efforts of Cranmer. In 1538 Cromwell ordered it to be placed so that it would be open to the public in every church. With the exception of the Lord's Prayer, the ten commandments, and the litany, which were translated into English and so taught, Latin remained in use during the lifetime of Henry VIII. In 1539, Parliament passed the Six Articles Act which made death by fire the penalty for denying the doctrine of transubstantiation. Marriages of clergy were forbidden. Communion was not permitted in both bread and wine. In part, Henry was trying to show the world that he was really an orthodox Catholic in spite of his disagreement with the pope. But the pope called on the sons of faith in Spain and France to join forces to put down the insolent heretic, Henry VIII of England. The emperor needed Henry's aid, however, and nothing came of the pope's request.

When Henry died, most of his subjects were with him in matters of the church and faith. Two other factions wanted to push in opposite directions; the Catholics wanted to return to what they had known, and the Protestants wanted to move in the direction of what was taking place on the Continent. Henry's successor, Edward VI, was only nine years old, and Somerset was the Protector. Somerset's sentiments were with the Protestants. It was in this period, under the Act of Uniformity in 1549, that a Book of Common Prayer in English was required. It applied to everyone in England regardless of private personal preferences. There was only one church *of* England and *in* England.

In 1553 Edward VI died. He was succeeded by Mary, who married Philip II of Spain. She reestablished papal control and set about destroying the leading clergy of the Church of England. This persecution by Mary Tudor was severe enough to earn her the title for all time of "Bloody Mary."

Mary was succeeded by Elizabeth who had little choice except to be Protestant regardless of her personal preferences. The pope regarded her as an illegitimate child of Henry so she had no standing as a monarch as far as Rome was concerned. In 1559, Parliament passed another Supremacy Act which rejected papal claims to authority and money. The queen was described as Supreme Governor of the Church of England. In 1563, the famous Thirty-nine Articles were published as the statement of faith for the Church of England.

These brief accounts do not do full justice to the major reformers and they certainly do not do justice to the developments in other countries. Dozens of other leaders participated, making their contributions in ink or in blood and sometimes in both. But enough has been said to indicate the foundations of a fundamental split in the great Catholic Church. Other splits continued to develop among denominations. But the Church of Rome also reexamined its position.

SUGGESTIONS FOR ADDITIONAL READING

Bainton, Roland H. *Here I Stand: A Life of Martin Luther.* New York: Abingdon-Cokesbury Press, 1950.

Bainton, Roland H. *The Reformation in the Sixteenth Century.* Boston: The Beacon Press, 1952.

Bettenson, Henry. *Documents of the Christian Church.* New York: Oxford University Press, 1960.

Calvin, John. *Institutes of the Christian Religion.* Edited by J. T. McNeill and F. L. Battles. Philadelphia: Westminster Press, 1960.

Constant, G. *The Reformation in England.* Translated by R. E. Scantlebury. New York: Harper and Row Publishers, 1966.

Elliott-Binns L. *The Reformation in England.* Hamden, Conn.: Archon Books, 1966.

Harkness, Georgia. *John Calvin.* New York: Abingdon Press, 1958.

Haugaard, W. P. *Elizabeth and the English Reformation.* Cambridge: The University Press, 1968.

Latourette, K. S. *A History of Christianity.* New York: Harper and Brothers, 1953.

Luther, Martin. *Luther's Works.* Edited by Jaroslaw Pelikan and others in 53 volumes. Saint Louis: Concordia Publishing House, 1958.

Walker, Williston. *A History of the Christian Church.* New York: Charles Scribner's Sons, 1959.

CHAPTER 24

ISABELLA, IGNATIUS, PAUL, AND TRENT

Protestant Christians were not the only ones who had to fear the Catholic Church. Even before Luther and Calvin had published their works Jews and Muslims began to experience the wrath of devoted Catholics in Spain.

The reform of the Catholic Church of Rome began before the Reformation in central Europe. Strangely enough, it began in a country which was less purely Christian than most others and which contained within its borders large groups of Muslims and Jews. Perhaps due to the compromises of Jews, Muslims, and Christians who modified their views in order to make life more harmonious, the Spanish Catholics were among the most conservative and orthodox of all Roman Catholics. They were loyal to the past institutions of the Church and to the power of the Pope. In the time of King Ferdinand and Queen Isabella, the same ones who sent Columbus on his way to find a new material world, the spiritual purity of the Catholic faith was given a strong boost.

The instrument through which the monarchs of Spain accomplished their reform was Cardinal Ximenes, appointed confessor to the Queen in 1492. He was loyal to the Church, somewhat reluctant about his post with the Queen, and actually critical of the Pope's sale of indulgences to finance the building of St. Peter's church in Rome. A bull from the Pope in 1494 gave the Spanish monarchs permission to reform the lax friars and nuns within their kingdom, and the task was turned over to Ximenes. He began his reform with his own order and had largely completed the task by the time the Franciscans began their missionary work in the Indies.

Isabella had little use for Moors and Jews and made sure that they knew it. She revived the Inquisition, which had been around since the days of Pope Innocent III and Pope Gregory IX. Members of the Inquisition held that heresy was treason against God, even more serious than treason against a king. They had appointed the Dominican order as watch dogs against heresy, with the responsibilities for investigation and accusation. Under Isabella the Inquisition was brought to such a fierce and severe art of persecution that the term "Spanish Inquisition" came to stand for persecution at its very worst. Isabella's inquisitor general was Tomas de Torquemada, who sought out Jewish and Moorish converts to Christianity and investigated their orthodoxy. It has been estimated that he may have burned to death some two thousand persons.

The reform in Spain was not simply a campaign of hatred against human beings who might differ on matters or religious faith. It was also famous for the lives and literature of devotion to God which it produced. The devotion was to God at the expense of the worshiper's comfort and ego exaltation. Generally it was in support of the Pope and the established teachings of the Church, submissive to the examinations of the Inquisition, and devoted to constructive reform.

A fine example is seen in the life of Ignatius Loyola. He was born about 1491 in Azpeitia, Spain, into a noble family of somewhat restricted financial means. Little is known of his life before he was twenty six years old, except that he learned to read and write and that he served as a page to the household of Juan Velasquez de Cuellar, Governor of the fortress of Arevalo. By his own accounts he engaged in the activities of young men of noble birth—hunting, fighting, and women. He seems to have been normally amorous, of a quick temper, and of a ready will to fight. He was not beyond having scrapes with the law either.

Ignatius went into military service with the Duke of Najera near Pamplona, a powerful man who had a military force of some four thousand men. Several years passed before Ignatius saw combat, but when he did something happened which changed his life forever. There was an attack by a vastly superior French force. The terms they offered the Spaniards for surrender were unacceptable and Ignatius participated in the defense. During the bombardment which followed, a cannon ball shattered the bone in the right leg of Ignatius and made a flesh wound in his left. After several days he was at the point of death. He did survive and recovered 'enough to ride and walk for great distances.

During his convalescence he read two books which influenced the rest of his life. One was the *Life of Christ*, and the other was the *Lives of the Saints*. He knew after reading them that his life was about to make a significant change. At first the impression that he would offer his life in service to some great lady, was vague. But then one night he had a clear vision of the Virgin Mary with the child Jesus. It was enough to make him hate his past life and vow to break with his former sins. He devoted his time to writing about Christ and "Our Lady" and to prayer. He wanted to do something sacred with his life but he was floundering for a direction.

In preparation for his journey to Jerusalem he went to Montserrat. At that time he confessed his sins and his determination to go to Jerusalem. He shed his customary clothes and put on a garment fashioned from sack cloth. On one occasion he kept watch with his armaments all night before the altar of Our Lady of Montserrat. He decided that from that time on he would be clothed only with the arms of Christ. On the 24th of March, 1522, he began his pilgrimage to Jerusalem as a new man in Christ. He lived entirely by what he could beg, and he gave Christian charity to all whom he met in need.

In all things Ignatius intended to remain in the good graces of the church. He journeyed with his companions to Paris and, among sordid conditions, pursued his education in spite of the immature and sometimes weird behavior of his superiors. He was constantly under suspicion and even accusation for his practices of devotion and for his extreme asceticism which included living in a poorhouse. He was not only out of step with the practices of the other students, but he was also too severe in his practice of the Christian faith. It would be many years before his style of Christian living would be recognized as valid.

In 1537 things began to change for the better for Ignatius and his friends. They won the support and favor of the Pope. He blessed their going to Jerusalem, gave them alms to help their journey and work, gave the priests among them power to hear confessions and to absolve all cases of episcopal jurisdiction, and for those who were not priests he gave a letter permitting any bishop to ordain them without benefice. The papal legate gave them authority to preach, teach, and interpret scriptures throughout the Venetian territory. At last the companions were respectable.

Besides the story of his personal spiritual pilgrimage, on which the account in this chapter had been based, Ignatius left two other documents of vital importance in understanding his contributions to Christianity. One was the *Spiritual Exercises,* a kind of manual of arms for a soldier of

Christ. The other was the *Constitutions,* an outline of administration for the Company of Jesus, otherwise known as the Society of Jesus and later as the Jesuits.

Officially the Company was not recognized as an instrument to reform the church. According to a bull of institution issued by Pope Julius III in July of 1550, the purpose was to defend and spread the Christian faith. Souls were to be helped to Christian life through preaching, Scriptures, teaching, hearing confessions and administering the sacraments. The Company was also to appease quarrels and to minister to prisoners and the sick. Everything was to be done without pay. And yet, in the purity of their teaching by word and example, they were an influence for correcting many of the abuses of the church. The ferment of reform within the church was taking place, and until his death in 1556 Ignatius exerted a steady influence from his position as the first general of the Company of Jesus.

Aside from the Inquisition and the Jesuits, a third factor was at work in the reform of the Roman church. It was the Council of Trent. Its first meeting was in Trent in December of 1545, with only 31 bishops present for the opening ceremony, out of the 700 who were eligible to attend. Pope Paul III had been reluctant to call the council insisted on by Charles V, who had hopes of bringing in the Protestants later and effecting a reconciliation within the Church. But from the first session the Italian and Spanish bishops worked on procedures which would protect the power of the Pope. By April of 1546 the Council had reaffirmed the Church's authority in interpreting scriptures and, in fact, its authority in all major practices of the church. The authorized version of the Scriptures for Catholics was the Latin Vulgate by St. Jerome. Individual interpretation of scriptures was ruled out for the church was to remain the sole interpreter of scriptures. Contrary to Luther the Council of Trent held that man could, through the sacraments of the church, obtain salvation through his own efforts. The merits of Christ were available to believers to help them in their efforts. The concept of salvation through faith alone, as Luther taught, was rejected. Any possibility of reaching agreement with the Lutherans and Calvinists was eliminated.

The results of the Council of Trent did not mean that significant reforms were omitted within the Roman Catholic Church. There was a possibility that one could come to know the contents of the Scriptures as they were officially interpreted by the Roman Catholic Church. The practice of Bishops drawing their income without performing clerical duties was changed and bishops were expected to preach. The parish clergy, who had often been occupied with pursuits of their own devising, were now expected to teach plainly what is required for salvation. Not only that, men who held parishes were expected to live in them and to work with their people, not collect their income and then live in more comfortable regions. Regular training programs for the clergy were established in theological seminaries, and care was given to supervision of the clergy. In particular, efforts were made to end the practice of priests having secret marriages.

At the same time, a step was taken to control what books were acceptable to the Roman Catholic Church and which were forbidden to Catholics. In 1571 the Congregation of the Index was created in Rome to list censured books. The practice of approving or disapproving books continued into the middle of the twentieth century.

The clergy were not the only ones reformed. There was a wave of pietism running through the whole church. The quiet life of devotion, sometimes rewarded by visions, was eagerly sought by many people. Teresa de Jesus of Avila was the inspiration of many women in the church. Her life of perfection was too high for many, but she set an example for others to imitate as best they could. In all things she kept her spirituality within the bounds of the Catholic control, realizing that visions could come from the devil as well as from God. The soaring verses of love to God from John of the Cross inspired many lesser lives to seek something of that warm personal devotion to God in their own experiences. Francois de Sales, a bishop of Geneva, had something of the same devotion and expressed it in terms of love for the Church and the sacraments. The Catholics had their own heroes of the faith whom they could follow, rather than the bombastic Luther or the systematic Calvin.

The missionary concerns of the church were again awakened. The discovery of the new world by Columbus, who was sponsored by Queen Isabella, opened virgin territories for the activities of Spanish Christians. The Catholics had millions of new souls to win who had never heard of Christianity. While Calvinists and Lutherans were fighting over the old countries in Europe, the Catholics were hard at work converting pagans in the new world.

So intense were the efforts of Catholic missionaries that rivalries and excesses crept into their work. It was necessary for the Pontiff to take charge and supervise their work in the new world to prevent heresy creeping into their products. The administrative channel for their supervision was established by Pope Gregory XV in 1622 as the Congregatio de Propaganda Fide.

In spite of the struggles which accompanied it, the Catholic Church was reformed. It responded to the Reformation and clarified its own position against those positions of Luther and Calvin.

SUGGESTIONS FOR ADDITIONAL READING

Bettinson, Henry. *Documents of the Christian Church*. New York: Oxford University Press, 1960.

Brenan, Gerald. *St. John of the Cross*. Cambridge: University Press, 1973.

Brodrick, James. *The Origin of the Jesuits*. Westport, Conn.: Greenwood Press, Publishers, 1971.

Latourette, K. S. *A History of Christianity*. New York: Harper and Brothers Publishers, 1953.

Loyola, Ignatius. *St. Ignatius' Own Story*. Translated by Young. Chicago: Loyola University Press, 1956.

Peers, E. A. *Saint Teresa of Jesus*. London: Faber and Faber, 1953.

Schurhammer, Georg. *Francis Xavier*. 2 volumes. Translated by M. J. Costelloe. Rome: The Jesuit Historical Institute, 1973.

Van Dyke, Paul. *Ignatius Loyola*. Port Washington, N. Y.: Kennikat Press, Inc., 1968.

Walker, Williston. *A History of the Christian Church*. New York: Charles Scribner's Sons, 1959.

CHAPTER 25

PIRATES, PILGRIMS, AND PLANTERS

The discoveries in the new world were made mainly by people who were of the Christian faith, and their explorations and settlements nearly always had a religious dimension. But almost never was religion the only dimension. If nothing else settlers had to find ways to shelter, clothe, and feed themselves and that inevitably involved them in economic activities. Moreover, wherever they went they found natives who already had established economic systems involving use of water and land. It was not always immediately recognized, but the new peoples were in competition with the old in using available resources. When the purpose of the new arrivals was not so much on settling and working for a living as stripping the wealth of the new land as soon as possible and shipping it back to Europe, conflicts of interest were quick to develop.

By 1519, Hernando Cortez had made Mexico and Montezuma, king of the Aztecs, his possessions. A few years later, after 1539, Fray Marcos of Nice, a Franciscan friar, traveled north some three thousand miles into the territories of Arizona and New Mexico. Claiming the territory for the king of Spain, he tried to claim the souls of the Indians for Christ. He promised that the Indians would not longer be enslaved by the conquistadors. Pope Paul II in *Sublimis Deus*, 1537, decreed that Indians were not to be deprived of their liberties and possessions even though they were outside the faith of Jesus Christ. Of course the Christian faith was to be made available to them, for as the pope understood it they were most eager to receive it.

St. Augustine was established in Florida in 1565 by Menendez. That settlement in turn became a launching place for Spanish missions to the rest of the area. Protestants too were tolerated in the new world, and Huguenots, French Protestants, settled at the mouth of the Johns River in 1564 at Fort Carolina.

The French were active in the North and in the central areas of North America. Samuel de Champlain explored the coast of Maine and pushed inland to the region of the Great Lakes. The most significant of the lasting French settlements was Quebec. The Franciscans were active missionaries in this region too, but they soon sought the aid of the Society of Jesus in such an enormous task of reaching the Indians for the Church.

Things went better for the settlers of the London Company who landed at Cape Henry, Virginia, in the spring of 1607 and settled further up the James River at Jamestown later that year. They were definitely Church of England people who established Virginia firmly in that tradition for the ensuing centuries. But they were primarily an economic group and it was on that basis that the new colony developed. The first winter began with only half of the more than a hundred settlers of the spring still alive. At the end of the winter even fewer remained. New colonists arrived and gradually the settlement prospered. A new settlement sprang up in Henrico, and in that church an act took place which symbolized a different kind of relationship with the Indians. An Englishman named John Rolfe married an Indian maiden, Pocahontas, in a Christian ceremony. Colonists continued to arrive and expand the land under cultivation. With them the Church of England grew, drawing their clergy from England. It was many years before they had either a bishop or clergy who had been born in the new world.

The second company chartered by James I in 1606 was the Plymouth Company, which was to settle somewhat north of the first. For some reason, the settlers landed on what is known as Cape Cod in Massachusetts. The purpose of the people who came to Plymouth Plantation in the Mayflower was primarily religious. The organizers were Puritans who had fled England for Holland to escape persecution in England for their non-conformity to the Church of England. They had wanted to go further into the Bible and further away from the practices of Rome which remained in the English church. Their Mayflower Compact was patterned after the voluntary church covenant, which became typical of the covenants of the Congregational churches of New England. Those who were accepted by vote of the congregation, after having applied and having agreed to keep the covenant, were members of the established church of the town where they lived. They lived in a theocracy, a people ruled by God. However· they also established a civil government which also was ruled by God. Church and state were separate, but supposedly not in disagreement with each other since both were under the direct rule of God. The church was ruled in each congregation by the democratic vote of its members. The town was ruled by the town meeting in which the citizens had democratic participation.

The fact that the Pilgrims had endured intolerance in England did not make them more tolerant of new settlers who disagreed with their ways. They were too afraid that some other group would gain power and deprive them of their newly gained freedom to worship God in the way they thought best. Their way was the only way tolerated in Massachusetts. Those who disagreed in the early days had to find their own place to live and worship. Roger Williams was told to leave the colony because he denied that King Charles ever owned it and said that it had never been bought from the Indians. He settled in a wilderness of Narragansett Bay; and he called his new settlement "Providence." At once it attracted hordes of dissenters from the old country and from Massachusetts, among whom were the Baptists. John Clarke founded Newport, Rhode Island. George Fox and his Quakers were tolerated in Rhode Island, but even the tolerant Roger Williams disputed their opinions.

It was a long way back to England to acquire an education for sons of Englishmen in the new world. The churches needed clergy badly but it was hard to attract competent men from the relative comforts of the home country. So they founded their own colleges. Harvard College was founded in 1626 along the strictest of Puritan tenets. One was to know the Latin and Greek languages extremely well before being considered for admission, and after admission one was expected to pursue a Christian life and knowledge with great diligence. Mr. Elihu Yale, an Anglican, was persuaded that it would be a better memorial than an Egyptian pyramid to make a gift to Yale University as a center for learning for dissenters. The first college in Virginia was chartered by William and Mary in 1693. The Baptists chartered Brown University in 1764. Thereafter, wherever colonies prospered, the most able denominations established colleges for the training of leaders in the communities.

Pennsylvania became another haven for dissenters. Wherever people were persecuted for their faith, they thought of the land which King Charles II had given to William Penn in 1681 as payment for a debt. Penn established his land as a place for a holy experiment. The first land holders were prosperous Quakers but Lutherans and Mennonites also came. Catholics were permitted and George Whitefield was active there. Not only instrumental in establishing the University of Pennsylvania, Whitefield was such a powerful speaker that he led Benjamin Franklin, America's foremost politician and scientist, to give all the money from his pockets for Whitefield's cause—when he had entered the meeting firmly resolved not to give a single penny.

At the end of the colonial period the Jewish community in Philadelphia was the largest in America. In 1761 the Jewish congregation received a Torah from the congregation in New York where Jews were firmly established.

The Roman Catholics were not left out of the English colonies either. Cecil Calvert, Lord Baltimore, received a charter in 1632 from King Charles I for land around the Chesapeake Bay. Since he was the only Catholic among the proprietors in the colonies, he made provision for the Catholics who were undergoing persecution for their faith at the hands of Protestants. Three Jesuit fathers accompanied the first expedition up the Potomac in 1634 and celebrated the landing with a mass. A permanent chapel was built at St. Mary's, the first capital of the Maryland colony.

John and Charles Wesley visited Georgia and left an influence that far exceeded the time of their stay. One can only speculate on what strength the Methodist church would have had, had not John sailed for home before facing a trial for denying holy communion to a young woman to whom he had been engaged. In 1758 the Georgia Assembly created eight parishes of the Church of England, but the churches existed primarily in the cities of Augusta and Savannah. The Moravians, who had impressed the Wesleys on their journey to Georgia, soon left the colony for more promising territories in Pennsylvania and North Carolina.

There was plenty of land in the new world. Hundreds of groups could form, divide, and reform as their readings of the Bible and their consciences might lead them. Not since the early days of St. Paul had there been such ferment and such variety of practice and belief in the Christian churches. For the most part, unlimited by decisions of councils or popes, the Protestants gave full range to the possibilities of interpreting the doctrines of Christianity. Theocracies and utopias abounded as new groups sought to imitate the communities of faith under guidance from new Abrahams and new Moseses.

The blacks, who had been imported as slaves to develop the plantations of the south, were also recognized as candidates for conversion to Christianity. For the most part, the Indians had gone from the coastal settlements, so attention could easily turn to the newest group unfamiliar with the religions and cultures of the white people. Although some planters resisted the missionizing of their blacks, the response of blacks to the Christian message was generally favorable. Some planters resented the time off from work that the meetings cost, and others disliked the spirit of freedom which some forms of Christianity inspired. Blacks were attracted to the story of the Children of Israel enslaved in Egypt and the wonderful way in which God intervened with a Moses to set them free. Their spirituals told of their desires for freedom in the language and imagery of the Bible. "Go Down Moses," "Ezekiel Saw the Wheel," "Swing Low, Sweet Chariot," and "Steal Away," are samples of themes which their religion expressed. Other planters liked the lessons of morality that Christianity gave to their blacks so they helped to foster their faith by encouraging their preachers and donating to the construction of their church buildings. In earlier days it was common for blacks to worship in the same church buildings with their masters' families, sitting in the balconies reserved for them.

The nineteenth century brought crowds of new immigrants. All the children of Abraham were represented, although few Muslims were among them. Jews in masses came to New York. Protestants of every imaginable sort came seeking new land to farm. The established cities were overcrowded. Competition for the vast farm and ranch lands of Midwest intensified and the best lands were taken. The immigrants formed their social life around their own people and their own religions. The Greeks and the Russians brought the Orthodox church with them. Everywhere one could find strange people, languages, customs, and religions. The settlers who had come first grew alarmed that their own ways might be threatened. Would America turn into another Europe? Would persecutions break out here too? In the name of preventing intolerance, intolerant groups formed to eliminate those who could be potential threats.

The increasing numbers of Catholics led to problems for them. They competed for jobs already held by Protestants in the New England region. They represented peoples who owed allegiance to a foreign potentate, namely the Pope of Rome. They also kept to themselves, preferring to establish and pay for their own parochial schools rather than to send their children to the community schools. They were different and their ways were not known and understood by many Prostestants. An Ursuline convent was burned in 1834 in Massachusetts. The churches of St. Michael and St. Augustine were destroyed in riots in

Philadelphia some ten years later. Propaganda pieces against Catholics included a work reputed to be by a former nun, Maria Monk, entitled *Awful Disclosures of the Hotel Dieu Nunnery of Montreal*, published in 1836. In politics, the expression against Catholics took the form of the Know-Nothing or American Party, which was formed in 1854.

Congregationalists and others sent missionaries to the Hawaiian Islands in the nineteenth century. Before the American Civil War the Hawaiian Islands were mainly English speaking and were regarded as a home mission project rather than a foreign one by the American Board of Commissioners for Foreign Missions. The Mormons established their work there too, and the Book of Mormon was translated into Hawaiian by 1854. It was not Christians or religions of the descendants of Abraham alone who came to these islands. The religions of Asia were also active, among them the Buddhist faith of the Japanese.

The new world offered a novel change to the children of Abraham. There was enough space, enough time, and enough freedom to allow most groups within any faith an opportunity to express themselves in their faith as they thought it should be, rather than what it had been. Judaism held its own well in the early centuries in the new world. Catholicism remained remarkably orthodox until the twentieth century. The Orthodox churches were conservative too. The Protestant Episcopal church remained close to its Church of England roots. But the Protestants and the Reformed groups who were guided only by the Bible, the Holy Spirit, and individual interpretation, gave rise to literally hundreds of different denominations and sects. It is in them that one can see clearly the richness and variety of the faith which began simply in the life of one man, Abraham.

One cannot possibly do justice to all the major religious groups in America in such a short sketch; many other books would be required. But in the new world, the richness of the three religions can be seen clearly. Time has brought the Protestant and reformed groups closer together. Both they and the Catholics have voluntarily changed as they have interacted in the new world. Judaism has also made its accommodations to the new culture of the new world. And Islam has been brought in too, not only by immigrants who have come from the African and Mediterranean countries, but also in the black Americans who have searched for a religion of their own, one that does not discriminate, and particularly one that is not that identified with white Americans.

SUGGESTIONS FOR ADDITIONAL READING

Braden, C. S. *Varieties of American Religion*. Freeport, New York: Books for Libraries Press, 1936; reprint 1971.

Hardon, John H. *The Protestant Churches in America*. Garden City, New York: Doubleday and Company, Inc. Image Books, 1969.

Latourette, K. S. *A History of Christianity*. New York: Harper and Brothers, 1953.

Littele, F. H. *From State Church to Pluralism*. Chicago: Aldine Publishing Company, n.d.

Myers, Gustarius. *History of Bigotry in the United States*. New York: Random House, 1943.

Olmstead, C. E. *History of Religion in the United States*. Englewood Cliffs, N. J. Prentice-Hall, 1960.

O'Neill, James N. *Catholics in Controversy*. New York: McMullen Books, Inc., 1954.

Smith, H. S., Hardy, R. T. and Loetscher, L. A. *American Christianity*. New York: Charles Scribner's Sons, 1963.

Sperry, W. L. *Religion in America*. Cambridge: The University Press, 1946.

Sweet, W. W. *The Story of Religion in America*. New York: Harper and Row, 1950.

CHAPTER 26

MODERNISM IN ISLAM

None of the children of Abraham escaped the effects of Modernism. Modernism was an attempt by religious faith to respond to the impact of science and philosophy and, subsequently, technology and industrialization.

The earlier theories of Copernicus, Galileo, Newton and Harvey had been noticed by Christianity and they had been contained, refuted, or ignored in ways which blunted their impacts upon beliefs of the faithful. However, industrialization of the nineteenth century gradually placed a strain on orthodox beliefs. Especially did new philosophies of the nineteenth century disturb traditional faiths.

Charles Darwin's theory of evolution was eventually seen as a challenge by science to religion, with one having to choose which is true. Karl Marx flatly condemned religion for lulling people to sleep while they ought to prepare to revolt against oppressive industrialists. Friedrich Nietzsche saw the death of God in the new scientific order, and John Dewey applied the test of pragmatism to established institutions and ideas, being willing to discard those which did not have usefulness in the contemporary world.

Religions had to respond when these challenges reached them. One could not be involved with the industrialized countries of the West without being challenged by these new ideas. Young people and intellectuals saw that their traditional ideas of religion had to reexamined. They could reject the scientific, technological way of dealing with the world and retreat into the fortress of established religion. Or they could ride on the new bandwagon of industrialization and leave the old religious ideas behind. Or more difficult, they could try to make a synthesis by borrowing from science, technology, and religion. All of these approaches were possible and in each faith all were tried.

Islam escaped the influence of the industrial revolution longer than did Judaism or Christianity. Indeed, in the opening of the nineteenth century, Karbala and Mecca were both attacked by traditionalists who insisted that those cities needed to be purified of innovations which had been introduced into practices of the faith. The leaders of the puritanical reform were followers of Muhammad ibn-Abd-al-Wahhab, who had begun his reform movement around 1744 in central Arabia. One factor in their success was their political alliance with the house of Saud. The Wahhabis thought that the innovations of the Sufis, which had been accepted along with the more orthodox rites of Islam, had to be purged.[1]

In the opening of the nineteenth century the Saud family conquered central and eastern Arabia and attacked Arab settlements even in Iraq. In 1802 they destroyed the shrine of the Shiah of Karbala. They also attacked the Sharifs of Mecca and managed to capture and purify Mecca in 1806. Through the intervention of the Ottoman sultan of Istanbul and Muhammad Ali of Egypt, the Saud family was defeated and replaced in strength by the Rashids. But the example set by the Wahhabis inspired zeal for tough methods among other Muslims who thought their faith needed reform. According to one theory, the emphasis upon uncompromising monotheism against the transcendentalism of the Ghazali synthesis was one of Arab preference against the preferences of non-Arabs.

Muhammad Abduh (d. 1905) took an approach to Islam that could be compared to the Protestant movement in Christianity.[2] Essentially he wanted to get back to the teachings of Muhammad and his companions. The various traditions that had crept into medieval Islam had to go, for they were not only unessential, but also they were making Islam a laughingstock in the modern world. Practices such as polygamy, quick divorces, and condoning of slavery were not essentials of the faith of Islam, said Abduh. These accretions and others could be separated from the essentials of the faith taught in Quran.

Two ways of handling modern thought emerged in Islam. In one, which was exemplified later in Turkey, the secular world was separated

---

[1]H. A. R. Gibb. *Modern Trends in Islam* (New York: Octagon Books, 1972), p. 26.

[2]*Ibid.*, begin on page 29.

from the sacred. That is, the state was to be operated on purely secular principles which partook heavily of the styles of governments of the industrialized nations in the West. The other way was that of Salafiyah, that is, one based on the positions of the founding fathers. The Salafiyah uphold the faith of the Companions of the Prophet and of the orthodox Caliphs without giving equal weight to the practices which came during the medieval period.

An essential part of the work of Abduh was a commentary on the Quran. He died before he could finish the project, so it was continued by Rashid Rida (d. 1935), a Syrian. Rida was publisher of a journal known as the *Lighthouse,* or *Manar,* which was widely read in Muslim countries. While not so heavy handed in his ideas of reform as the Wahhabis, he was attracted to the ideas of an enthusiastic political reformer named Jamal-al-Din al-Afghani.

Al-Afghani was a colorful figure in the nineteenth century.[3] A Persian, he was led to India in 1869 and then back to Istanbul, whence he was expelled by 1871. He was alo expelled from Egypt in 1879 because he made trouble against English involvement there. He published a periodical known as *The Firm Bond, al-Urwah al-Wuthqa,* an advocate of a new Islam. In spite of his rejections elsewhere he returned to Persia in 1889 to become prime minister. His revolutionary companions and he did not last long, nevertheless, and he was taken to Turkey, whence he escaped to London in 1892. He returned to Istanbul before he died in 1897.

Whereas Abduh was a spiritual reformer, Al-Afghani was best known as a political reformer. He was, however, more a preacher of reform ideas than he was a person who administered reform in a government. He was intensely aware of the intrusions upon Islam of politics, economics, and philosophies from the industrialized nations of England and Europe. The individual nations of Islam might be at the mercy of the great powers to the North, but if all of the Muslims could assert their ideals and their strength as one people perhaps they could stand firm against the modernism and other ideals of the Europeans. He did not hesitate to advocate the use of force to bring about the kind of Islamic unity that could stand up to the colonial powers. On the other hand, he believed in the use of reason in religion, agreeing with the modernists on that point, and in education to bring the thinking of the Muslim up-to-date.

In India a movement began which was considerably more liberal, for

---

[3]*Ibid.,* p. 27.

it started with a bold new assumption. Sayyid Ahmad Khan (1817-98) went beyond the belief of Muhammad Abduh that science and Islam could not be at odds in the long run by asserting that Islam was justified only so long as it was in conformity with the laws of science.[4] With that principle, Khan opened the door for students to question and discard anything that did come into conflict with the latest teachings of science. To carry out his bold assumption, he founded a college in 1875 at Aligarh, an institution to bring the religious teachings of Islam into the modern world. The modern sciences were to be taught along with religion and the two brought into a single world view, with religion changing where it did not agree with science. It is obvious that such a program was to cause problems for the founder. Students who studied the sciences not only questioned practices that had arisen in medieval times, but they also went so far as to question the very authority of the Quran and of the Prophet. Revelation did not seem consistent with the naturalistic and materialistic world of sciences, and reason and scientific method seemed opposed to revelation and illumination. As enemies of the new college were quick to see, such a program, if unchecked, could lead to the sciences wiping out the faith of Islam.

But the ethics of the liberal Islam were attractive to intellectuals who had become embarrassed by slavery, polygamy, and easy divorce. The person who helped circulate the ideas and popularize them was Sayyid Amir Ali of India. A Shiite jurist, he published a book in 1891 on *The Spirit of Islam*. The trouble was, as the conservative could see, that Ali was using Western thought, that is, the whole thought system of the industrialized countries, which meant predominantly Christian, to serve as a framework into which he interpreted Islam. Essentially the life and teachings of Muhammad were explained in a humanistic and not supernatural manner. The Quran was accepted as being a product of Muhammad. A similar process was to take place in Christianity as part of the quest for the historical Jesus. The teachings of Muhammad were described in terms of modern social ideals.

The practices of Muslims that had offended the moral sensibilities of persons in the modern industrial countries were rigidly examined. Blame for them was placed upon the successors of Muhammad who were over-come by past cultural practices and did not really understand his radically new teachings. Muhammad's example of his life was against divorce. The teachings of Muhammad about the equality of all mankind before Allah

---

[4]*Ibid.*, p. 59.

certainly had to be against the practice of slavery. Polygamy, when practiced by Muhammad, was not for lust but out of social concern for the welfare of the widows of his fallen companions.

Bridging the nineteenth and twentieth centuries was the life of Muhammad Iqbal (1876-1938) who carried the process of modernism to a new pinnacle.[5] Using the vital forces in the philosophies of Nietzsche and Bergson as a framework, he expressed his Sufi philosophy. His work published in 1928, *The Reconstruction of Religious Thought in Islam*, was of considerable influence upon younger generations. Sir Hamilton Gibb gives it credit for the forces which led to the establishment of Pakistan as a Muslim state in 1947, although he admits that Iqbal was not well known outside of India and Pakistan.

One way of modernizing Islam was to refashion it in terms of the new thought world of the industrial countries; yet, another was also open. The other way was to admit that while Muhammad was the Prophet of Islam and that the Quran was the greatest of books, revelation and prophecy had not ended with Muhammad. Revelation could continue, and indeed has continued, to be received by chosen men in the modern world.

Mirza Ghulam Ahmad Qudiyani, who died in 1908, claimed that this was the mission to which he had been divinely called.[6] He was charged with the task of bringing Islam into the modern world. Although he started out modestly enough with doctrines that were not far from the orthodox reformers, he became broader in his claims as his followers increased. Ahmad went so far to claim that he was the promised Messiah of the Christians and the Mahdi, or coming prophet of Islam, and the Krishna of Hindus. Naturally he met opposition to his claims, not only by outsiders but also by people in his own ranks. His followers came to be known by his name, the Ahmadiyah. Although they had their divisions in early years, they were strongly motivated as missionaries to proclaim their syncretistic doctrines especially in the regions south of the Sahara and in the East Indies.

The Ahmadiyah think that the Quran is the greatest book, and they translate it and spread it abroad. But there is a kind of mysticism in their teachings which permits a wide range of interpretation in the Quran. In addition, they believe in using reason and in accepting the teachings of modern science. Remarkably, they defend the faith and practices of the Sufis.

---

[5]Malek, Hafeez, ed. *Iqbal* (New York: Columbia University Press, 1971).

[6]H. A. R. Gibb, *Modern Trends in Islam*, p. 61.

Another group based upon fresh revelation is the Babi sect. Although their founder was named Sayyid Ali, the name of the sect is taken from the term he gave to himself, the "Bab." "Bab" means "gate," and Sayyid Ali thought of himself as the gate through which new divine truth would be given to his believers. He proclaimed his mission to the Persians in 1844, beginning in the city of Shiraz where eighteen prepared hearers received him.[7] He considered himself a preparer of the way for someone to come after him. He went to Mecca in 1844 to declare himself but was rejected by the Shiah teachers since he had no armies they expected in a Mahdi. In July of 1850 he and a companion were executed by a firing squad of Armenian soldiers.

Baha'ullah, the one for whom the Bab prepared the way, was born in Teheran in 1817.[8] His title meant, "Glory of God." He spent much time in prison when a crazed follower attempted to assassinate the Shah. Baha'ullah wrote many world leaders and outlined his doctrine that all people are one, there is one God and there should be one commonwealth of all nations, races and creeds. He lived to the age of 75 and is buried in Haifa.

His son Abdul-Baha was also imprisoned for a time but was successful in visiting Europe and the United States. In 1920 he had knighthood bestowed upon him by the military Governor of Haifa. He was buried beside the Bab on Mt. Carmel.

The Bahai religion continues well into the twentieth century, presented as a hope for the unity of mankind in one faith. The leaders had seen themselves as the promised ones forseen by the Jews, the Christians, and the Muslims. Under them, all of the divided faiths of the children of Abraham could be healed. They had only to acknowledge the one true God whom all of them worshipped. Men only had to accept the teachings of the one true prophet which the earlier prophets of Judaism, Christianity, and Islam had announced would come before the final arrival of the rule of God. God was to be worshipped by all and anything that was not God was to be given a subservient place. Bahai is a religion of love, toward God and toward one's fellow man. It is a religion of the brotherhood of man, of service and of involvement of devoted persons. There is no formal priesthood, although teachers can be supported by the

---

[7]Esslemont, J. E. *Baha'u'llah and the New Era* (Wilmette, Illinois: Bahai Publishing Trust, 1950).

[8]*Baha'i World Faith* (Writings by Baha'u'llah) (Wilmette, Illinois, U. S. A.: Baha'i Publishing Committee, 1943).

faithful so that they can devote full time to teaching.

The great bulk of traditional Muslims did not follow the leadership of the Bab and the Bahai way. They tried to remain with their traditional beliefs and practices as long as possible. Nevertheless, the more they had contact with the Europeans, the more they saw the difference between laws of society there and the laws of society based on the Sharia. The Sharia rested upon the revelation in the Quran, the sayings and practices of the Prophet, the consensus of the Medina community, and the opinions of the followers of the Prophet. To a large extent it was a part of the theocratic faith and practice of Islam. Whole countries were expected to keep the Muslim law. But that law was slow to change, and it reflected conditions of centuries before the scientific and industrial revolution which had taken place in Europe and in America. When some Muslims tried to strengthen their ties with European ways, they soon came to realize how much the Sharia reflected pre-industrial conditions and societies, and how strange it seemed to persons who had grown up with the revised, modern system of laws of the industrial powers. At no place was it more striking than in the Muslim treatment of women.

One solution was that taken in Turkey where the law of the land was openly declared to be European and the Sharia was relegated to the background, handling only questions of religious dispute. Laws borrowed from Europeans became the rule of the land, bringing Turkey into the industrial age insofar as its laws were concerned. To a certain extent Egypt went down a similar path through its ties with Britain.

Other nations have had to come to terms as they have become more involved in trade with the Americans and the Europeans. The colonial nature of their relationships has shifted dramatically to one of mutual independence. To a certain extent, Westerners have had to live on terms of the Muslims countries. But the presence of so many prosperous Europeans and Americans and such a mighty influx of money and goods could not be without influence upon Muslim men and women. There is tremendous pressure upon them to accept American and European values, rights, and freedoms along with the benefits of their trade and technology. Where the Sharia remains in force on a large scale, it cannot help but undergo pressure for substantial change.

In 1979, Iran took a different approach. The masses of people overthrew the Shah who had brought Western industries, customs, and military hardware into the country. He was replaced by Ayatullah Khomeini who was for all intents and purposes the sole human head of a theocracy. Subsequent elections of other officials occurred to establish an Islamic republic but initially the real power rested with one clergyman.

All things Western were despised and an attempt was undertaken to restore pure Islamic customs of the Shiite faith. Modernism was rejected in a stampede to return to orthodox Islam as seen by Shiite Muslims.

SUGGESTIONS FOR ADDITIONAL READING

Lewis, Bernard. *Islam in History.* London: Alcove Press, 1973.

Rodinson, Maxime. *Islam and Capitalism.* New York: Pantheon Books, 1974.

Rosenthal, Erwin I. J. *Islam in the Modern National State.* Cambridge: At the University Press, 1965.

CHAPTER 27

JUDAISM IN AMERICA

America and Judaism have developed an interrelationship which has had profound effects upon each of them. While the relationship has not been without its cyclical nature, on the whole it has been extremely fruitful. Perhaps the same could be said for the Irish, the Italians, the Germans and others who came in large numbers in the nineteenth and twentieth centuries. But Judaism has not only undergone fundamental changes in America; it has, in turn, profoundly influenced America, and through America, much of the world.

The sporadic episodes of intense persecution which punctuated the long periods of racial discrimination against the Jews by various European countries motivated Jews to seek a new homeland. The land of the Bible would have been the first choice of many of them if it had been available. However, it was a part of the Turkish empire and not open to settlement by Jews. Holland was usually tolerant of Jews as it had been for the Protestant Christian dissenters from England. A tolerant spirit, however, could not always be coupled with adequate territory and economic opportunity. The United States of America was, in the nineteenth century and the early twentieth century, the land of opportunity.

As the pathetic, humorous, and heart-warming accounts of famous Americans who were raised in the Jewish communities of New York have demonstrated, life for Jews in the new world was a severe struggle. The streets were not paved with gold and in spite of the sentiments expressed on the Statue of Liberty in the harbor new arrivals were more likely to be resented than welcomed. The climb up the long ladder to success usually began with the very bottom rung of socio-economic acceptance. Family cooperation and community support might give moral encouragement, but in the end every person had to fight one's own way to the ladder and make one's own climb.

While there were notable exceptions, for the most part the Jews who came in great numbers to America after the Civil War had a lot working against them. Their language, Yiddish, was a curious mixture of Hebrew and German, and while they could manage to earn a living or run a house with it, it was not a standard language of ordinary citizens or of intellectuals. The clothing which they wore because of their faith or because of their segregated living in European counties appeared to some people ridiculous in America. Long deprived of owning land or attending schools in European countries, they had not the traditions of farmers so that they could proceed to the frontier of America and build a life of farming or ranching on cheap land. They were city people, so many of them stuck together near the port of entry, New York. Without formal education in the ways of the world outside Judaism, and lacking capital to start their own trades, professions, or businesses, they were limited to the most disagreeable sorts of labor. They could burn out their lives night and day in labor or they could starve. To their everlasting credit they poured themselves into any industry that would give them an opportunity. And in a generation or two their devotion to hard work and determination to succeed usually gave them leadership in both labor and management of the industries they served.

With their children raised in America it was different. Although some of them had to spend most of their lives working at home or in sweat shops for pennies a day, others, through sacrifices made by their families, were able to attend the public schools. They quickly learned the new language, the new customs, and which of the Jewish practices made them objects of ridicule to gentiles. It was less painful to adapt to new ways of doing things. A two-dimensional life began for the younger Jews. They tried to please their Jewish parents and honor their Jewish traditions; they also tried to be successful in America, which meant, it seemed to many of them, compromising their traditions in order to acquire the new customs of other Americans.

The compromise with customs of America involved much more than accommodating the theories of scientific methods. It went beyond Darwinism or literary-historical criticism of the Bible or the changing of Yiddish for American idioms. It was a shift of an inward directed life to an outward directed life. No longer was the center the Bible and the

Talmud interpreted by the elders of the Jewish community. The center was the American dream, a dream of unending technological progress, of man over nature, of man over the problems of man, of steady climbing up the ladder of success in terms of business and professional prominence, social elevation, and economic rewards. Education, a pragmatic philosophy of life which recognized the material values of society, and aspiration with perspiration were the forces which could lift one not only out of the ghettoes of Europe but also out of the slums and stigmas of being a poor foreigner in America.

There arose a division of practices within the communities of Jews, based not so much on an acceptance of science as upon a question of how much traditional Jewish beliefs and practices could be compromised to allow Jews to function successfully in the new milieu of America.

The Jews from Germany were the ones who seemed most eager to bring the philosophy and practices of Judaism into line with the philosophies and lifestyles of America. They found a leader in a young rabbi from Austria, Isaac Meyer Wise (1819-1900), who wanted to bring the Reform ideas of Germany to the free congregations in America. He was not a radical, yet Rabbi Wise aroused such antagonism among his congregation in Albany, New York, that some members bodily attacked him in his pulpit. Although Gentile friends urged him to forget the rabbinate and enter law as a profession, Rabbi Wise decided to try again by accepting a call to a congregation in Cincinnati, Ohio.

Part of his success in reforming Judaism for America was in his publishing a journal known as *The Israelite*. Another part was also a publication, a prayer book called *Minhag America*, or the custom in America. It was a kind of common prayer book for Jews in America, designed to replace the diverse customs of Jews from so many countries who came to the new land. A third part of his effort was the organization, in 1855, of a conference around articles of "Union of American Israel." The conservative position of Wise himself was that the Bible is of divine origin and that the Talmud is a traditional development of the laws in the Bible.

The position of Rabbi Isaac Meyer Wise was too liberal for many Orthodox Jews in America and far short of the liberalism advocated by Einhorn, based on Geiger. So the organization of Jewish congregations in 1873 did not become specific about what was and was not to be believed and practiced. In 1873 the Union of American Hebrew Congregations respected the authority of each member congregation but agreed to cooperate in promoting institutions for higher learning in Hebrew literature and Jewish theology, of religious instruction and relief for Jews who were politically oppressed. The weakness of the system was that the authority for Judaism was shifted from the Law to the individual congregation, resulting in many different and changing authorities rather than one, central authority for all Jews. This arrangement had its parallels with certain Protestant Christian groups such as the Congregationalists and the Baptists.

The unity of Jewish Congregations was next approached by Wise through the establishment of an institution for the training of rabbis, the Hebrew Union College, which was founded in 1875. Since it was to be interdenominational, as were its Protestant Christian counterparts, it had a homogenizing effect upon the wide variety of students who studied there. The groups might retain their different names and creeds, but a greater degree of similarities in understanding, proclamation, and practice crept into the students who graduated from the college. It prepared a group of leaders who could adapt Orthodox Judaism to the life of Jews in America, a conservative position.

It did not go far enough for some young rabbis. The trouble with Orthodoxy was not merely adapting the Bible and the Talmud to America. There were serious problems in the doctrines of the Bible and the Talmud in terms of intellectual development of mankind. Certain beliefs and philosophies were no longer intellectually respectable among educated people whether in America or in any other part of the world. This led to a third major group in America, Reformed Judaism.

The Reformed group of 19 rabbis came together in 1885 under the leadership of Kaufmann Kohler. The essential points on which they agreed were listed in a document known as the Pittsburgh Platform. Judaism was not based on a fixed nation or a fixed historical experience. It was part of an ongoing, ever-changing experience. Revelation did not stop with the Bible or with Torah. Laws that were binding for past ages are not necessarily binding in subsequent ages, for ongoing revelation requires changes in conceptions and practices. The Platform of 1937 stressed a bit more that Judaism had a desire in building up a homeland in Palestine, for by that time the Nazis of Germany were making the need for such a provision extremely clear. The Pittsburgh platform, however, had stressed humanism as opposed to supernaturalism. It had played down Jewish nationalism and had emphasized religious practices. While accepting the Bible and the Talmud as ethical guides, it did not hold them binding in terms of diet. It had denied resurrection of the dead and it also denied any "hereafter" or life after death. There was nothing to offend the sensibilities of Jews who were leaders in science, medicine, law, business, or the labor movement.

Reform Judaism has done much to reach out to the Gentile community and show how they have a common moral, humanist tradition. They have worked against prejudice in all kinds of situations. There are lectures open to Jewish and to Christian clergy. Some rabbis and Protestant pastors exchange pulpits once a year and some congregations even meet for a common service on occasions such as Thanksgiving. Through the Jewish Chautauqua Society rabbis are made available to speak on college campuses, and books on Judaism are donated to college libraries. Such a positive approach to American society by Reformed Jews has done much to develop a more positive attitude in Americans toward Judaism and Jews of all congregations.

There is much to be said about the positive position of Jews in America. They are regarded as Americans rather than as foreigners. Under the law they are not in any way second class citizens. They can generally buy property where they please, enter the schools and professions they please, and take part in government at all levels. However, as good as that picture is, there are facts that indicate a residual prejudice even in America.

SUGGESTIONS FOR ADDITIONAL READING

Hardon, John A., S. J. *American Judaism*. Chicago: University of Chicago Press, 1971.

Martin, Bernard. *A History of Judaism*, Volume II. New York: Basic Books, 1974.

Trepp, Leo. *A History of the Jewish Experience*. New York: Behrman House, 1973.

CHAPTER 28

TWENTIETH CENTURY CHRISTIANITY

Christianity, whether Protestant, Catholic, or Orthodox, has faced some significant challenges in the twentieth century. Sciences and technologies have led to questions about traditional beliefs. Different social conditions have brough forth new interpretations of the role of the Christ and the church. New political and economic philosophies, translated into military forces, have led to divisions and upheavals even within the same major body of Christians. And above all, secularism, the way of the good life without the necessity of God, has been a tide which has washed in and out decade after decade, leaving the sands of faith a little thinner after each cycle.

The great variety of sects in American Protestantism came about, in part, through individual interpretation of the Scriptures as the word of God. However, there were among Protestant Christians in America people who regarded themselves as Christians, although they did not regard the printed words of the Bible as the absolute word of God. There were scholars who studied the ancient Greek and the ancient Hebrew and who knew that the meaning of some passages of Scriptures were different from what they seemed to imply in translation. After the middle of the nineteenth century, there were scholars who dealt with "higher" criticism, that is, the origin of the original documents themselves. About the same time that Darwin' theory of evolution was unfolding, theories were developing about the evolution of the Bible.

Of tremendous influence, in a popular sense, for the liberal cause was the preacher of the famous Riverside Church in New York, Dr. Harry Emerson Fosdick. He was always Bible centered in his pulpit and in his national radio programs, but his interpretation of the Bible was along the lines developed by the liberal scholars of the Scriptures. There was a distinctively human and ethical emphasis in all that he did. There was also an emphasis upon the humanity of Jesus that failed to emphasize equally the divine nature of the Christ which had been included in the early councils of the church. Fosdick's popular book, *The Man from Nazareth*, made the point that Jesus was a human being of highly developed ethical sense.

There was a large group of Protestants who resented that kind of erosion of supernatural authority of the Bible and formed a solid front against the liberal theologians and preachers. This movement was that of the fundamentalists, led in part by the very able John Gresham Machen. By 1919, there was organized a World's Christian Fundamentals Association. Their archenemy was the spokesman for liberalism, Harry Emerson Fosdick, who countered their position in public through the newspapers and other media. One famous sermon against them was his "Shall the Fundamentalist Win?" The doctrines of the fundamentalists which he challenged were their views that the Scriptures were inerrantly dictated by God to man, the insistence that Jesus had to be born of a virgin, and that Christ is literally coming back on the clouds of heaven to set up his kingdom on earth. Dr. Fosdick did not object to Christians holding these historical views; he did object to their trying to remove from the churches as unchristian all persons who did not agree with these "fundamentals" of the Christian faith.

A third position in Scriptures was advocated by the Swiss theologian Karl Barth. Although he rejected philosophy as the spectacles through which Scriptures should be approached and insisted that the Scriptures should speak for themselves, Barth did not identify the written words of Scripture as the very word of God. The word of God speaks through the Scriptures as it does in no other writings, but the word of God is not to be identified with the words of Scripture. Thus his position and that of other Neo-orthodox theologians is neither liberal nor fundamentalist. Rather it attempts to go back to the kind of position taken by the Protestants and Reformed theologians of the sixteenth century. It looks upon the community of Christians in the church as part of the means of interpreting the Scriptures rather than depending upon isolated individuals, rigid literalism, or selective reading in light of the latest fads in science or philosophy. The community of the faithful is important in the understanding of the meaning of the Scriptures.

The quest of the historical Jesus came together nicely with the Social Gospel. Its greatest leader was Walter Rauschenbusch, a Baptist minister who served a poor parish in New York City. Salvation which the church was called to provide, thought Rauschenbusch, was something more than saving an individual soul for heaven when one died. The gospel had meaning for human lives here and now. Jesus was seen more as a social worker and a social reformer. The church was called upon to help change human living conditions for the better both by direct action to assist individuals and families and to change the directions, concerns, and programs of governments. Rauschenbusch wrote the first of several books on his preachings in 1907, *Christianity and Social Crisis*. It was followed by two others in the next ten years. Many liberal Christian groups began to work toward the Kingdom of God on earth in terms of improved economic and social conditions rather than by emphasizing the second coming of Christ on the clouds or waiting for individual salvation upon death. To the fundamentalists the Social Gospel was a distortion of the Bible. To the liberals it was the very essence of the teaching of Jesus. The concern for human beings in industrial situations led to cooperation among some denominations who sought to carry out the social implications of the gospel.

Neo-orthodox theologians, such as Karl Barth and Emil Brunner, indicated that the hope of liberal theologians of ushering in the Kingdom of God on earth through social reform was doomed to failure. The problem was not in social conditions, at the root, but in the human soul which had been permanently warped through the sin of Adam. Without the direct intervention of God to restore the distorted image of God in man, the "do good" programs of the "social gospelers" would only issue in distorted "good." Emphasis needed to be placed upon the Christian community and being open to God's grace, which could alone save individuals, who then in turn might be capable of good deeds. God's kingdom would come as God might give it but it could not be built by human beings no matter how good their intentions.

The giving of the Holy Spirit on the day of Pentecost during the days of Simon Peter, the chief apostle, was an exciting, dramatic event in the life of the church, and a very large group of people came into the church at that time. Since that time there have always been Christians who looked back in history to that event as a model for an ideal Christian experience.

In the large cities of America, the charismatic experience was kept alive through the means of a city-wide crusade for Christ or "revival."

One of the early stars of this kind of evangelism was Billy Sunday, who talked tough in his fight against the devil. Women were effective too, and Amy Semple McPherson drew thousands to her meetings where men came to Christ through the beautifully gowned evangelist. The techniques of modern advertising, mass media, and political organization combined to give Billy Graham of Charlotte, North Carolina, a world-wide reputation as a leader of crusades for Christ. Although Mr. Graham was somewhat more subdued than many evangelists and differed in that he tried to work with established churches, his evangelism was more that of the charismatics than that of the sedate rituals of the established Protestant churches.

All of the Protestant groups have had access to the mass media, and many of them have used printing, radio, television, and films with great effectiveness. Nevertheless the dominant use of the most effective media, namely radio and television, has been by the evangelical charismatics. In addition to the stations that regularly carry some religious programs, there are others that carry, along with local advertising, a full schedule of gospel singing and radio preachers. A much more sophisticated ministry is operated and carried by various stations by evangelists such as Oral Roberts and Billy Graham. The Christian Broadcasting Network of Portsmouth, Virginia, carries not only the ministry of Pat Robertson, but also a full line of other ministers and types of services. The success of these ministries is a testimony not only to the personalities and skills of the founders, but also to the desires and needs of millions of Americans which have not been adequately met by the ministry of the established Protestant churches.

While divisions of Protestant denominations have been the rule, there have been some exceptions. In almost every major denomination, there have been groups that were once separated by doctrine which have overcome their differences enough to agree on the essential principles of the denomination. Baptist, Methodist, and Presbyterian denominations can all cite such overcoming of separate groups. Mergers across denominational lines have been, however, slow to come. When they have developed, they have involved smaller denominations rather than larger ones.

The concern over church union has not led most Protestant churches to contemplate return to the Church of Rome, which they perceive to be ready to receive them any time they will agree to repent and become good Roman Catholics. Anglicans, however, and some Episcopalians in the United States, do think seriously about means of restoring the full union of the old Church of England and the Roman Catholic Church. Questions of clergy and of communion are still vital points of separation of these two groups, which are in many ways so close. The Orthodox have been historically more willing to discuss cooperation than have the Roman Catholics, but they too have a concept of what the true church is, and it will not allow them to agree with the lowest common denominator as a basis of merger.

Cooperation among Protestant groups has strongly increased in the twentieth century, and some of the rivalry that prevailed in earlier days has diminished. Relationships with Orthodox churches have been improved through the ecumenical councils. Protestants and Catholics have moved closer together in that cooperation is possible under some circumstances. The bigotry and prejudice that each used to have toward the other have diminished considerably in the United States. Protestant relationships with Jews varies from one group to another, but bigotry on religious grounds alone is seldom openly preached. Relations with Muslims are likely to be on economic and political grounds rather than on religious grounds. Certainly there is almost no serious consideration among Protestant groups of union with either Jews or Muslims. The spirit of toleration for the religion of others rather than a compulsion to convert the heathen has come over some Protestants, but by no means over all. Protestantism is at the stage where greater acceptance of other faiths and peoples could take place with little internal resistance.

Authority was an important question for Catholics as well as Protestants in the twentieth century. Whereas Protestant authority has centered around the Scriptures, Catholic authority has centered primarily around the Papacy. Each authority was challenged by masses of believers who gained new knowledge of the sciences. They were not content to leave the old doctrines alone, but sought to bring them up-to-date with the latest teachings of the sciences and other branches of knowledge outside the teachings of the church. And as the Protestants had split into liberal and conservatives on the challenge, so the Catholics split into those who favored "modernism" and those who wanted to keep intact all of the old dogmas.

The Pope accepted the primary role for protecting the doctrines of the church against the new theories. Bishops were stressing humanitarianism, cooperation with other Christians, and sharing the authority of the pope with the bishops. Some Catholics questioned the right of the church to teach what a Christian must believe in order to attain salvation. To some of them, it seemed that intelligent persons would have to change the teachings of the Catholic Church that were based on outmoded sciences and philosophies.

Popes have been firm in their resistance to the concept that doctrine was a matter of individual preference or individual conscience. Christ had entrusted his teachings to Peter, and through him to his successors, the popes of Rome. Even the authority of the bishops was derived from the pope and that of the clergy was derived through the bishops. The Church of Rome is a hierarchical institution—not a democratic one.

Perhaps no issue has focused attention on the question of papal authority more than has that of papal pronouncements on the nature of marriage and sex. Early in the century, Pope Pius XI declared that marriage between two baptized persons is a sacrament, symbolizing the permanent union between Christ and His church, and cannot, therefore, be broken by any separation. Anyone who leaves one's spouse to marry another is guilty of adultery. Moreover, he asserted that the purpose of marriage is primarily that of begetting children, and that anyone who interferes in that natural process is committing evil. The view on abortion has been that it is murder of innocents.

Priests and bishops who had to work with the laity felt growing pressure as the twentieth century advanced. It was increasingly difficult for them to defend the stance of the church as laymen and laywomen grew in education and freedom in other areas of their lives. Humanism has taught a secular compassion for human beings which has led some Catholics to regard the teachings of the pope as lacking in compassion. The Catholic teachings seemed not only set apart from the real world, but also from the teachings of the other churches. By the middle of the century there was a rash of priests and nuns leaving the church orders because they believed them to be hopelessly out of touch with the human condition in the twentieth century.

With the beginning of the pontificate of John XXIII, a breath of hope inspired both Catholics and Protestants. Although he was completely orthodox, he had a saintly spirit and love for all Christians. He called the Second Vatican Council to deal with many of the problems facing the church at that time. Catholics from all over the world were in attendance, and other Christian groups, including Protestants, were invited to send observers. Perhaps, at last, there was a sign that the separatism of the Roman Catholics and the traditional conservatism of their theological and ecclesiastical positions were to be brought into the twentieth century.

With regard to their attitude toward other Christians, there was some marked progress. The document, *De Oecumenismo,* published in 1964, gave hope that Christians might eventually form a united church. In the meantime, the Catholic Church conceded that all who believe in Christ and have been properly baptized are true Christians and are to be treated with love and respect by Catholics. That was a radical reversal of the early days when persecution was the order of the day for those whose communion with the Catholic Church was imperfect. It was a major step in healing attitudes of hatred which had existed from the days of Luther and Calvin. The Catholic Church made it clear that its own position was the one Christ had established and that in time, it hoped all Christians would be fully in communion with that order. However, conversations on church cooperation could take place. Catholics did not have to shun Protestants as enemies of the church. Protestants, however, according to Catholics, lack the full blessings of the covenant available only through the apostolic college with Peter as its head.

On July 25, 1968, Pope Paul VI issued *Humanae Vitae*, a strong document defining the position of the Catholic Church on birth control. It was issued before it was discussed with the bishops, who would soon be meeting in a second session of a synod. This act by Pope Paul VI, successor to Pope John XXIII, destroyed the hope of some bishops for a more open church, one that could meet changing human needs and changing times.

The bishops reacted strongly to *Humanae Vitae*, perhaps because the issues on which it spoke had been under fervent discussion for five years. Pope John XXIII had called a Commission on Population and Family Life in 1963. It was continued by Pope Paul VI, who issued his document in 1968. During those five years, the issues of contraception, sterilization, and abortion were widely and deeply discussed in papers and journals. Sides were taken and recommendations were made. Pope Paul made it clear when he issued *Humanae Vitae* that there was no question of where the Catholic doctrine stood. He stated again the traditional teachings of the church.

If Pope Paul VI was conservative on matters of sex and marriage, he was innovative in his reaching out to human beings of the world. He traveled by airplane outside of Italy and tried to reach as many countries where there were Catholics as he could. He greatly increased the diplomatic relations with other countries and tried to establish, with some success, friendly personal relations with Russian leaders in order to seek a better treatment of Catholics behind the Iron Curtain. He held an historic meeting with Bishop Athanagoras of the Orthodox Church, beginning an effort to heal the schism that had divided the church East from the church West since medieval times. In the use of media he was modern. As was true of Fundamentalist Protestants, the orthodox and rigid nature of the Catholic doctrines was circulated with the most advanced of technologies.

Revolution was present in the religious orders of the church. From the earliest days institutions were provided for men and for women to live lives of strict obedience, in order, in chastity, and in poverty. By the late 1960's, there were strong currents of unrest. In the modern world, just how servile must one be to be obedient to Christ? Does chastity mean total abstinence or does it mean responsible marriage? How much merit is there in archaic rules and dress of monastic orders? Could some priests and some nuns contribute more to the world by living apart from the rigid rules of orders?

In time, reforms came. The most obvious change was in the dress of nuns. The habits were redesigned in some institutions. Other nuns were permitted to dress in "civilian" clothes of good taste.

As expected, the Roman Church held fast to celibacy for priests and for nuns. Those who wanted to marry had to leave and give up their vows. Exceptions were not made. One who married was no longer a priest or no longer a nun of the Catholic Church. Although the flow of priests and nuns out of the church was not great in light of the number who remained, a more serious consequence was that far fewer men and women became available to enter the religious life. It was no longer appealing to young men and young women in the last half of the twentieth century—at least not to enough of them to replace those who were leaving either through choice or through death.

Another division of opinion in the church came over what language should be used in the church, particularly in the Mass. Latin had traditionally been the only language allowed so that a Catholic could attend a Mass anywhere in the world and know exactly what was taking place. Now Latin has largely been replaced by the language of the people who are worshiping, much to the consternation of some older Catholics. To some of them the Mass is no longer the Mass. Protestants are welcome at Catholic services and it is not strictly forbidden for good Catholics to attend worship in a Protestant church. Traditional chants of the church are sometimes replaced by the folk music of the current generation, giving rise to the Folk Mass, an attempt to appeal to the younger generations which have been alienated by traditionalism.

The Orthodox churches have moved toward cooperation with Protestants and Catholics. But it has been sorely tried in those countries where Marxism has become the dominant political force. It is no longer possible to move freely at home and participation in activities abroad can be difficult. The faithful continue, but repression in many areas makes corporate religious expression extremely difficult.

As the twentieth century draws toward a close Christians are being introduced to different relationships with Muslims. For many of the people of both faiths this is a new experience. Each is almost a stranger to the faith of the other and where there is some opinion, it is as likely as not to be based on misinformation as upon facts. Many opportunities exist for them to study each other and perhaps discover not only their differences but also those great ideas of faith which they both share. Christians and Jews have made progress in tolerance for each other and occasionally have been able to cooperate in projects. Perhaps Muslims and Christians can make progress, using as a model the work between Jews and Christians.

SUGGESTIONS FOR ADDITIONAL READING

Abbott, Walter M., S. J., Editor, *The Documents of Vatican II.* New York: Herder and Herder, 1966.

Brauer, Jerald C. *Protestantism in America.* Philadelphia: The Westminster Press.

Ferm, Vergilius. *The American Church of the Protestant Heritage.* New York: Philosophical Library, 1953.

Gaustad, Edwin Scott. *A Religious History of America.* New York: Harper and Row, 1966.

Hardon, John A. *Christianity in the Twentieth Century.* Garden City, N. Y.: Doubleday and Company, Inc., 1971.

Sperry, Willard L. *Religion in America.* New York: The Macmillan Company, 1946.

Sweet, W. W. *The Story of Religions in America.* New York: Harper and Brothers, 1930.

CONCLUSION

The children of Abraham are, without doubt, products of the same father, but each descendant is different, and special in its own way. How these descendants can relate to each other in the next century is of vital interest to the peace and prosperity of the world. Warfare between any two of them could have disastrous results for the economic prosperity of the entire world. Through peaceful cooperation, on the other hand, their rich resources could lead to a much higher standard of living not only in the developed countries of the world but also in the second and third world countries.

A giant step toward cooperation could take place if members of each of the religions had a better factual knowledge of its roots. Most members of each religion are, for the most part, uninformed of the common ground of faith they share with the other two religions. They are largely unaware that they are descended, in faith, from the same ancestor and that they share a rich heritage which is not the exclusive property of any one of them. When they make that discovery, that they are a family which belongs together and is distinguished from other families of the world, such as the atheistic communists, a foundation might then be recognized for peaceful coexistence if not for fervent cooperation. It would be a situation where everyone could win.

The heritage that the children of Abraham have in common is very great. Their roots go back to a common figure whose life was a symbol of faith in God. Abraham left his home and his kinsmen to wander the earth wherever God would lead him; he placed his life in the hands of God, to do His will as it might be revealed to him. Life was not to be guided by custom or the greatest good for the greatest number determined by some opinion poll or vote. The excellent way in life was not to be determined by the strongest who could impose their will on the weak, or by slaves, or capitalists, or laborers, or any particular race or nationality. The values of life were to be determined apart from the pleasure or the displeasure of individuals. There was, above all of these, the will of God which set the proper course of human beings to travel.

Although the Muslims' heritage divides from the Jewish during the time of Abraham, that same faith has been retained. The continuing heritage of the Jews, especially the great prophets, was recognized by Muhammad as extremely valuable. Even the prophet Jesus, who led to a separation from the Jews by the Christians, is recognized by Islam. So the long heritage of religious and moral teachings of the great Jewish prophets is recognized by all three religions. All have societies under law which are believed to be based upon, or influenced by, revelations from God.

There are, nevertheless, points of separation. The Jewish tradition makes it clear that Jews are the chosen people of God. Various prophets differed in just what being chosen meant, whether it was for privilege alone or also for a special mission of example and teaching for the service of mankind. There have been periods when some Jews did not think that the occupation of the Promised Land was extended in perpetuity; but others have believed it so strongly that they have fought and died to possess it.

Christians and Muslims are not of uniform opinion about those Jewish claims. Many Christians believe that Jews are special to God and that He means for them to have the Promised Land even today. They believe, however, that Jews failed to serve God by receiving Jesus as His Son and that Christians have succeeded Jews as God's chosen people, both for blessing and for responsibility. Other Christians do not think Jews, who are no longer the chosen people of God, are intended to have the Promised Land, since they did not receive the new covenant in the Christ but rejected him. Christ has given a more complete revelation of God and a new covenant based upon baptism rather than upon circumcision. The new covenant is based upon grace rather than law. Since the Jews have rejected that new covenant and Christians have entered into it, Christians think they are more pleasing in the sight of God.

Muslims, however, while regarding Jews and Christians as recipients of the revelation of God, have found the revelations of those peoples incomplete and their practices distorted. Muhammad was a later true prophet of God and had the latest authoritative message. All the prophets before him, including the great prophet Jesus, were valid teachers of God's will, but God's latest and clearest revelation was to Muhammad. Because many Jews and many Christians have refused to recognize Muhammad as a true prophet of God, treating him, instead, as an infidel, many devoted Muslims have an animosity, or at least a coolness, towards Jews and Christians.

Christians make claims that Jews and Muslims cannot accept. Most Christians hold it essential that Jesus was the promised Messiah, or Christ, the only begotten Son of God, born of the Virgin Mary. There is salvation only in Him. Such a doctrine excludes Jews and Muslims, as well as some who believe themselves to be liberal Christian, from salvation, making them at best second or third rate persons, if not hopelessly lost souls. It is understandable that Jews and Muslims have not warmed to friendship with persons who rigidly hold such beliefs.   How, then, is any sort of cooperation and mutual benefit possible, when feelings run so strong? Much tension comes about through people who do not understand the faith of the other religions. And, unfortunately, some of it comes about through persons who neither know nor understand the great teachings and spirit of their own faith. A person who has grasped the teachings of his own religion, who has been open to the greatness of his own religion and who has been exposed to the greatest doctrines and practices of the other two is much more likely to welcome understanding and cooperation than a person whose knowledge is more limited.

One purpose of this introduction has been to promote understanding of the great dimensions of these three religions of the Near East and the West. For the author believes that in such understanding lies the common ground for peaceful coexistence, and even more, for cooperation in all sorts of beneficial endeavors whether political, economic, humanitarian, or religious.

A fact of life is that Jews, Christians, and Muslims are thrown into interaction in many endeavors of life. The question remains how these interactions will affect persons and nations. The author believes that the interactions will have a greater chance of positive results when persons from each religion understand and appreciate the beliefs and practices of the others.

The first principle should be not to offend. It is easy to offend a person of any of these religions if one does not know what is considered sacred and what is forbidden. It is easy to offend if one does not know the dietary customs, the worship customs, the holidays, or the social customs of initiation, of marriage, of contracts, and of death. It takes a basic amount of knowledge, then, just to avoid offending a person one wants to work with successfully in politics or economics.

If one is interested in establishing a positive friendship, it is helpful to have a better understanding of the other person's deepest values and highest hopes. These may well come from the religion that person professes. To know and appreciate the values of a person's religion is to go a long way in understanding and appreciating the person. This kind of appreciation is contagious, and is likely to be reciprocated among people of good will.

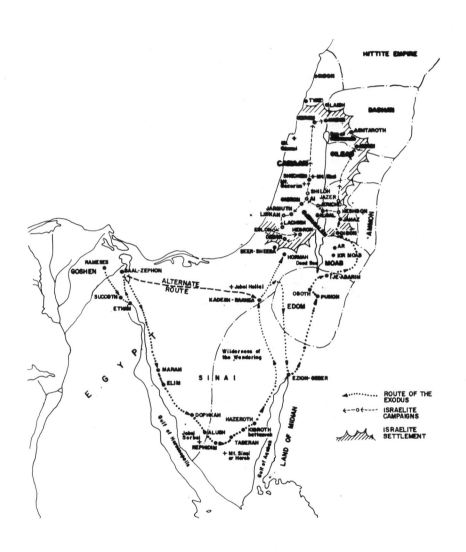

HITTITE EMPIRE

BASHAN

ASHTAROTH

CANAAN

GILEAD

AMMON

EDOM

MOAB

RAMESES

GOSHEN

BAAL-ZEPHON

ALTERNATE ROUTE

+ Jabal Halhil

SUCCOTH

ETHAM

KADESH-BARNEA

OBOTH

PUNON

IJE-ABARIM

AR

KIR MOAB

Dead Sea

HORMAH

BEER-SHEBA

SHECHEM
Mt. Gerizim

SHILOH
JAZER
JERICHO
HESHBON
JAHAZ
GILGAL
DIBON
HEBRON
LACHISH
LIBNAH
JARMUTH
EGLON
DEBIR

TYRE
LAISH

Wilderness of
the Wandering

EGYPT

SINAI

MARAH

ELIM

EZION-GEBER

DOPHKAH

HAZEROTH

Jabel Serbel

ALUSH

KIBROTH
hattaavah

REPHIDIM

TABERAH

+ Mt. Sinai
or Horeb

Gulf of Suez

Gulf of Aqaba

LAND OF MIDIAN

▶•••••• ROUTE OF THE
        EXODUS

◀─○─○─ ISRAELITE
        CAMPAIGNS

ᗗᗗᗗᗗ ISRAELITE
        SETTLEMENT

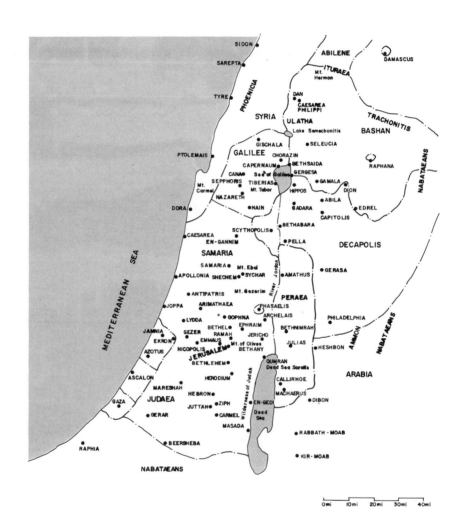

SIDON

ABILENE

DAMASCUS

SAREPTA

ITURAEA

Mt. Hermon

TYRE

PHOENICIA

DAN

CAESAREA PHILIPPI

TRACHONITIS

SYRIA

ULATHA

BASHAN

Lake Semechonitis

NABATAEANS

GISCHALA

SELEUCIA

PTOLEMAIS

GALILEE

CHORAZIN

CAPERNAUM

BETHSAIDA

RAPHANA

CANA

Sea of Galilee

GERGESA

Mt. Carmel

SEPPHORIS

TIBERIAS

GAMALA

DION

NAZARETH

Mt. Tabor

HIPPOS

ABILA

EDREL

DORA

NAIN

GADARA

CAPITOLIS

BETHABARA

CAESAREA

SCYTHOPOLIS

PELLA

DECAPOLIS

EN-GANNIM

SAMARIA

SAMARIA

Mt. Ebal

GERASA

APOLLONIA

SHECHEM

SYCHAR

AMATHUS

MEDITERRANEAN SEA

ANTIPATRIS

Mt. Gezerim

PERAEA

River Jordan

ARIMATHAEA

JOPPA

PHASAELIS

PHILADELPHIA

LYDDA

GOPHNA

ARCHELAIS

GEZER

BETHEL

EPHRAIM

BETHNIMRAH

RAMAH

JERICHO

JAMNIA

EMMAUS

JULIAS

HESHBON

EKRON

NICOPOLIS

Mt. of Olives

AZOTUS

JERUSALEM

BETHANY

BETHLEHEM

QUMRAN

ARABIA

Dead Sea Scrolls

ASCALON

HERODIUM

CALLIRHOE

MARESHAH

HEBRON

MACHAERUS

GAZA

JUTTAH

ZIPH

DIBON

JUDAEA

EN-GEDI

GERAR

CARMEL

Dead Sea

MASADA

Wilderness of Judah

BEERSHEBA

RABBATH-MOAB

RAPHIA

KIR-MOAB

NABATAEANS

AMMON

NABATAEANS

0mi   10mi   20mi   30mi   40mi

ITALY

ADRIATIC SEA

ILLYRICUM

MOESIA

BLACK SEA

ROME
THREE TAVERNS
APPII FORUM

THRACE

BITHYNIA

PONTUS

PUTEOLI

TYRRHENIAN SEA

MACEDONIA

PHILIPPI

PROPONTIS

ASIA MINOR

GALATIA

CAPPADOCIA

BEREA
AMPHIPOLIS
APOLLONIA
THESSALONICA

TROAS
ASSOS
MYSIA
MITYLENE

ASIA

ANTIOCH
TARSUS

SICILY

RHEGIUM

ACHAIA

ATHENS

LYDIA
PHRYGIA

LYSTRA

SYRACUSE

CORINTH
CENCHREA

EPHESUS
MILETUS

PISIDIA

DERBE

TARSUS

SELEUCIA

CNIDUS

ATTALIA
PERGA
MYRA

PAMPHYLIA
CILICIA

ANTIOCH

MELITA
(MALTA)

PATARA

SYRIA

CRETE

RHODES

PAPHOS
SALAMIS
CYPRUS

PHOENICIA

SIDON

LASEA

MEDITERRANEAN   SEA

TYRE
PTOLEMAIS

CAESAREA

JERUSALEM

50   150   250
  100   200   300

EGYPT

ARABIA

·········· ▸ JOURNEY TO ROME
- - - - - ▸ FIRST COMMISSION
·············▸ SECOND COMMISSION
————▸ THIRD COMMISSION
▨▨▨▨▨ LIMIT OF ROMAN EMPIRE
— ·· — ROMAN PROVINCIAL BORDERS

INDEX